From Foraging to Agriculture

The Levant at the End of the Ice Age

DONALD O. HENRY

 UNIVERSITY OF PENNSYLVANIA PRESS   *Philadelphia*

Permission is acknowledged to reproduce the following figures.

Figure 7.15: D. A. E. Garrod and D. M. A. Bate, *The Stone Age of Mount Carmel,* vol. 1 (Oxford: Clarendon Press, 1937); Figures 7.16, 7.19: F. R. Valla, Centre de Recherche Français de Jérusalem; Figure 7.18: A. E. Marks, ed., *Prehistory and Paleoenvironments in the Central Negev, Israel,* vol. 1 (Dallas, Tex.: Southern Methodist University Press, 1976); Figure 7.22: A. E. Marks, ed., *Prehistory and Paleoenvironments in the Central Negev, Israel,* vol. 2 (Dallas, Tex.: Southern Methodist University Press, 1977).

Library of Congress Cataloging-in-Publication Data
Henry, Donald O.
  From foraging to agriculture.

  Bibliography: p.
  Includes index.
  1. Neolithic period—Middle East. 2. Agriculture, Prehistoric—Middle East. 3. Paleoclimatology—Middle East. 4. Middle East—Antiquities. I. Title.
GN776.32.M628H45 1989   939.4   88-27848
ISBN 0-8122-8137-3

Designed by Adrianne Onderdonk Dudden

To my mother Katherine
and in memory of my father Owen.

CONTENTS

5 The Mushabian Complex   125

8 Considering a Universal Cause for Agriculture   229

FIGURES

TABLES

ACKNOWLEDGMENTS

While I assume full responsibility for the contents of the book, I find in retrospect that its completion was more a team than an individual effort. First off, I would like to thank Tony Marks for introducing me to Levantine prehistory some 18 years ago and for continuing to offer his encouragement and criticism of my research.

In that my perception of the issues addressed in this work has been shaped mostly by my field experiences, I think it is important to acknowledge the organizations and individuals that made the field research possible. Grants from the National Science Foundation, the National Endowment of the Humanities through the American Schools of Oriental Research, and the Office of Research of the University of Tulsa supported field projects between 1972 and 1984. Subsequent to working on Tony Marks' Negev Project, Ofer Bar-Yosef and Jim Phillips gave me the opportunity to gain experience in the Sinai and later in the western Galilee. In 1977, Jim Sauer (then Director of ACOR) assisted me in starting up a project in southern Jordan which was supported by the Office of Research of the University of Tulsa. His continued help along with that from David McCreery, Director of ACOR, and Adnan Hadidi, Director of the Jordan Department of Antiquities, enabled me to enlarge upon the investigations on the southern flanks of the Jordanian Plateau during field seasons in 1979, 1980, 1983, 1984. A grant from the National Endowment of the Humanities allowed me to spend my sabbatical year in Jordan. And it was during that time that I was able to start work on the book between field sessions.

Much of the synthetic work in the book was made possible by colleagues who were generous in giving me access to their artifact collections and keeping me informed of their own on-going research. Diana Kirkbride, Hans-Peter

Uerpman, Hans-Georg Gebel, Andy Garrard, Brian Byrd, Alison Betts, Phillip Edward, Geof Clark, Mujahid Muheisan, Gary Rollefson, Nigel Goring-Morris, and Dan Kaufman are all to be thanked for their professional courtesies.

I would also like to offer my appreciation to Tony Marks, Robert and Linda Braidwood, Frank Hole, Geof Clark, and Jim Peoples for taking the time to read and comment on earlier versions of the manuscript.

My thanks are also extended to those "people in the trenches" who assisted me in getting the book to press. Dorothy Gaston, Sally Fowler, and Cindy Hale performed various wizardry in typing the manuscript, while Lucy Addington, Kim Raptou, and Liesa Stromberg showed their talents in artifact illustration and drafting. Jon Sellars, Marsha Peachey, Freida Odell-Vereecken, and Jaymi Bouziden cheerfully helped in the onerous general editing chores.

Tony Marks and Francois Valla are also to be thanked for allowing me to use their published and unpublished illustrations and photographs. And I'm grateful to Mark Newcomer for finding me a copy of Waechter's dissertation.

And finally, I offer my sincere gratitude to Nancy who, aside from helping me with the library research, showed remarkable patience and sensitivity throughout the project.

From Foraging to Agriculture

1
Changes: Causes and Consequences

In the history of human development it is hard to overemphasize the importance of the economic transition from foraging to food production. After enjoying some 3 to 4 million years of success through foraging, the human species adopted a radically different adaptive strategy that within the last 10,000 years has replaced foraging in virtually every part of the world. With the shift to producing food the human adaptive system was fundamentally changed. Settlement mobility, population stability, conservation of resources, low energy requirements, and general system equilibrium were replaced by settlement permanence, population growth, intensified exploitation of resources, escalation of energy needs, and general system disequilibrium.

As we shall see, most scholars have viewed this transition as a result of groups being forced into higher levels of productivity either because of a growth in population or a decline in resources. Explanations vary in detail, but most contemporary thinking holds that at the end of the Ice Age, hunter-gatherers were pushed toward intensifying their exploitation of resources because of scarcity and that this trend ultimately culminated in food production. In contrast to this interpretation, I will be arguing that, at least in the Levant, foraging groups were attracted or pulled to new resources that demanded intensified exploitation. More importantly, it is proposed here that the adaptive ramifications of this economic shift were destabilizing in the long term, for they increased the vulnerability of groups to perturbations and shortfalls in resources. Again, this interpretation runs contrary to popular opinion concerning intensive or complex foraging communities. The greater size and permanency of such communities along with their richer material culture (e.g., architecture, cemeteries, storage pits) have prompted most archaeologists to associate them with secure, stable adaptive systems.

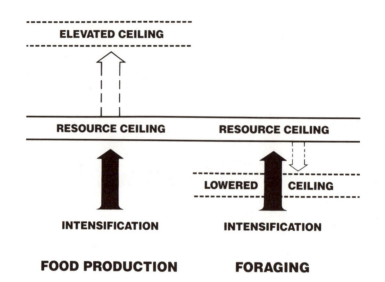

Figure 1.1. *Diagram comparing the effect of intensification on systems of food production and foraging. Note that intensification acts to lower the resource ceiling in foraging while elevating the ceiling in food production.*

The terms "simple" and "complex" foraging are used throughout the book to distinguish between the two radically different kinds of hunting-gathering adaptive patterns that were employed by the terminal Pleistocene populations of the Levant. In many ways, the two patterns parallel those contrasted by Binford (1980). He describes a "foraging" strategy characterized by high mobility and movement to resources in contrast to a "collecting" strategy in which greater residential permanence is maintained through storage and the logistical acquisition of resources. The simple-complex foraging dichotomy also parallels Gould's (1982) distinction between "risk minimizers" (simple foragers) and "resource maximizers" (complex foragers).

In the Levant, the intensive collection of wild cereals and nuts prompted the emergence of complex foraging. This is associated with the Natufian archaeological complex. Natufian communities were much larger and more permanent than their simple foraging contemporaries or predecessors. Through their strategic placement and the development of storable surpluses, these communities took on the general appearance of early farming villages some 2,000 to 3,000 years before the first evidence of agriculture. But with the changes in economy and settlement, the inhabitants of these communities had given up the principal means by which foragers cope with shortages in resources—mobility. On the other hand, they had come to adopt an essentially agricultural strategy insofar as they were dependent upon storable surpluses developed through intensive collection.

In the context of foraging, however, such a strategy lacked the essential element upon which agriculturalists depend; that is, the ability to elevate the resource ceiling through greater investment of energy or technological advances. In this light, complex foraging is seen as an adaptive strategy that was ripe for failure. "Intensification" and "foraging" are contradictions from the perspective of successful long-term adaptation. Ironically, the long-term stability of foraging was in part dependent upon inefficiency in the exploitation of resources, at least to the degree that sufficient resources remained unexploited in order to renew themselves. Through a dependence upon storable surpluses for security, complex foragers like the Natufians were confronted with the paradoxical situation of actually lowering their resource ceilings while attempting to increase their security by intensifying their exploitation of such resources (Figure 1.1). It is not surprising then to find that complex foraging societies are rare and short-lived in both archaeological and ethnographic contexts. Furthermore, from various archaeological sequences, we find that such societies were often transitional between simple foraging and agricultural systems.

It will be argued here, therefore, that the key to solving the puzzle of agricultural origins in the Levant rests in understanding the development and dissolution of complex foraging. This is the rationale for tracing the rise and evolution of the Natufian. But it should be emphasized that tracking the development of other, often ignored, Levantine populations is of near equal importance. A comparison of the Natufian to contemporary populations that failed to adopt complex foraging and agriculture helps to isolate those factors that were responsible for the Natufian's emergence and evolution. In this light, we can better understand the adaptive changes that occurred at the end of the Ice Age and ultimately gave rise to agriculture.

A History of Ideas

These adaptive changes and their material consequences have long fascinated archaeologists and other scholars. Much of their attention has been focused on the Near East, perhaps because the transition occurred earlier and was more dramatic there than elsewhere in the world. Whatever the reason, since the early part of this century there has been a steady stream of ideas concerned with explaining the origin of agriculture in the Near East. In reviewing the evolution of these ideas, three intervals can be defined. These mainly consist of episodes of theoretical movement separated by a period of data collection.

CHILDE'S CONTRIBUTION

Thinking on the subject was initiated during a period of arm-chair theorizing as expressed in the works of Smith (1923), Peak and Fleure (1927), and most notably V. Gordon Childe (1928, 1934). It is during this period that the economic importance of the Neolithic was recognized and the Near East was identified as a region of agricultural origin. Childe (1934) was responsible for bringing specific focus to the Levant, as opposed to the Nile, as a likely area for the emergence of agriculture. He cited the recovery of sickle blades and grinding stones from the Natufian horizons of the Carmel Caves of coastal Palestine as evidence for the collection of wild cereals. In addition to addressing the question of where the transition to agriculture was most likely to have taken place, Childe (1928, 1934) advanced ideas on when and why the event occurred. In synthesizing the works of Pumpelly (1908) and C. E. P. Brooks (1926), Childe (1928) suggested that the earliest steps toward food-production began at the end of the Pleistocene when the onset of drier conditions forced man and potential domesticants into close proximity in well watered areas around oases and rivers. Childe's propinquity or desiccation theory lacked detail and sound empirical support, but it did provide a framework for linking the time and place of early food-production with climatic change.

By the mid-1930s, Childe had integrated environmental, technological, and economical evidence into a synthetic regional model that supported his general theory of human adaptation and cultural evolution. His effort takes on particular significance when one considers that most of his peers were engaged either in developing local cultural chronologies or in advancing sweeping theories. By introducing to Near Eastern prehistory a level of general inquiry that was based upon an explicit model, Childe established the level and the parameters of research that would influence his successors. This is not to suggest, however, that all subsequent work reached the synthetic and theoretical levels achieved by Childe. A number of Near Eastern prehistorians contributed little to testing Childe's theory and supportive evidence.

CONCENTRATION ON FIELDWORK

For almost 20 years following the publication of *The Most Ancient East* (1928), Childe was alone in attempting to examine his ideas in the light of newly acquired archaeological evidence. The absence of involvement by other scholars in evaluating Childe's theories is particularly surprising given the large numbers of excavations at sites containing terminal Pleistocene occupations during the 1930s and 1940s. Excavations by Garrod (1954), Turville-Petre (1932), and Stekelis (1942) of caves located in the Mount Carmel area complemented the inland fieldwork conducted along the hilly spine of Palestine at the cave of Shukbah (Garrod, 1932) and at several sites in the Judean Hills (Neuville, 1934, 1951). These studies provided important chronological, technological, economical, and environmental evidence that was clearly pertinent to Childe's ideas of terminal Pleistocene adaptive changes.

In leading the field studies, Garrod and Neuville were committed to establishing cultural chronologies and identifying climatic successions in the Levant through artifact seriation, stratigraphic comparisons, geologic studies, and faunal analyses. Although their field methodologies and analytic techniques were quite good for the day, these researchers failed to recognize the significance of the evidence that they had recovered. These data clearly meshed with Childe's theories, but neither Garrod nor Neuville attempted to integrate their findings into the broader context of explaining terminal Pleistocene adaptive changes. Childe, actually having little field experience in the Near East (Trigger, 1980), nevertheless utilized the new evidence to support his ideas as advanced in *New Light on the Most Ancient East* (1934, 1952) and *Man Makes Himself* (1939). Surprisingly, he failed to incorporate the climatic findings of Garrod and Neuville into his writings even though these reconstructions actually supported his desiccation theory.

Following World War II, fieldwork in the Levant was resumed at a strong pace. Excavation of the important Natufian open-air site of Ein Mallaha (Perrot, 1962, 1966), along with work at Jericho (Kenyon, 1959), Nahal Oren (Stekelis and Yizraeli, 1963), and Beidha (Kirkbride, 1966), furnished significant new information. Ein Mallaha provided important evidence on the internal layout of a Natufian hamlet, and the deposits of Jericho, Nahal Oren, and Beidha yielded evidence from Natufian and succeeding Neolithic horizons. However, except for Perrot's (1962) discussion of the general economic and settlement trends that accompanied the transition from the Natufian to the Neolithic, research focused on gathering facts with few attempts at explanation theory.

BRAIDWOOD'S ECOLOGICAL APPROACH

The next major theoretical push came from outside the Levant in Iraqi Kurdistan (Braidwood and Braidwood, 1950; R. Braidwood, 1951a, 1951b; L. Braidwood, 1952). Although Robert and Linda Braidwood questioned the transitional status of the Natufian, as proposed by Childe, they were nevertheless convinced that such a transition did take place, but elsewhere, in the natural habitat of the wild cereals.

While Braidwood and his colleagues were admittedly strongly influenced by the writings of Childe, new methodological and theoretical perspectives were introduced by the Iraq-Jarmo Project. Through the project, Braidwood initiated the first effort to research the terminal Pleistocene transition through a field investigation. Previous studies had lacked continuity between research design and field inquiry and, as Wright (1971:456) has noted, "at this point, testing of hypotheses about food-production began." Perhaps as a result of Childe's influence, Braidwood had a strong ecological perspective of the problem and incorporated this approach into his field methodology. A multi-disciplinary team of scientists participated in the Iraq-Jarmo Project in order that the wide variety of cultural and environmental evidence could be recovered, analyzed, and interpreted.

Braidwood's ecological orientation and explicit testing of previous hypotheses, particularly those of Childe, resulted in the introduction of new concepts that would form the foundation for contemporary theories concerning the terminal Pleistocene transition. The most significant ideas advanced by Braidwood dealt with his concept of a "nuclear area," the question of terminal Pleistocene climatic stability, and his notion of an intensified economy.

Braidwood proposed that the transition from hunting-gathering to food-production took place in a nuclear area:

Within the hilly-flanks zone occur in nature (or, in the case of some of the larger animals, occurred until recently) a remarkable constellation of the very plants and animals which became the basis for the food-production pattern of the Western cultural tradition (Braidwood and Howe, 1960:3).

In many ways Braidwood's nuclear area was an environmentally better defined and geographically more restricted version of his predecessors' "fertile crescent," the name first introduced by the historian James Breasted for the mountainous arc stretching from the southern Levant to Iran; but the term also carried a "cultural area" connotation commonly held by anthropologists in North America:

on one hand culture can be understood primarily only in terms of cultural factors, but that on the other hand no culture is wholly intelligible without reference to the noncultural or so-called environmental factors with which it is in relation and which condition it (Kroeber 1939:205).

The cultural area concept served Braidwood's ecological interest better than Childe's more environmentally deterministic interpretations of the fertile crescent. It also encouraged scholars to begin examining the problem of the terminal Pleistocene transition from various regions within the nuclear area. Through this concept, Braidwood emphasized a problem oriented approach that allowed scholars to compare evidence from different prehistoric provinces within a cultural area:

Regardless of dating problems, these archaeological efforts in the Jordan Valley and those in Iraqi Kurdistan will prove to be interdependent and related. Regardless also of the question of specific ecological niches, both efforts lie within the general area that we feel may be crucial to the great transition (Braidwood and Howe, 1960:6).

As a result of the initial paleoenvironmental studies associated with the Iraq-Jarmo Project, Braidwood concluded that no significant climatic changes had occurred at the end of the Pleistocene (Braidwood and Howe, 1960:181). By the late 1960s, however, palynological evidence (Wright, 1968) obtained from Pleistocene lakes in the Zagros caused Braidwood to alter his interpretation (Braidwood, 1969, in Wright, 1971). Although the notion of terminal Pleistocene climatic stability was shortlived, it nevertheless became entrenched in the literature and strongly influenced subsequent thinking.

Without climatic change as a prime mover, prehistorians began to search for other factors that might have been responsible for the social and economic transition. In relying upon Braidwood's dismissal of climatic change as a causal factor, Binford (1968) and Flannery (1969) employed models of population pressure and population-subsistence disequilibrium to explain the economic changes among terminal Pleistocene populations in the Near East. Before exploring these models in detail it is important to examine Braidwood's "settling-in period," for both of these population and subsistence models rest on the demographic assumptions implicit in this concept.

Braidwood (1960a, 1960b) proposed that toward the end of the Pleistocene man had successfully occupied most of earth's environments and was in the process of more intensively exploiting local environments through broader subsistence patterns. Although he did not directly speculate about demographic changes, increased population density is implied by his (1960a:131) suggestion of greater efficiency in the exploitive patterns of terminal Pleistocene societies:

As technologic competence increased, it became possible to extract more food from a given environment; or, to put the matter the other way around, increased "living into" a given environment stimulated technological adaptation to it.

During the 1950s and 1960s, excavations in Israel, Jordan, and Iraq furnished a considerable body of evidence in support of Braidwood's proposals. Excavations at the Natufian open-air sites of Ein Mallaha (Perrot, 1960), Jericho (Kenyon, 1959) and Nahal Oren (Stekelis and Yizraeli, 1963) revealed permanent or semi-permanent village communities that were supported through foraging. Research at the site of Zawi Chemi Shanidar (Solecki and Rubin, 1958; Solecki, 1981) complemented Howe's work at Karim Shahir and indicated a parallel development of preagricultural village communities in Iraqi Kurdistan and in the Mediterranean littoral, thus reaffirming Braidwood's cultural area concept.

The effect of Braidwood's conclusion, that terminal Pleistocene populations began to intensively exploit the local environments of the hilly flanks of the fertile crescent during a climatically stable interval, fundamentally altered the manner in which scholars searched for the factors responsible for the "great transition." Prior to Braidwood's investigations in Iraqi Kurdistan, prehistorians relied upon the dynamic element of climatic change and concomitant environmental adjustments to account for the terminal Pleistocene cultural transition. Their concern with the dynamic and diachronic aspects of the environment drew their attention from the complex static and synchronic ecologic relationships that existed in such an environmentally diverse area as the Near East. In stressing the synchronic interaction between man and environment at the end of the Pleistocene, Braidwood influenced other researchers to begin detailed examinations of regional cultural histories and environmental settings (Perrot, 1962). And this induced scholars to assess the processual character of the terminal Pleistocene transition from a more ecological and less environmentally deterministic perspective (Flannery, 1969; Binford, 1968).

THE ROLE OF CLIMATIC CHANGE

Near the end of the Ice Age, some 10,000 to 13,000 years ago, environmental changes induced by worldwide climatic oscillations caused significant adjustments in the adaptive strategies of prehistoric populations. These changes in man-land relationships are commonly viewed as having been most pronounced in those areas of the world adjacent to continental glacial masses because of the dramatic terminal Pleistocene shifts in biotic zones of the peri-glacial regions. In the lower latitudes, however, certain arid regions of the world—such as the Near East—appear to have experienced equally significant movements of biotic zones during this period. Although the variations in terminal Pleistocene climate may not have been as marked in these lower latitude arid belts as in the periglacial zones, the environmental expressions of sustained shifts in the temperature and moisture parameters of these regions were undoubtedly striking. In these regions today, even subtle shifts and relatively brief climatic changes have pronounced environmental consequences, due to the inherent sensitivity of such marginal zones to slight alterations in temperature and moisture level.

Reaction to the early ideas of Childe (1928), with their strong flavor of environmental determinism, has caused most scholars to ignore or at least de-emphasize the role of environmental change in shaping cultural evolution in the Near East. Alternative stances have been adopted that rely upon other forces such as population pressure and economic adjustments to account for the rapid social changes that occurred during the terminal Pleistocene. In contrast to these prevailing views, an examination of prehistoric evidence from the Levant—the best researched region of the Near East for this period—confirms that significant climatic-environmental oscillations did occur. And, of even greater importance, these changes can be shown to have been relevant in shaping the tempo, mode, and direction of cultural evolution for the inhabitants of the region.

Unlike Childe's environmental determinist view of this succession, the environmental changes can be shown to have had different kinds of impact upon the inhabitants of the region depending upon their local ecologies. Differing economic, demographic, social, and ideological adjustments by the populations can be traced to a common environmental change. These ecologically specific responses also can be shown to have resulted in the development of alternative paths and trajectories of cultural evolution among contemporary populations. Not only does this multilineal view of cultural evolution for the region differ from Childe's early unilineal stadial view, but it also differs from most recent thinking, which accepts a multistage unilineal sequence of development (Moore, 1985). While some populations did experience a succession leading from highly mobile foraging to sedentary foraging and ultimately to food-producing societies, other coeval populations continued to persist as simple foragers.

The archaeological evidence from the Levant also refutes another commonly held view of the cultural evolution of the terminal Pleistocene Near East—namely, that developments were always cumulative and unidirectional. In this regard, the evidence points to some populations that adjusted to environmental changes by adopting *less* as opposed to *more* complex economic and social patterns. This is reflected in some sedentary foragers who returned to mobile foraging while others adopted agriculture.

Conflicts Between Notions and Evidence

A review of contemporary ideas concerning the adaptive changes of terminal Pleistocene populations in the Near East reveals a disturbing trend: thinking has become based principally on high level abstraction rather than on primary evidence. In addressing the question of terminal Pleistocene adaptation, specific cultural chronologies, site distributions, paleoenvironmental data, and economic evidence have been generally ignored or at least examined uncritically.

In many ways recent studies have continued the highly theoretical approach established by Childe, but there is one important difference. Whereas Childe really had little primary field evidence by which to check his ideas, contemporary researchers have access to an abundance of primary data, particularly that accumulated over the last two decades. As noted by Hole (1971), contemporary theoretical advances can provide a structure by which primary data can be ordered and evaluated, but this generally has not been done. Instead, a whole series of untested notions have taken on the character of fact with the result that the contemporary view of the adaptive changes occurring at the end of the Pleistocene is based more upon the logical relationship of ideas than on the critical evaluation of evidence. The tendency to over-generalize the problem, the reliance upon secondary sources, and the failure to examine critically many of the ideas that have become entrenched in the literature have obscured our view of the topic in several ways.

UNILINEAR VERSUS MULTILINEAR EVOLUTION

First, by ignoring the complexity of the cultural and economic mosaic of the Levant between 14,000 and 10,000 B.P., scholars have focused on and overly emphasized only one of a number of important linked relationships—namely, the transition from foraging to food-production, as exemplified by the evolution of the Natufian to the Neolithic. A brief overview of a more holistic picture of the region during this period reveals the parallel and partially synchronous development of two simple foraging societies (represented by the Mushabian and Geometric Kebaran complexes). These societies were apparently composed of small, highly mobile, materially impoverished, and probably socially egalitarian groups. Around 12,500 years ago, one of these societies, the Geometric Kebaran, evolved into a complex foraging society, the Natufian, with a concomitant emergence of large, sedentary, materially rich, and socially stratified communities.

support a key notion? And second, if so, when does this evidence first appear in the archaeological record? This second question has generally been ignored, although the sequence or order of these phenomena is particularly crucial to a model's verification or rejection.

Depending upon the model, the triggering mechanism of the first transition precipitated the replacement of small, highly mobile groups by larger, sedentary communities. In the cultural-historic context of Levantine prehistory, this transition is reflected in the development of Natufian communities some 12,500 years ago.

In timing, the various models suggest that some combination of broad-spectrum subsistence, population growth and expansion, or resource stress preceded the first transition, whereas the expansion of cereals occurred nearly concurrently with the emergence of complex foraging. With the exception of cereal expansion, the notions rest on the concept of gradual cumulative change occurring over millennia. The cereal expansion notion, however, is associated with the concept of a rapid and dramatic change in subsistence induced by the availability of a new resource. Therefore, in checking the models against real-world data recovered from Levantine prehistoric deposits, evidence for cereal expansion should be principally associated with the Natufian, whereas evidence in support of the key notions of the other models should be found in pre-Natufian times. As will be shown in the critical review of the evidence, however, these notions, if confirmed at all, first find support during the Natufian. Thus, apart from the cereal expansion idea, such factors could not have caused the transition to complex foraging.

BROAD-SPECTRUM SUBSISTENCE: FACT OR FICTION

Since the period was described by Braidwood (1960a; 1960b) as an "era of intensive hunting and collecting," the concept of an intensive broad-based subsistence pattern has formed an important part of most models of terminal Pleistocene adaptive changes in the Near East. When viewed as a precipitating factor, a broad-spectrum subsistence strategy has been seen as emerging first in the late Pleistocene among Upper Paleolithic populations of the region and ultimately leading to sedentism and population growth (Binford, 1968; Flannery, 1969). Binford (1968:332) favored a broad-spectrum subsistence pattern derived from "the harvesting of fish, molluscs, and migratory 'fowl'," while Flannery (1969:77) suggested "a trend toward increasing use of small game, fish, turtles, seasonal water fowl, partridges and invertebrates." From a different perspective, Hayden (1981:525) has recently characterized the development of a broad-spectrum economy as a trend of increasing use of r-selected as opposed to K-selected species. The categories of r- and K-selected species are based upon an ecological concept that distinguishes populations according to reproduction and growth patterns (Pianka, 1970). Hayden (1981:525) notes that:

The effects of this change in exploitation strategy were much more far-reaching and fundamental than the number of species involved in this "broadening" of the resource base would indicate.

K-selected species normally consist of large-bodied animals that, although furnishing a high energy return, have lower rates of productivity and are hence potentially unreliable as food resources. In contrast, r-selected species—for example, mice, many fish, shellfish, and grasses—typically are small, short-lived, highly productive, and resistant to eradication through overexploitation. Their numbers and density often provide for a very high and, perhaps more importantly, a dependable energy return for labor investment. In short, a movement toward greater exploitation of r-selected species is thought to have resulted in a much more reliable subsistence strategy allowing for sedentism and population growth.

The adoption of a broad-spectrum subsistence pattern should be directly evidenced by a higher ratio of small to large organisms in the food residue recovered from prehistoric deposits. Even though this, at first, appears to be a rather straightforward procedure in determining the relative breadth of prehistoric dietary patterns, there are a number of factors that could bias such a relationship. For example, the remains of microfauna are more likely to be introduced to a site, particularly a cave or rockshelter, by natural agencies than are megafaunal remains. Remains of rodents, amphibians, reptiles, fish, and molluscs are commonly brought into caves and rockshelters by predatory birds and mammals. Some of these organisms may also inhabit caves and rockshelters, or they may be attracted to the organic residue left by human inhabitants. Different recovery procedures, as governed by the coarseness of the mesh in screening and whether or not wet-sieving and flotation techniques were employed, also strongly influence the proportion of large to small organisms attributed to a deposit.

With these cautions in mind, a comparison of faunal assemblages from several Near Eastern (mostly Levantine) prehistoric deposits points to little, if any, broadening of the diet prior to the Natufian some 12,500 years ago (Table 1.1). From Middle Paleolithic through pre-Natufian Epipaleolithic times, small animal species ranged from being nearly equal in number to about twice as common as large animal species. During this interval the evidence for the processing of plants is rare. Beginning with the Natufian, we see a marked shift in this ratio, with small animals becoming some three to eight times more common than large animal species. It is also at this time that we see a marked increase in plant processing technology. These data, therefore, indicate that the gradual development of a broad-spectrum pattern did not in fact take place during the Late Pleistocene of the Near East but seemingly occurred dramatically and simultaneously with the emergence of complex foraging.

At this point, it is important to underline the difference between the diversity of species and the contribution of different species to a prehistoric diet. Whereas

TABLE 1-1
A comparison of the subsistence resources associated with selected late Last Glacial and terminal Pleistocene occupations in the Near East. Similar levels of recovery and analysis were employed at all of the sites.

	Late Last Glacial (18–13,000 B.P.)				Natufian (13–10,000 B.P.)		
	Ein Gev I[a]	*Ein Aqev*[b]	*Hayonim Cave*[c]	*Pale-gawra*[d]	*Hayonim Cave B*[c]	*Hayonim Terrace B, C, D*[2e]	*Rosh Horesha*[f]
Large mammals[1]							
Gazelle	1	1	1	1	1	1	1
Goat/sheep	1	1		2	1	1	1
Cattle	1		1	1	1	1	1
Pig	1			1	1	1	
Deer	3		3	1	3	3	
Other	2	1	1	1		1	1
Total	9	3	6	7	7	8	4
Medium and small animals[1]							
Sm. Mammals	1	1	6	16	19	9	5
Fish					1	1	
Birds	4	1	1		27	6	4
Reptiles	1	1		6	4	4	2
Total	6	3	7	16	53	20	11
Ratio of large to medium and small animals							
	.7	1.0	1.2	2.3	7.6	2.5	2.8
Plant processing technology							
Mortars	+				+	+	+
Pestles						+	
Handstones		+			+	+	+
Grinding slabs					+	+	
Sickle sheen					+	+	+

[a]Davis, 1974:453–62.
[b]Tchernov, 1976:70.
[c]Bar-Yosef and Tchernov, 1966:121–39.
[d]Turnbull and Reed, 1974.
[e]Henry and Davis, 1974; Henry, et al., 1981.
[f]Butler, et al., 1977.
[1]Number of species.
[2]The remains of birds from Hayonim Terrace have not been analyzed.

even a narrow spectrum subsistence pattern may show as many or more small species than large ones, when the actual contribution to the diet is considered, large-bodied animals contribute an overwhelmingly greater proportion of the diet than do the small-bodied species. Not only do the large animals contribute a greater part of the diet because of their size, but in these pre-Natufian deposits they also appear in greater absolute numbers. For example, at Palegawra Shelter (Turnbull and Reed, 1974:96) over 70% of the minimum number of individuals within the faunal assemblage are represented by six species of megafauna (*Equus hemionus*, *Cervus elephus*, *Ovis orientalis*, *Capra hircus aegragus*, *Sus scrofa*, and *Bos primigenius*), with these same six species providing 99.5% of estimated meat yield. For small animals to have made a significant contribution to a prehistoric diet, they would have had to have been harvested in quantities so huge that they should be readily apparent in archaeological deposits. While such small animals do appear in Near Eastern deposits beginning in Middle Paleolithic times, their small numbers imply that they never formed a significant part of the diet.

Flannery (1969:78) remarks that small mammals would not have provided a reliable food source in the Near East but that "water fowl, fish, mussels, snails, and plants . . . are readily and predictably available in some quantity." Of these resources, however, only land snails (*Helix sp.*) are reported in any number and these from only two sites—Ksar Akil in Lebanon (Ewing, 1949) and Palegawra Cave (Reed, 1962) located in the Zagros Mountains of Iran. Even in these areas, it is hard to imagine that snails, unless occurring in tremendous numbers such as in the snail middens of the Capsian of North Africa, could have significantly augmented a prehistoric diet. Even though relatively rich in calcium, snails are a poor source of calories and protein. Also, snails may well have been attracted to human occupations, particularly caves and rockshelters, because of the higher humidity levels and cultural residue present in such settings. Although this idea has not been examined in the Near East, clear correlations do exist between inedible snails and prehistoric midden locations in North American rockshelters (Hall, 1980).

With respect to plants, another resource suggested as broadening the diet, there is no evidence for their intensive use until Natufian times. Both Hole (1984, in press) and Moore (1982, 1985) argue for a long and gradual growth of plant use that culminates in cultivation, but the dramatic appearance of a wide range of plant processing equipment with the Natufian points to a sudden shift in subsistence practices. This is not to suggest that plants, snails, fishes, reptiles, and other r-selected species were not incorporated into the Late Pleistocene diet, but the intensity by which these resources were exploited could not have supported sedentary communities nor induced a growth in population. Empirical verification thus is really not available for Flannery's (1969:79) proposition of over a decade ago that

data tentatively suggest that a "broad spectrum revolution" was real, that it was nutritionally sound, and that it originally constituted a move which counteracted disequilibria in less favorable hunting areas.

The proposition of an emergent, broad-spectrum diet has undergone a clear evolution, as with many such reasonable notions, from a tentative idea to an accepted concept without the benefit of reexamination.

Although the notion of a gradual broadening of the subsistence base during the Late Pleistocene cannot be supported, the question remains whether a broad-spectrum subsistence is appropriate for describing the economic pattern of Natufian communities. As the broad-spectrum pattern is presently understood it does not seem to have been followed even during Natufian times. The Natufian economy, as reflected in subsistence evidence from archaeological deposits, was based upon increased specialization in the hunting of megafauna—especially gazelle—and upon an intensive exploitation of cereals and nuts. Although present, small game, fish, fowl, and invertebrates were unimportant to the overall Natufian subsistence base.

Small animal species are much better represented in Natufian deposits than before, but the absolute numbers of small game, fish, turtle, fowl, and invertebrate remains indicate that they could not have made a significant contribution to the overall diet. Even in those excavations where all minute faunal remains were recovered through fine-mesh water sieving and froth-flotation, the quantity of the remains of r-selected species implies that, relative to the large species, they contributed less than 1% of the meat to the diet.

At the Natufian site of Hayonim Terrace (Henry, et al., 1981), for example, the recovery of hare, squirrel, mole rat, various lizard, tortoise, bird, snake and fish remains attest to the inclusion of a wider range of small animals in the diet. But all these animals combined account for an exceedingly small proportion of the meat diet. In using a generous estimate of 400 individuals from the remains at Hayonim Terrace and an average meat yield of 0.1kg per individual, only 40kg would have been furnished by the small animal portion of the diet. The more than 200 individuals represented by the megafaunal remains (86% of which are gazelle) would have provided over 4,000kg of meat. The inclusion of a slightly greater range of small animals in the Natufian diet, therefore, seems to be an unlikely explanation for the observed demographic changes within the Natufian, certainly not to the extent of supporting large sedentary communities.

Rather than being an explanation for the emergence of sedentism in the Natufian, the greater diversity of small animals in Natufian middens may have actually been a consequence of sedentism. Two factors may account for the introduction of a greater range of small animal species into the Natufian deposits. First, the emergence of large sedentary communities in the Natufian is likely to have resulted in a more intensive exploitation of site catchments, so that a wider range of foodstuffs would have been incorporated into the diet. Second, the development of a year-round occupation at a single location would have brought together the residue of all the foodstuffs that were formerly contained within individual segments of a mobile annual cycle; thereby effectively enlarging the diversity of the sample. In comparing faunal assemblages from Natufian hamlets, representative of the totality of resources obtained over a year, with pre-Natufian sites that contain resources obtained from only a portion of the annually exploited territory over a relatively brief interval, it is not surprising to find that the Natufian assemblages reveal a marked increase in the diversity of small species over earlier assemblages.

Interestingly, when megafaunal remains are considered, Natufian assemblages actually show a reduction in the diversity of species when compared to earlier assemblages. This more narrow range of megafauna is attributable principally to the intensive exploitation of gazelle, which account for 50–90% of the assemblages (Henry, 1975; Bar-Yosef, 1981a). The high frequencies of gazelle remains in Natufian deposits have been interpreted as evidence for communal hunting through surrounds and ambushes (Henry, 1975), the clearance of woodlands through burning, and the control of gazelle through a kind of incipient domestication (Legge, 1975). Regardless of the reason for the emphasis upon gazelle exploitation, the practice represents a change toward specialization—as opposed to diversification—of subsistence activities by Natufian hunters.

The most important change in subsistence activities during the Natufian was the adoption of the intensive harvesting of wild cereals and nut crops. As discussed in detail later, this economic adjustment appears to have led to the formation of the large, sedentary villages that characterize the Natufian. The importance of wild cereals to the Natufian economy was recognized over half a century ago by Childe (1934). The presence of silica lustre, "sickle sheen," on Natufian blades and microliths prompted him to suggest the harvesting of wild cereals, but recent critics of the idea have pointed to the fact that silica polish can be produced by the cutting of other plants such as reeds (Vita-Finzi and Higgs, 1970). The argument that Natufians were engaged in the intensive collection of wild cereals, however, is based upon much more than the presence of silica lustre. The distribution of Natufian sites, unlike earlier sites, shows a strong correspondence to the natural habitat of cereals some 10,000–12,500 years ago. Not only do the Natufian hamlets have a geographic distribution limited to hill and plateau regions of the Levant, but the sites reveal a clear trend of increasing elevation to the south and east (Henry, 1973a, 1983). These distributional patterns follow the range of the Mediterranean woodlands, the wild cereal habitat, which are similarly confined to the uplands of the Levant. They increase in elevation to the south and east in order to compensate for the regional decline of moisture in these directions.

In addition to artifacts bearing silica polish, several other artifacts and features related to plant processing first become common with the Natufian. Mortars, pestles, querns, grinding slabs and storage pits are typically found in Natufian sites and attest to the emphasis on plant-processing activities. The recovery of cereal pollen from Natufian deposits (Henry, et al., 1981; Henry and Turnbull, 1985) reinforces the argument for intensive cereal harvesting, as does direct evidence in the form of carbonized remains of wild cereal and nuts (Moore, 1975; McNicoll, et al., 1985). Given the many extensive excavations of Natufian sites it may seem odd that cereal remains should be so rare if they in fact had been intensively exploited. The rarity of carbonized remains may be explained by the nature of the sediments in Natufian deposits that are not conducive to the preservation of organics (Smith, et al., 1985). For example, hearths and other evidence of burning are abundant, but charcoal is quite rare in most

Natufian sites. This paucity of charcoal is reflected by the relatively few numbers of radiocarbon dates based upon charcoal, as opposed to bone samples, that have been obtained for the industry (Henry and Servello, 1974).

Other evidence pointing to a large cereal and nut component in the Natufian diet comes from the analysis of skeletal remains. Based upon dental attrition scores, Pat Smith (1972) suggests that stoneground foods formed a significant and increasing part of the Natufian diet through time. Through the study of strontium-calcium ratios, other researchers have concluded that Natufians incorporated a large proportion of plant material in their diets (Schoeninger, 1981, 1982; Sillen, 1981; Smith, et al., 1985). Interestingly, the results of Schoeninger's (1981) research indicate that the Natufian diet showed a significant increase in plant foods over earlier Late Glacial populations, while Sillen's (1981; Smith, et al., 1985) study shows a higher proportion of plant consumption for the Natufian than for later food-producing populations.

To summarize, two conclusions can be reached about the notion of a broad-spectrum subsistence pattern in the cultural evolution of the Levant. First, the proposal of a gradual broadening of the economy leading to a more secure subsistence base, the emergence of sedentary communities, and a growth in population can be rejected. Such a trend is not indicated by pre-Natufian subsistence evidence. Secondly, the emergence of large sedentary communities, as represented by the Natufian, can best be explained by the intensive exploitation of cereals and nuts. Specialization, as opposed to diversification, characterized the Natufian economy. Although small animal species did form a larger portion of the diet in Natufian times than earlier, these food sources furnished an exceedingly small, almost negligible, part of the overall diet. Instead, the specialized hunting of gazelle and the intensive collection of cereals and nuts contributed the greatest part of the subsistence base.

POPULATION GROWTH AND EXPANSION

The notion of population growth and expansion has also been advanced as an explanation for the marked economic and social changes that took place among the terminal Pleistocene inhabitants of the Levant. Two kinds of population stress models have been proposed: population growth and population expansion. Models of population expansion reject the concept that human groups would have reproduced to levels that would have exceeded their resources. Instead, they favor the idea that an expansion of groups from the rich to the poor environments of the Near East taxed the resources of the marginal areas and thus induced changes in subsistence (Binford, 1968; Flannery, 1969). Binford (1968) suggested that the rich coastal environment with its aquatic resources precipitated sedentism, population growth, and ultimately expansion into the marginal steppe-desert zones. With this expansion, he thought, a population-subsistence tension zone developed as immigrants expanded into the territory of indigenous groups, disrupting the balance between their population levels and their existing resources. Flannery (1969) adopted a similar argument. He proposed that the rich environment of the Mediterranean woodlands promoted population growth and expansion into the marginal steppe-desert zones, where a broad-spectrum subsistence developed to stabilize the imbalance induced by an elevated population dependent upon meager resources.

Although these models have been criticized (Meyers, 1971; Cohen, 1977; Redman, 1978), they have not been questioned at the level of the primary evidence furnished in their support. The presence of bone harpoons, and turtle and fish remains, from Natufian deposits are mentioned to uphold Binford's (1968) contention that aquatic resources were important to the emergence of the Natufian. Very small quantities of fish remains have been found at Ein Mallaha, Hayonim Terrace, and Hatula, but, as previously discussed, the quantity of remains could not have made a significant contribution to the overall diet. A few "strangled stones" were recovered at Abu Hureyra (Moore, 1975), and barbed points (harpoons) have been found at five other sites. But fewer than ten harpoons have been found in all of the Natufian excavations, and there is no direct evidence to imply that they were even used for spearing fish. Their recovery from sites (e.g., Erq el Ahmar) distant from lakes, rivers, and the sea indicate that the notched bone points may even have been used for hunting terrestrial game.

Gary Wright (1971) also notes, in support of Binford's model, that the temporal and spatial distribution of Natufian sites reflects an expansion from coastal to inland areas. Until recently, the oldest radiocarbon dated Natufian sites were found near the Mediterranean coast (Hayonim Terrace) and Lake Hula in Upper Jordan Valley (Ein Mallaha), but an even earlier site is now known from southern Jordan (Wadi Judayid). And Wadi Judayid, located about 60km north of the Red Sea coast at an elevation of over 1,000m, is not associated with any variety of aquatic resource. Clearly, the proposed coastal to inland expansion cannot be supported.

In summarizing his model, Flannery (1969:76) notes that

it would appear that the mixed oak woodland of the Levant coast supported higher upper paleolithic populations than some of the treeless inland steppe areas, at least where survey has been comparably extensive.

This observation is not substantiated by more recent systematic surveys conducted in Sinai (Bar-Yosef and Phillips, 1977), the Highland Negev (Marks, 1976, 1977c), and southern Jordan (Henry, 1981). In these regions, Upper Paleolithic sites show considerably higher densities than areas of equivalent size within the Mediterranean woodlands. In short, both population expansion models can be rejected on the basis of the empirical evidence available today.

An alternative population model has been presented by Mark Cohen (1975, 1977) who, following the ideas of Boserup (1965), argues that populations reproduced to levels that exceeded food resources. This led to the adoption of alternative subsistence strategies, manifested by broad-spectrum subsistence patterns and ultimately agriculture. As an overview of his model, Cohen (1977:14) states:

that human population has been growing throughout its history, and that such growth is the cause, rather the simply the result, of much human "progress" or technological change

With regard to the Levant, he draws upon two lines of support for his model. One is based upon his assumption that changes toward a broader subsistence is indicative of the increases that are thought to have occurred in population. This reasoning is potentially circular; in any event, as we have seen, this broad-spectrum notion cannot be supported for the Levant.

Cohen's second line of support, based upon the relative numbers of sites through time, is more direct and tangible. In relying upon Perrot's (1962) review of the prehistory of Palestine, he proposes that the trend of increasing broad-spectrum subsistence is paralleled by:

independent evidence that the absolute population density of the Middle East was increasing at least from the Upper Pleistocene through the early post-Pleistocene period (Cohen, 1977:137).

and that

beginning as early as the Upper Paleolithic Aurignacian industries and extending through the period of Natufian occupation there is a buildup in the numbers of sites (Cohen, 1977:137).

A major problem in using the relative numbers of archaeological sites as a direct measure of changes in population levels is related to differences in their preservation and exposure. This is an especially important problem with Pleistocene sites, for the probability of the burial or erosion of paleosurfaces tends to increase with the age of the surface. Therefore, in order to measure accurately the relative numbers of sites for a given area through time, it is critically important to have some understanding of the geomorphic history of the area.

For example, in disregarding the region's geomorphic background, Cohen (1977:137) cites as evidence for a rising population the absence of Upper Paleolithic sites in the Upper Jordan Valley followed by the appearance of Epipaleolithic sites. This apparent rise in population, in fact, can be explained by the valley's inundation by the ancient Lisan and Beisan lakes during Upper Paleolithic times (Koucky and Smith, 1986). Upper Paleolithic sites were present just above lake level but in lateral tributaries of the valley as documented by sites in the Wadi Fazael (Bar-Yosef, et al., 1974) and Wadi Hama (McNicoll, et al., 1985). With the late Pleistocene recession of the lakes, Epipaleolithic and later Neolithic sites made their appearance on the shoreline of the lake, but at lower elevations near the present floor of the valley.

TABLE 1.2
The percent distribution of occupations by Paleolithic interval recorded within the deposits of 21 major cave/rockshelters in the Levant.

Lower Paleolithic	Middle Paleolithic	Upper Paleolithic	Epipaleolithic Pre-Natufian	Natufian
10	36	22	12	20

When attempting to trace the relative numbers of prehistoric occupations through time, one way of overcoming the problem of differential preservation is to limit the scope of the survey to protected sites that have functioned as natural sediment traps. Although caves and rockshelters are certainly not immune to the natural factors that may influence the presence or preservation of a prehistoric occupation, such settings are less subject to natural biases than open sites. Erosion is less common in protected sites, and buried occupations are more likely to be discovered because of the archaeological practice of deeply sounding such settings. In short, it is suggested that a survey of protected sites furnishes a better measure of the occupational intensity of the Levant through time than a similar survey of open sites. In reviewing such a survey (Table 1.2), it is apparent that the proposed increase in number of occupations beginning "as early as the Upper Paleolithic" cannot be supported.

A similar rejection of the idea is called for by data from those areal surveys that have attempted to control for the geomorphic history of study areas. In the Gebel Lagama area of Bar-Yosef and Phillips's (1977) Sinai study, Upper Paleolithic sites greatly outnumber later ones. In Marks's (1976, 1977a) investigation of the Avdat area in the Highland Negev, Upper Paleolithic sites again outnumber later occurrences. In my own work in southern Jordan (Henry, 1981), the number of sites discovered for a specific prehistoric period show, as might be expected, a direct correlation with the size of the area of sediments exposed for that period. More importantly, when the density of sites is calculated for the area of exposure of sediments of the same antiquity, there is no significant change from the Lower Paleolithic until the Natufian. Surprisingly, this change during the Natufian actually shows a decline, not a rise, in site density. These data indicate a near stable population from the Lower Paleolithic until the Natufian, when a population increase occurred. Although the number and hence the density of sites decline with the Natufian, the Natufian sites are markedly larger and relate to permanent occupations, not multiple occupations over the course of a year. They therefore indicate a greater number of residents per site on a year-round basis.

In summary, the ideas of population growth and expansion as currently presented cannot be supported by the evidence related to changes in subsistence patterns or in the numbers of sites. Population increase did occur, but during

Natufian times and not before. Thus, neither population growth nor expansion could have precipitated the evolution to complex foraging but were apparently by-products of complex foraging once it had developed.

RESOURCE STRESS

As with the notions of population growth and expansion, resource stress has been viewed as a factor that "pushed" populations toward broadening their subsistence patterns and ultimately to adopting agriculture. In his account of various "origins," Marvin Harris (1977:35) argues "that the extinction of Pleistocene megafauna triggered the shift to an agricultural mode of production in both the Old and New Worlds." In the same vein but on a more regional scale, Moore (1985:12) suggests that under stress from the late Last Glacial steppic conditions "some groups may have eaten, perhaps for the first time, the seeds of wild grasses as well as other plants." And Brian Hayden (1981) has recently advanced a comprehensive model that ties periodic episodes of resource stress to technological innovations and subsistence changes during the course of the Paleolithic. Harris' proposal could not have accounted for the adoption of agriculture in the Near East since the extinction of important megafauna did not take place there at the end of the Pleistocene. Gazelle, wild cattle, onager, deer, and wild goats formed the principal sources of meat for prehistoric populations from early Last Glacial times (i.e., 90,000 B.P.) until the adoption of animal husbandry. Moore's argument does not explain why steppe settings, both earlier in the Last Glacial and coeval with complex foraging societies, failed to promote intensive plant use.

Central to Hayden's model is the notion that "periods of resource stress inevitably occurred because of long- and medium-term cyclical fluctuations in natural resources" (Hayden, 1981:522). These episodes of resource stress are thought to have affected prehistoric populations in two ways. First, there was an effort to balance the morbidity/mortality related to resource stress with the cost of maintaining population controls at acceptable levels. Second, groups attempted to minimize the effects of resource stress through increasing the reliability of the exploited resources. Hayden proposes that, in an effort to increase the reliability of resources, human populations evolved through four technological subsistence stages, each representing an expansion of resources. This gradual economic evolution is thought to have culminated at the end of the Pleistocene in a "change from large-bodied easily handled and captured foods" to "diminutive and unobvious resources such as rodents, grass seeds, snails, fish, insects . . ." (Hayden, 1981:525). As previously discussed, this change might better be described as a shift from K-selected to r-selected species. Hayden goes on to suggest that this final stage was accompanied by two trends. One led toward an increasing diversification of exploitation in those areas of poor-to-moderate resource richness. The other resulted in more specialized exploitation practices in those areas that were resource-rich.

In order to test the applicability of Hayden's model to events during the terminal Pleistocene in the Levant, three bodies of evidence need to be considered. These include evidence for resource diversification, resource specialization, and environmental deterioration. As already discussed, the proposed trend of increasing resource diversification cannot be supported by data recovered from terminal Pleistocene deposits. There is, however, considerable evidence in support of the argument for the development of a specialized exploitation pattern in the Natufian, specifically in the context of gazelle and cereal/nut procurement. The specialized economic pattern of the Natufian seemingly corresponds to Hayden's proposition that in resource-rich environments populations would have responded to resource stress through specialization, as opposed to the diversification of resources. But, when paleoenvironmental evidence is reviewed, as is done in Chapter 3, there is a clear picture of an episode of environmental amelioration during the Early Natufian and pre-Natufian times.

During this period, around 13,000−11,000 years ago, the Levant experienced an elevation in temperatures and moisture budgets that triggered an expansion of the Mediterranean woodlands into areas that are today within the steppe zone. And even in those areas within the arid zone peripheral to the Mediterranean woodlands, there is abundant evidence for greater available surface water and a generally richer environment. The paleoenvironmental data accompanying the period of specialized economic patterns within the Levant thus leads to the rejection of the idea that populations were "pushed" into new and specialized subsistence practices as a result of a stress on their resources. I will argue to the contrary that populations were attracted to or "pulled" toward the exploitation of newly available set of resources that accompanied the expansion of the Mediterranean woodlands near the close of the Pleistocene.

2
An Alternative Explanation: A Composite Model

The notions of broad-spectrum subsistence, population growth and expansion, and resource stress are reasonable. They may be appropriate for explaining the transition to complex foraging in other parts of the world. But they do not fit the evidence recovered in the Levant. An alternative model, which in many ways is a composite of a number of existing ideas, is proposed in order to better accommodate the environmental, economic, and demographic evidence available from the region. Its most distinguishing feature is that climatic changes are viewed as the triggering mechanisms that led to the development of complex foraging and subsequently prompted the adoption of agriculture.

Unlike the other notions, which see populations as having been "pushed" into complex foraging, a climatic change is thought to have initially "pulled" populations toward the intensified harvesting of plant resources found in the Mediterranean woodlands. It thus induced sedentary lifeways, population growth, and expansion. Subsequently, a second climatic change caused a retreat of the Mediterranean woodlands, at the expense of expanding steppe and desert zones, and thereby created a situation of declining resources in the face of a growing and expanding population. These conditions overloaded the complex foraging system that, unlike simple foraging, was inherently vulnerable to resource stress. This setting induced alternative adaptive responses. People living in the core Mediterranean zone adopted agriculture; those occupying the more arid, marginal environments returned to a simple foraging pattern.

Climatic change has not been favored as a prime mover of the cultural succession of the Near East since being challenged by Braidwood's pioneering work in Iraqi Kurdistan (Braidwood and Howe, 1960). In relying upon the initial field evidence recovered by Braidwood's team, most subsequent research efforts have accepted the idea that the Near East experienced a stable climate at the end of the Pleistocene. Researchers have incorporated this assumption into their explanatory models (Binford, 1968; Flannery, 1969; Cohen, 1977). More recent fieldwork, especially in the Levant, confirms that significant climatic changes occurred near the close of the Pleistocene. As described in detail in Chapter 3, diverse lines of evidence (pollen, faunal, and geologic data) agree in defining major climatic oscillations between some 14,000 and 10,000 years ago. However, the important question is not whether such changes occurred, but whether they were pertinent to the cultural evolution of the region.

In addressing this issue, Charles Redman (1978:104) touches upon the central considerations for determining the relevance of climatic change to cultural evolution. He suggests that one means of ascertaining the importance of the environment is through a detailed comparison of areas that "seem to share the same crucial environmental factors, but in which agriculture did not develop" (Redman, 1978:104). Alternatively, Redman (1978:104) suggests that:

Explanations for the different course of development should also be sought because, if they were convincingly related to certain environmental variables, then the case for the environment playing a deterministic role would be considerably strengthened.

Although Redman's remarks principally focus upon questions related to the emergence of agriculture, they are equally pertinent to addressing the role of environment in the transition from simple to complex foraging. The composite model, presented here, shows that diverse evolutionary paths did develop among terminal Pleistocene populations in the Levant because of diachronic changes and synchronic differences in environment.

With the expansion of the Mediterranean woodlands out of Pleistocene refugia some 13,000 years ago, cereals and other plant foods acquired a new economic significance. Although these plant foods were exploited within the refuge areas before their expansion into their optimum habitat, they did not have sufficient economic value to promote intensive collection, sedentism, or other characteristics of complex foraging. Similarly, following the expansion of the Mediterranean woodlands, the populations living in steppe and desert settings were engaged in the exploitation of plants. But because of the nature of these arid land plant resources, these groups never achieved the levels of intensive collection common to the complex foraging communities of the Mediterranean woodlands. Therefore, the factors that are correlated with complex foraging, in both synchronic and diachronic contexts, are the Mediterranean woodland resource zone and its distribution within an optimal habitat.

As discussed in detail later, only when the Mediterranean woodlands colonized the higher elevations of the Levant were food sources found in this environment sufficiently attractive to promote complex foraging. The economic importance of these foods was enhanced by the Mediterranean woodlands' expansion onto the lime-rich, clayey *terra rossa* soils of the hills and uplands of the

Levant. Such a setting provided the ideal edaphic conditions for cereals and nut crops.

The wider elevational amplitude of the woodlands after colonizing the uplands had important economic consequences as well. The greater elevational ranges of cereal grasses and nut-bearing trees acted to ameliorate the impact of short-term weather perturbations on the productivity and survival of these plant populations. Whereas annual variations in temperature and precipitation patterns would have significantly affected the vigor of a plant population occupying a narrow elevational belt, a similar population occupying a much wider belt would have been relatively immune to such fluctuations. Perhaps of even greater importance, the colonization of the uplands extended the period of maturation of various plants. The elevationally staggered maturation of cereals, for example, would have stretched from April at 200–300m above sea-level to early August at 1,500m. With the inclusion of nut crops from stands of oak, almond, and pistachio, a wide range of easily collected and storable foodstuffs were available from late spring through autumn.

The second part of the composite model is related to the emergence of agriculture in the Levant. This part of the model again satisfies Redman's critical test of an environmental prime mover. It relates alternative adaptive responses of a complex foraging society to those changes in the distribution of the Mediterranean woodlands that occurred with the onset of arid conditions about 11,000 years ago. The drier conditions, inducing local and regional shifts in the woodlands, caused a decline in the critical storable resources upon which Natufian communities relied. Within the core Mediterranean zone, those communities adjacent to dependable water sources could have augmented wild foodstuffs with cultivated cereals and thereby maintained the basic fabric of a sedentary society. Other communities located within the encroaching arid zone or adjacent to less secure water supplies failed, and their inhabitants returned to a mobile simple foraging strategy. Alternative adaptive responses to a common climatic change were therefore dictated by the local environmental expressions of that change.

The composite model does emphasize the role of climatic changes and their environmental consequences as prime movers in the terminal Pleistocene cultural evolution of the Levant. But it also takes into consideration differences in the flexibility and stability of alternative adaptive systems. In this regard, the model is at odds with the prevailing view of complex foraging systems. Rather than being secure stable systems, they appear to be relatively unstable when compared to simple foraging patterns. Complex foragers relinquished the principal means of adaptive flexibility and success enjoyed by simple foragers (mobility) while not having achieved the principal adaptive mechanism of agriculturalists (the ability to raise the ceiling of their carrying capacity through food-production). Given this perspective, it is not surprising that complex foraging adaptations are relatively rare, short-lived, and so often transitional between simple foragers and agriculturalists.

The transitional nature of complex foraging is exemplified clearly by the Natufian. Most of the demographic, social, and even ideologic features common to early agricultural villages were in place in the Natufian some 2,500 years before the first evidence of food-production. With their evolution from a simple foraging base, however, Natufians gave up the adaptive flexibility afforded a mobile society and adopted a strategy linked to intensified collection and storage for adaptive success. This new economic strategy permitted and demanded sedentism, promoted community and regional population growth, significantly altered settlement structure, and induced major changes in social organization and even ideology. These changes, when viewed in conjunction with the greater material wealth of complex foraging communities, seemingly denote an adaptive strategy that offered greater stability and security than simple foraging. Each of these changes, however, increased the rigidity of the adaptive system. In combination, they rendered it subject to disruptions by environmental changes on a long-term scale. The Natufian, then, like other complex foraging societies, was particularly susceptible to the kinds of destabilizing forces represented by the onset of the drier conditions about 11,000 years ago. Those Natufian communities resting within the better watered Mediterranean zone were able to maintain a strategy of intensification and storage through incipient horticulture. But those communities in the arid zone failed and were abandoned, their inhabitants returning to the more secure strategy of simple foraging. Therefore, according to the composite model, the earliest attempts at agriculture were not merely the mechanical result of a climatic change. Rather, climatic shifts interacted with an unstable system's sensitivity to such changes to produce two distinct adjustments.

The First Transition: Ideas and Evidence

The transition from simple to complex foraging within the Levant, I claim, was triggered by a worldwide elevation in temperature that in turn caused an expansion of the Mediterranean woodlands out of Pleistocene refugia and into the uplands about 13,000 years ago. The idea that the Mediterranean woodlands assumed their contemporary distribution only after a terminal Pleistocene temperature elevation was advanced initially by Herbert Wright (1977). He based his proposal on a review of geomorphic and pollen evidence from the eastern Mediterranean basin. In elaborating upon Wright's idea, it is proposed here that the expansion of the Mediterranean woodlands had a number of economic consequences beyond the mere extension of woodland resources over a larger area.

In using various paleoenvironmental data from the Mediterranean basin, Wright (1970) proposed that a cold and relatively dry continental climate was replaced by the modern Mediterranean climate at the end of the Pleistocene. The effect of the depressed Pleistocene temperatures on the distribution of the Mediterranean woodlands, however, is the significant factor to be considered. Geologic and palynologic data indicate that during the last glacial episode the snow lines of the mountains around the Mediterranean basin were some 600−1,300m below the snow lines of today (Wright, 1977; Erinc, 1978), and along the coast sea level dropped over 100m (Shackleton, 1977). Herbert Wright (1977:291) concludes that the lower snow lines denote a mean annual temperature that was depressed at least 8°C for late Last Glacial times (i.e., oxygen isotope stage 2) in the Levant. This is consistent with other estimates of Last Glacial temperatures for similar latitudes elsewhere in the world (Emiliani, 1972:400; Flint, 1971:439; Emiliani and Shackleton, 1974:513; Roberts, 1982:246).

These depressed Last Glacial temperatures would have confined cereals and other food resources associated with the Mediterranean woodlands to low elevations and warmer latitudes in the Levant. Wright (1977) noted that cereals would have been restricted to refuges along the Mediterranean coast, the Rift Valley, and perhaps northwest Africa. A more precise reconstruction of the distribution of cereals can be developed by comparing the critical parameters of their modern habitats with those of the past.

Wild barley, the most widespread of the Near Eastern cereal grasses, also evinces the widest environmental parameters. It grows best on well drained, deep loam, calcareous soils of high nitrogen content (Renfrew, 1973:80−81). Wild barley does not tolerate extreme cold and is confined to elevations below

TABLE 2.1
Correlation of annual mean temperatures with various elevations in the Levant. Pleistocene estimates are based upon a reduction of 8°C from modern correlations.

Altitude (m)	Modern Temperature (°C)	Pleistocene Temperature (°C)
0	21.5	13.5
131	21.0	13.0
207	20.5	12.5
283	20.0	12.0
359	19.5	11.5
435	19.0	11.0
511	18.5	10.5
587	18.0	10.0
663	17.5	9.5
740	17.0	9.0
815	16.5	8.5
892	16.0	8.0
967	15.5	7.5
1043	15.0	7.0
1119	14.5	6.5
1195	14.0	6.0
1271	13.5	5.5
1347	13.0	5.0
1423	12.5	4.5
1500	12.0	4.0
1576	11.5	3.5

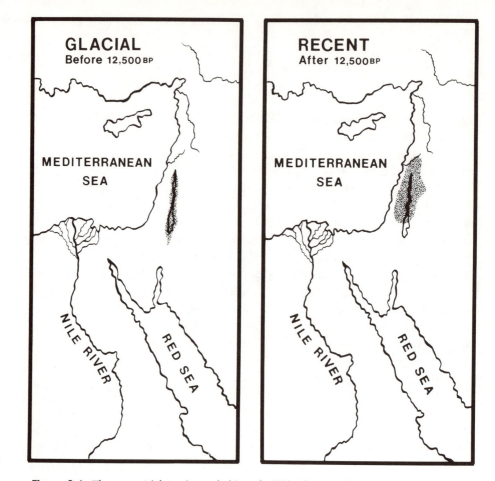

Figure 2.1. *The recent (right) primary habitat of wild barley* (Hordeum spontaneum) *within the Levant (after Harlan and Zohary, 1966) compared to a reconstructed (left) habitat for late Last Glacial times.*

1,500m where the ripening season is relatively long and cool (Renfrew, 1973: 80–81; Zohary, 1969:53–55). Although wild barley is the most arid-tolerant of the cereals, often penetrating warm steppe and desert settings, it thrives under conditions of moderate rainfall, not exceeding 890mm (Renfrew, 1973:80–81).

Wild emmer wheat grows in abundance on well-drained clay loam, calcareous soils and thus shows a particular preference for basaltic and limestone regions (Renfrew, 1973:66). In the Levant, wild emmer shows the most restricted primary habitat of the cereal grasses, for dense stands are restricted to the slopes and uplands of the Galilee and Golan Plateau overlooking the Upper Jordan Valley. Although the best areas for emmer are at elevations under 900m with relatively high mean winter temperatures, elevations as high as 1,600m on the east face of Mount Hermon support a slender late-maturing variety (Zohary, 1969:49). Emmer wheat, less arid-tolerant than barley, thrives in areas receiving between 500 and 750mm of rainfall annually (Redman, 1978:123).

A correlation of elevations with isotherms for Israel (Orni and Efrat, 1966: 106) and with mean annual temperatures for other points in the Levant (Zohary, 1962; Bender, 1968) reveals a drop in mean annual temperature of 0.66°C for

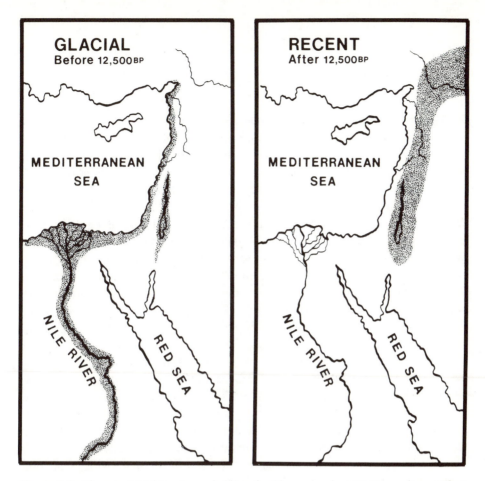

Figure 2.2. *The recent (right) primary habitat of wild emmer wheat* (Triticum dicoccoides) *within the Levant (after Harlan and Zohary, 1966) compared to a reconstructed (left) habitat for late Last Glacial times.*

about every 100m (Table 2.1). Therefore, the maximum elevation for wild barley and emmer wheat of 1,500m shows that these cereal grasses do not thrive in areas that experience a mean annual temperature of under 12°C. Although the critical lower temperature limits for cereal growth is actually minimum winter temperature, mean annual temperature should provide a conservative measure of the *minimum* temperatures tolerated by the cereals. To reconstruct the elevational limits for cereal growth during the Pleistocene, 8°C (representing the temperature depression during the Last Glacial) is subtracted from the modern mean annual temperatures. The temperature-elevation correlations, subsequent to the −8°C correction, indicate that the critical mean annual temperature of 12°C would have been encountered at only 283m above sea level during the last glacial episode. Although such a temperature depression would have excluded most of the contemporary geographic range of cereals as a habitat (Figures 2.1 and 2.2), it should be stressed that this is a conservative reconstruction. The real elevational depression, relative to the modern cereal habitat, was probably of an even greater magnitude. The 1,500m and 12°C threshold denotes the extreme range of cereals and not their optimum range, which lies between 0−900m and

21.5–16.0°C. Reduction in the annual temperature of 8°C therefore would have entirely excluded wild cereals from their optimum habitats, except in those sections of the Jordan Valley well below sea level. Also, the lower sea level during the Last Glacial would have acted to reduce the moderating effect of the Mediterranean on temperature extremes along the coastal Levant.

The glacial temperature depression and associated exclusion of wild cereal grasses from their modern habitats in the Levant would have had an important impact upon the density, vigor, and predictability of cereal resources. Not only would wild cereal grasses have been restricted to the predominantly sandy soils of the coastal Levant and Rift Valley, but their elevational amplitude would have been limited to between ca. 200m above modern sea level and fluctuating glacial sea levels. To complete the germination cycle, cereal grasses require soils with a capacity for relatively high moisture retention. The calcareous clay soils of the Mediterranean hill zone optimally satisfy this requirement, and cereals thrive within the zone. Given the porosity and low moisture retention of sandy soils, wild cereal grasses would not have done well in the sandy lowlands of the Levantine coast. Renfrew (1973:66,81) notes that both wheat and barley grow poorly on such sandy soils. Furthermore, the restricted elevational range of wild cereal grasses would have amplified the impact of annual or short-term fluctuations in precipitation and temperature on the overall cereal population. The wide elevational range over which cereals are presently distributed insures that some part of the population will experience near optimum conditions, despite marked short-term fluctuations in weather patterns.

Cereal grasses, no doubt, existed in low elevational refuges in the Levant and at lower latitudes in northeast Africa during the Last Glacial, but wild cereal stands would have achieved high densities only after they had invaded their modern habitats in the Levant. Before they could have become an important resource, stands of wild cereal grasses had to have been established in relatively high densities with reasonably predictable annual yields. With rising temperatures toward the end of the Pleistocene, wild emmer wheat and barley expanded out of low elevational refuges in the Jordan Valley and coastal lowlands into the Mediterranean hill zone. The climatic changes that prompted the elevational shifts of cereal grasses in the Levant would also have induced a northward latitudinal retreat of barley in northeast Africa.

The expansion of the Mediterranean woodlands into the uplands of the Levant had economic importance beyond merely exposing cereals to optimal edaphic and meterologic conditions. The enlarged elevational range accompanying the expansion resulted in the elevationally staggered maturation of cereals and nuts over a much longer period of time. In the Levant, at low elevation near sea level, cereals ripen as early as April, and at elevations between 1,400 and 1,500m they ripen as late as July. When acorns and nuts (almond, pistachio) are considered, the seasonally staggered maturation of plant foods can be extended through October and November. Therefore, with the colonization of the uplands by the Mediterranean woodlands, several easily procured nutritious and storable food sources became available over several months of the year.

This colonization also would have introduced a new arrangement to what Flannery (1969) has called a vertical economy. That is, from a single site setting groups could have exploited several closely packed elevational belts that would have come into productivity over a period encompassing several months. The elevationally staggered maturation interval becomes important when one considers that these plant foods ripen quickly and must be harvested over relatively brief periods of time—perhaps only a few days to a couple of weeks. A timely harvest is necessary to avoid loss (in the case of cereals) or competition from other predators (in the cases of cereals and nuts). Not only did the harvest represent a labor-intensive activity, but the processing and storage of the plant foods also necessitated high demands on labor. With the exploitation of wide range of elevations, however, the harvest period was extended over several months, thereby enabling groups to tap those resources efficiently as they became available and thus not overtax their labor forces.

Ironically, the intensive exploitation of cereals and nuts both allowed for and demanded sedentism. On the basis of his classic experiment of harvesting wild wheat in Turkey, Harlan (1967) estimated that a family could have collected over a ton of wheat within a three-week period. Such a resource was undoubtedly attractive, but its effective, intensive exploitation required the establishment of long-term encampments devoted to processing and storage. While the elevationally zoned resources could have been easily collected and transported to a nearby camp, the resources required careful monitoring in order to determine the time for harvest. They were also likely to have been periodically examined for signs that other predators, ranging from herbivores to insects, were jeopardizing the harvest. Therefore, hamlets with year-round occupants are likely to have developed as a result of: (1) the extended period in which a single locus could be used to exploit the resources; (2) the bulk, necessary processing and storage requirements of these foodstuffs; and (3) the importance of monitoring the food sources during much of their growth cycles.

EVIDENCE FOR CEREAL EXPANSION

The proposal that cereal grasses invaded their modern habitats only at the end of the Pleistocene is supported by direct and indirect evidence of cereals appearing in the uplands of the Levant only after around 12,500 years ago.

Palynological studies in the Levant confirm the presence of cereal grasses throughout the late Pleistocene. But prior to about 12,500 years ago, cereals appear to have been restricted to elevations near or below sea level. Pollen of cereal grasses has been recorded in last glacial and even interglacial (Batroum) deposits of archaeological sites, but all these sediments are near sea level along the Lebanese coast. A core (studied by M. Tsukada) from the former Lake Hula, located near sea level in the northern Jordan Valley, has yielded pollen that indicates the presence of cereal grasses as early as 29,000 years ago (Bottema and Van Zeist, 1981). Cereal type pollen has been identified from Late Glacial pond deposits also located near sea level along the Nile in Upper Egypt (Wendorf and Schild, 1976:73–74). In addition to the pollen evidence, the physical remains of carbonized cereals have been recovered from layers dated to between 15,000 and 18,000 B.P. at the coastal site of Nahal Oren (Noy, et al., 1973). Once again the deposit is situated within a few meters of sea level.

Thus palynological studies of sediments dated prior to 12,500 years ago and found near or below sea level show the presence of cereals. What of contemporary sediments at high elevations? The series of diagrams developed for several Late Pleistocene sites in the highland Negev (i.e., elevations from 500–1,000m) shows no evidence of cereal pollen until after 12,500 years ago (Horowitz, 1976, 1977, 1979). Similarly, a series of diagrams obtained from Middle, Upper, and Epipaleolithic sites on the southern edge of the Jordanian Plateau (elevations from 800–1300m) shows minor percentages of cereal pollen in Upper Paleolithic sediments, but a marked increase is noted about 12,500 years ago in the Early Natufian (Henry, et al., 1985).

Although outside the Levant, Leroi-Gourhan's (1969) palynological investigation of Shanidar Cave (elevation 850m) in Iraq and Van Zeist's (1967) study of Last Glacial sediments of Lake Zeribar at 1300m in the Zagros Mountains of Iran show similar patterns. Both studies show that cereal pollen was absent or appeared in low frequencies until about 10,000 years ago, when it increased dramatically.

Another line of evidence in support of the proposed cereal expansion is the distribution of material culture elements that are associated with cereal processing. Sickle sheen and groundstone artifacts, like the direct evidence for the presence of cereals, were confined to low elevations until after 12,500 years ago, when they spread to higher reaches of the Levantine uplands (Table 2.2). In addition to this diachronic shift in distribution, these material culture items become more numerous and diverse after their appearance in the uplands. This probably reflects the increased economic importance of cereals once they had colonized the uplands.

The most abundant evidence of cereal processing prior to 12,500 years ago comes from a number of Late Paleolithic sites along the Nile in Upper Egypt. These sites have yielded various grinding stones and flint specimens with sheen (Wendorf, et al., 1979; Wendorf and Schild, 1976; Butzer and Hanson, 1968; Wendorf, 1968) and are well dated radiometrically to no later than 12,000 years ago (Wendorf and Schild, 1976:291).

In that the Nile is presently outside the range of the most arid-tolerant of the cereals (wild barley) because of inadequate moisture and excessively high summer temperatures, markedly lower temperatures are postulated for this interval during the Late Paleolithic (Wendorf et al., 1979). Such a proposal is consistent

TABLE 2.2
The elevational distribution of sites on the Nile and in the Levant that contain artifacts associated with cereal processing. Note that those sites dated after 12,500 B.P. are often higher and contain a more elaborate technology.

	Elevations	Artifacts[a]	Dates (B.P.)		
Late Last Glacial Sites (18,300–12,000)					
Levant					
Ein Gev	50	M, P, SS	15,700 ±	415	(GrN-5576)
Ein Aqev	390	HS	16,900 ±	250	(I-5494) to
			19,980 ±	1,200	(SMU-5)
Lagama North VIII	320	HS			
Mushabi XIV	390	M	12,900 ±	235	(QC-201) to
			13,900 ±	400	(RT-417)
Mushabi V	389	P	12,990 ±	110	(SMU-171)
Upper Egypt					
Tushka	140	HS, GS, SS	14,550 ±	490	(WSU-315)
Gebel Silsila 2B	97	HS, GS	13,560 ±	120	(WSU-Y1447)
			13,090 ±	120	(WSU-Y1395)
Series of Qadan, Affian, and Isnan sites near Isna	ca. 100	GS	12,000 to 12,608 years ago		
Wadi Kubbaniya Sites	ca. 100	GS, M, P, SS	17,000 to 18,300 years ago		
Terminal Pleistocene–Early Holocene (12,500–10,000)					
Levant					
Hayonim Cave & Terrace	250	M, GS, SS	11,920 ±	90	(SMU-231)
Ein Mallaha	72	M, P, HS, GS, SS	11,590 ±	540	(LY-1660)
			11,740 ±	590	(LY-1661)
			11,310 ±	830	(LY-1662)
Nahal Oren	55	M, HS, GS, SS	10,046 ±	318	(BM-763)
El Wad	100	M, P, GS, SS	11,920 ±	660	(UCLA)
			11,475 ±	600	(UCLA)
			9,795 ±	600	(UCLA)
Kebara	100	SS	11,150 ±	400	(UCLA)
Shukbah	250	M, SS			
Erq el Ahmar	650	M, P, GS, SS			
Rosh Zin	525	M, GS, SS			
Rosh Horesha	930	M, HS, SS	10,490 ±	430	(SMU-9)
			10,880 ±	280	(SMU-10)
Beidha	1,000	GS, SS			
Wadi Judayid	1,200	HS, SS	12,090 ±	800	(SMU-805)
			12,750 ± 1,000		(SMU-806)
			12,784 ±	659	(SMU-803)
Jericho	−200	M, SS	9,800 ±	240	(GL-72)
			9,850 ±	240	(GL-69)
			11,166 ±	107	(P-376)

[a]Grinding stone—GS, handstone—HS, mortar—M, pestle—P, sickle sheen—SS.

with local evidence from diatom flora (Wendorf and Schild, 1976: 72) and is also in agreement with the previously discussed temperature reconstructions of H. Wright (1977) and Emiliani (1972). It is noteworthy that the latest dated (ca. 12,000 years ago) evidence of the procurement of wild cereal grasses along the

Nile is coeval with the earliest evidence of the exploitation of cereal grasses in the uplands of the Levant. The rise in temperature at the end of the Pleistocene some 12,000–13,000 years ago appears to have synchronously induced the expansion of cereal grasses into their modern Levantine habitats while extirpating cereals from along the Nile.

Between 18,000 and 12,000 years ago, when utilization of cereal grasses along the Nile is clearly indicated, evidence of the exploitation of cereal grasses in the Levant is confined to elevations beneath 400m above sea level (Table 2.2). Only after the postulated temperature elevation of 12,000–13,000 years ago does an elaborate cereal processing technology, quite similar to that found in the Late Paleolithic sites of Upper Egypt, emerge in the Mediterranean hill zone of the Levant. At this time, a sophisticated technology associated with cereal procurement and processing coincided with the modern geographic distribution of wild cereal grasses, at elevations up to 1,200m above sea level.

The diachronic shift in the distribution of cereal grasses could be interpreted as a stimulant for the diffusion of a technology for intensive cereal exploitation, from northeast Africa to the hill zone of the Levant (Reed, 1977:548). An incipient technology for cereal processing, however, was apparently present at low elevations deeply within the Levant as early as 16,000–17,000 years ago. Furthermore, the widespread distribution of Early Natufian sites throughout the Mediterranean hill zone, from the coastal Galilee to the Jordanian Plateau, detracts from the diffusion model and more strongly supports a scenario of numerous indigenous, although initially unrelated, adjustments in the exploitation of a new, widespread resource.

EVIDENCE FOR SEDENTISM AND POPULATION GROWTH

Substantial evidence exists to support the proposed expansion of the Mediterranean woodlands and the attendant economic shift to the intensive exploitation of cereals and nuts. But what data support the emergence of sedentism and population growth?

Using their site catchment analysis, Vita-Finzi and Higgs (1970) concluded on theoretical grounds that the catchments surrounding Natufian hamlets could not have yielded sufficient resources to support year-round occupations. Their argument, however, excluded plant resources from consideration. Even if sedentism can be demonstrated, Hayden (1981) has recently questioned whether it would have inexorably led to population growth, a view commonly held by other scholars (Harris, 1977; Cohen, 1977; Harris, 1978). Although the linkage between sedentism and population growth can be debated theoretically, a number of lines of evidence unambiguously point to the longer duration of residence and a greater number of inhabitants in Natufian sites than in contemporary or ancestral simple foraging communities.

The permanence of Natufian communities is indicated by several lines of evidence. Architectural features (e.g., stone-walled dwellings, retaining walls, storage pits), cemeteries, thick cultural deposits, and very high artifact densities all suggest longterm occupations. Similarly, the high incidence of human commensals (e.g., house mice, house wrens) and faunal assemblages containing both warm and cold-season representatives imply year-round residence.

Architectural features are exceedingly rare in pre-Natufian contexts and are unknown from Epipaleolithic sites contemporary with the Natufian. Similarly, only two sites outside the Natufian have yielded burials. In addition to being normally much thicker, the cultural deposits of Natufian sites characteristically display artifact densities that are some five to ten times greater than those from other Epipaleolithic deposits (Bar-Yosef, 1982). It could be argued that these differences in artifact density result from different rates of deposition rather than different rates of artifact discard. But, in that this pattern holds across a variety of depositional contexts (cave-terrace, alluvial, and aeolian deposits), it is unlikely that the higher artifact densities of Natufian deposits are expressions of slower rates of deposition.

Faunal remains recovered from Natufian sites also point to long-term, even year-round occupation. In the excavation of Hayonim Cave (Bar-Yosef and Tchernov, 1966), human commensals (animals that are attracted to human settlements such as *Mus musculus* and *Passer domesticus*) were noted to have increased markedly within the Natufian horizons. Also, the excavations of Hayomin Terrace (Henry and Davis, 1974) and Ein Mallaha (Perrot, 1966) yielded the remains of various reptiles and amphibians that are active only in the warm season, along with migratory birds that are found in the area only during the winter months.

Regarding population trends, two general observations can be advanced. First, the relative numbers and the sizes of Natufian sites denote an increase in population density at both community and regional scales. Secondly, the temporal-spatial distribution of Natufian settlements reflects an expansion of the population from the core to the edge of the Mediterranean habitat.

A number of problems prohibit a precise determination of community and regional population levels (Hassan, 1981:90–93), but an obvious rise in population can be defined with the emergence of the Natufian. Natufian camps were large, averaging over 1,000m². The camps of their simple foraging predecessors (Geometric Kebaran) were considerably smaller, averaging about 200m² in area, with the largest extending over only 600m² (Henry, 1973a, 1985; Bar-Yosef, 1981a). Hassan (1981:93) estimates that Geometric Kebaran settlements averaged about 22 persons while the Natufian hamlets would have had over 150 residents. Even with the greater Natufian community population levels there was no appreciable change in overall number of sites between Geometric Kebaran and Natufian times within the core Mediterranean zone. In that the temporal durations of the two complexes are roughly equivalent (i.e., ca. 2,000 years), the site densities recorded for the two complexes are likely to mirror the real occupational intensities of the two populations. Regional population density is therefore likely to have increased concurrently with the rise in Natufian community population levels.

An expansion of Natufian settlements into a less productive habitat, represented by the marginal Mediterranean environment, was probably caused by the growth of population in the core Mediterranean zone. A coastal to inland expansion was proposed some years ago (Binford, 1968; Wright, 1971, 1978), but a much broader distribution in the Mediterranean core area is now indicated as a result of the discovery of a well dated Early Natufian site in southern Jordan (Henry, 1982). The colonization of the marginal Mediterranean environments, characterized by the transition from woodlands to steppe vegetation, is evidenced by the Late Natufian occupation of such areas as the Highland Negev of Israel, the Black Desert of northeastern Jordan, and along the Euphrates in northern Syria. Although dominated by steppe vegetation today, these areas rested on the very edge of the Mediterranean woodlands during Natufian times. After emerging about 12,500 years ago, the Natufian population of the Mediterranean core area had reached levels that demanded an expansion into these less productive areas by some 11,000 years ago. While Early and Late Natufian sites are found within the core zone, only Late Natufian settlements are known from these marginal areas (Henry, 1973a, 1983, 1985).

The Second Transition: Ideas and Evidence

The transition from complex foraging to food-production in the Levant was likely to have been prompted by the onset of drier conditions about 11,000 years ago. These conditions initiated a retreat of the Mediterranean woodlands at the expense of an expanding steppe-desert zone, thereby causing a marked reduction in the habitat and resources upon which the Natufian ecosystem depended. It should be underscored, however, that though this climatic change was of importance in the timing of the transition, it was not really a causal factor. The transition was caused by the inherent instability of the Natufian adaptive system. Had the climate not changed, it is likely that the Natufian ecosystem would have been upset by some other environmental perturbation or from population pressure alone.

The loss of mobility was the prime factor that rendered the Natufian adaptive system unstable. In contrast to mobile, simple foragers, complex foraging populations were more vulnerable to population pressure and perturbations in resources. And, the social responses to such threats were likely to have been counterproductive.

POPULATION PRESSURE

Natufian communities encountered two kinds of population problems. One was related to long-term growth, at community and regional scales, and the other was associated with the inability in the short term to reduce community size through fission. Once established, Natufian communities experienced rapid population growth. Hassan's (1981) population estimates indicate that Natufian hamlets reached levels some six to seven times greater than pre-Natufian settlements. What prompted this rapid growth and why did it threaten the Natufian ecosystem? In general, the Natufian population explosion can be attributed to the emergence of complex foraging accompanied by sedentism and the attendant loss of several fertility-dampening mechanisms related to mobility. Also, the shift from a high protein to a low protein-high carbohydrate diet may have further elevated fertility levels.

The low population densities of simple foragers have been attributed to various factors: long child-spacing intervals, delayed age at menarche, and low female fecundity. Recent studies suggest that these factors are directly linked to the lactation patterns, the diets, and the energetics of female foragers.

Simple foragers typically exhibit long child-spacing intervals of three to four years (Lee, 1972; Harris, 1978; Howell, 1979; Hassan, 1981). The exact physiological mechanism responsible for this long interval of postpartum infertility is debated (Bentley, 1985), but it is thought to be related to the extended period over which foraging mothers breastfeed. Among the !Kung, for example, infants suckle on demand and have constant access to their mother's breast normally to the age of three and occasionally to the age of five or six (Konner and Worthman, 1980; Lee, 1979:330). Several studies have defined a strong correlation between the length of the lactational period and the length of post-partum amenorrhea (Billewicz, 1979; Van Ginneken, 1974; Jelliffee and Jelliffee, 1974; Knodel, 1977). This correlation appears to be tied to the nursing stimulus, which triggers the secretion of the pituitary hormone prolactin that in turn suppresses ovulation (Mosley, 1977; Lee, 1979:328). As Lee (1979: 329) points out, the frequent stimulation of the breast by a carried child may provide an effective birth control device "rather like carrying your contraceptive on your hip."

The adaptive significance of such a mechanism is obvious in the context of mobile foraging. A single child, who must be carried for some 3 to 4 years, creates a heavy burden for the mother; a second or third child within this interval would create an unmanageable problem for her and also jeopardize her health. As noted by Lee (1979), the relationship between nomadism and long birth spacing has been recognized for some time (Carr-Saunders, 1922), but infanticide has been viewed as the mechanism for achieving the long intervals between children (L. R. Binford quoted in Pfeiffer, 1969; Birdsell, 1968).

Another factor acting to reduce population among foragers is delayed menarche. !Kung women reach menarche between 15 and 17 years (Lee, 1979:312), an age falling near the upper limit of the worldwide range of 12−17 years (Tanner, 1964:326). Frisch's "critical fatness" hypothesis (Frisch, 1974, 1975; Frisch and Revelle, 1970) has been advanced as an explanation for the late age of puberty (Howell, 1979). Frisch's hypothesis argues that critical levels of fatness (17% of total body weight) trigger the onset of menarche in adolescent girls, while a higher fat to body weight ratio (22%) is necessary for women to remain fertile. The theory has been widely criticized (Billewicz, et al., 1976; Trussell, 1978), and when applied directly to Howell's (1979) data for the !Kung it proved inconclusive (Lee, 1979:327; Bentley, 1985). Nevertheless, most specialists in human fertility agree that direct correlations exist between levels of fatness and fertility.

Bentley (1985) has recently argued that delayed menarche, as well as other factors that may lower !Kung female fecundity, is tied to their high energy expenditures. She cites numerous studies in sports medicine that show strong correlations between "endurance exercise" and gonadal disorders (Bentley, 1985:80). These include late or delayed menarche, dysmenorrhea, and secondary amenorrhea. Other dysfunctions include low gonadotropin levels, abnormal estrogen and progesterone levels, and a short luteal phase. Along these same lines, fertility experts have recently noted a connection between the "exercise ethic" of "Yuppies" and problems with female fecundity.

Though heavy exercise may act indirectly to reduce fecundity by lowering fat to body weight ratios, recent research has identified the direct and independent endocrine effects of exercise on reproductive function and menstrual cyclicity (McArthur, et al., 1980; Prior, et al., 1982; Shangold, et al., 1979; Warren, 1980). A study by Warren (1980), for example, found that delayed menarche and secondary amenorrhea were strongly associated with the degree of activity among young ballet dancers. While the dancers reached menarche much later than a non-dancing control group (15.4 ± 0.9 years compared to 12.5 ± 1.2 years), mean fat to body weight ratios reached an "acceptable" range 4–8 months prior to this event.

Other physiological fertility-dampening mechanisms that are apparently triggered by exercise have been recorded in clinical studies of female runners (Shangold, et al., 1979; Prior, et al., 1982). Both studies indicated shortening of the luteal phase (i.e., the period in which a fertilized egg can be supported). Prior, et al., (1982) noted decreased luteal phases evolving to anovulatory cycles, Shangold, et al. (1979) found a significant inverse correlation between the length of the luteal phase and the weekly distance run. The luteal phase lasted for 13–14 days when fewer than 8km/wk were run and was 9 days or less when 21km/wk were run.

The endurance exercises recorded for these female atheletes parallel the energy expenditures of contemporary female foragers as shown in Bentley's (1985) comparisons. In addition to traveling great distances (2,400km annually; 46km a week) !Kung women are burdened by equipment, gathered material, and most notably children. During camp moves !Kung women will carry 5–10kg of possessions and on the return leg of a day's foraging trip a woman will have gathered 7–15kg of plant food (Lee, 1979). Lee (1979:312) also has estimated that a !Kung mother will have carried her child some 7,800 km during its first 4 years of life. Translated to carried weight, this burden will range from birth weight of 3.1kg to 15.0kg at the age of 4 years.

It would appear then that a number of interrelated factors associated with a mobile foraging strategy are likely to have provided natural controls on fertility and perhaps explain the low population densities of the Paleolithic (Table 2.3). In mobile foraging societies, women are likely to have experienced both long intervals of breastfeeding by carried children as well as the high energy drain associated with subsistence activities and periodic camp moves. Additionally, their diets, being relatively rich in proteins, would have contributed to maintaining low fat levels, thus further dampening fecundity.

In the context of complex foraging, female mobility would have declined, resulting in shorter intervals of lactation and lower energy drains. As we shall see, in the Natufian this transition was also accompanied by a shift toward greater consumption of cereals resulting in a higher carbohydrate, lower protein diet. In addition to contributing to higher fat to body weight ratios, this dietary change would also have furnished soft foods (porridge or gruel) that are easily digested by infants. Availability of such food is likely to have lessened the dependency of sucklings and to have indirectly increased female fecundity. Lee (1979:330) has observed a similar phenomenon among settled !Kung who recently gained access to cereals and experienced a marked rise in fertility.

The physiology of simple foragers must have undergone several million years of selection for mechanisms that assisted in balancing population and resources. In that simple foragers typically responded to scarcity through higher levels of mobility, the adaptive advantage of gradational fertility controls that were adjusted by increasing degrees of mobility is obvious. The inverse linkage between

TABLE 2.3
A comparison of mobile and sedentary foraging strategies in regard to various factors that influence female fecundity. Note that "energy drain" and "diet" are both likely to affect the "fat:body weight ratio."

	Mobile Foraging	Sedentary Foraging
Lactation	Longer, more intense	Shorter, less intense
Fat:body wt. ratio	Lower	Higher
Energy drain	High	Low
Diet	High protein– low carbohydrate	Low protein– high carbohydrate

TABLE 2.5
**Frequency of enamel hypoplasia for Natufian skeletal populations. The popula-
tions are ordered chronologically based on seriation schemes presented by
Henry (1973) and Bar-Yosef and Valla (1981). The hypoplasia frequencies were
published by Smith, et al. (1985).**

Site/Phase	Frequency of Hypoplasia	Time
Nahal Oren/Late	61	Late
Ein Mallaha/Early	27	
Kebara/Early	23	
El Wad/Late & Early	15	
Hayonim/Early	10	Early

apparent high rate of female infanticide in Natufian communities as an expression of their attempt to control a dramatic growth in their population.

Another measure of the mounting stress on Natufian resources can be seen
in the frequency of enamel hypoplasia in Natufian skeletal populations. Hypoplasia frequencies provide a good indicator of the nutritional deficiencies experienced by infants and children (Goodman, et al., 1984). In a study of the dental
pathologies of Natufian skeletal populations from five sites, hypoplasia frequencies range from 10−61% (Smith, et al., 1985). More important, when these sites
are seriated, a clear pattern emerges in which the frequency of enamel hypoplasia can be seen to increase through time (Table 2.5). This pattern is also paralleled by a decline in stature seen between early (Ein Mallaha) and late (Nahal
Oren) Natufian populations (Smith, et al., 1985), but factors other than nutritional stress may have been responsible for the evolution in stature.

SENSITIVITY TO ENVIRONMENTAL CHANGES

If population pressure alone was not responsible for destabilizing the Natufian
ecosystem, the added burden of a decline in critical resources was too much for
the system to withstand. The two parts of this argument consist of evidence for
(1) a climatic change that significantly reduced the critical resources upon which
Natufian society depended and (2) the factors associated with complex foraging
that rendered the Natufian unstable as an adaptive system.

In that a detailed analysis of the climatic change and its environmental consequences is presented in Chapter 3, only a brief overview is presented here.
Following the worldwide elevation of temperature at the end of the Pleistocene,
some 12,500 years ago, the storm tracks that provided moisture to the eastern
Mediterranean basin began to migrate northward. From a position over the Sinai
Peninsula they steadily moved north, paralleling the retreat of high latitude gla-
ciers, until reaching their near-modern paths over southern Turkey and Syria
about 10,000 years ago. With this northward movement of the moisture-bearing
winter westerlies, the Levant experienced a general drying trend commencing

about 11,000 B.P. This was accompanied by a shrinkage of the Mediterranean woodlands to the northwest on a regional scale and their upslope migration locally.

A substantial body of paleoenvironmental data exists as a record of these events. But assumptions of synchronous, pan-Levantine climatic change have slowed the recognition of the temporal and geographic trends of this interval. For the Southern Levant, various paleoenvironmental data confirm the onset of drier conditions about 11,000 years ago, coincident with the transition from Early to Late Natufian times. Palynological diagrams from archaeological and natural deposits denote the declining moisture levels during the Late Natufian as evidenced by a general replacement of Mediterranean flora with steppe varieties (Henry, et al., 1981; Leroi-Gourhan, 1981; Bottema and Van Zeist, 1981). Faunal studies have yielded similar interpretations with woodland forms giving way to species adapted to more open habitats (Tchernov, 1981, Bar-Yosef and Tchernov, 1966; Henry, et al., 1981). Geomorphic data also point to an arid phase, sometimes in a dramatic fashion as evidenced by the 2–3 meters of drift sand that overlays Early Natufian horizons at sites in southern Jordan.

This climatic change and the associated shifts in the region's environments had important economic consequences. With the shrinkage of the Mediterranean woodlands, critical cereal and nut resources were greatly reduced. By the end of the Natufian, around 10,500 years ago, the Mediterranean woodlands covered roughly half the area they had enjoyed some 2,000 years earlier. This then induced economic stress of major proportions.

The magnitude of the loss of resources was great. But had the Natufians relied upon a simple foraging strategy they would have been able to adjust their economy and demography to meet the new distribution of resources. Several elements common to a complex foraging system were incapable of being reformed to meet the needs of a society confronted with such a loss of resources. Natufian communities were vulnerable to climatic-environmental perturbations because they were geographically fixed, they relied upon a few critical resources, and they had a social organization that functioned mainly to protect and elevate existing resources rather than open up access to new ones.

Natufians were obligated to live in sedentary communities in close proximity to the wild cereal and nut crops upon which they depended. These crops were bulky and they required processing before storage. They also had to be closely monitored during their maturation. These close ties between settlement and resources underline some of the major differences between complex and simple foraging patterns. Unlike simple foragers, who conservatively exploited large territories and enjoyed loosely defined boundaries, Natufians intensively exploited relatively small territories and maintained strong boundary definition. These differences are reflected in the "radiating" procurement-settlement pattern of the Natufians and the "circulating" pattern associated with Geometric Kebaran and Mushabian groups (Henry, 1975). Natufian hamlets were strategically placed so that they commanded access to a maximum number of critical resources (e.g., water, cereals and nuts, gazelle, flint, fuel) over an annual cycle at minimum distance. The resources within the immediate catchments of a hamlet were supplemented with resources from farther afield, which were obtained from specialized, nonresidential exploitation camps. In contrast, the circulating pattern of Geometric Kebaran and Mushabian groups was based upon mobility. When resources within a catchment were depleted to a level that demanded an expenditure of energy above a relatively low threshold, groups moved to establish new camps and catchments.

The archaeological manifestations of these contrasting settlement patterns can be seen in the sizes and locations of sites. Natufian sites vary greatly in size and content. Base camps or hamlets are large and normally contain architectural evidence, a diverse artifact inventory, and burials. Specialized exploitation camps are small, show a restricted range of artifacts, and rarely contain architecture or burials. Geometric Kebaran and Mushabian sites are much more homogeneous in site size and content. They range from about 100−600m² in area and yield roughly similar artifact inventories.

In regard to placement, Natufian hamlets were restricted to the Mediterranean environmental zone and they followed a specific pattern relative to the local setting. Hamlet sites are consistently found at the foot of slopes that divide hill and mountain regions from broad valleys or coastal plains. These topographic divides also form boundaries between the Mediterranean woodlands and open grassland. Hamlets established along this divide had access to the wild cereals and nuts of the uplands in addition to the gazelle herds occupying the open grassland. Futhermore, the hamlets were closely tied to the abundant water sources, represented by springs or rivers, that are concentrated along the edge of the hill and mountain zone. In contrast, Geometric Kebaran and Mushabian sites display a much wider environmental distribution, and local site settings vary greatly. Though found in the Mediterranean zone, settlement also extended into steppe and perhaps even desert zones. Local site settings vary from coastal lowland to mountain with no specific pattern emerging.

Natufians were able to exploit relatively small territories intensively from permanent, strategically placed hamlets. But the small sizes of their territories increased their vulnerability to severe shortfalls in resources. Unlike simple foragers with their larger territories and their access to neighboring catchments, Natufians were unable to level their shortfalls in resources through the exploitation of larger areas. The Natufian settlement-procurement system also relied upon the exploitation of a constellation of critical resources from a single locus. With shifts in the distribution of one or more of these resources, the entire Natufian settlement-procurement system was threatened. Simple foragers, on the other hand, were able to respond to such shifts by readjusting their scheduling and mobility patterns.

Natufians responded to a decline in their resources through other means, but these were inappropriate and unsuccessful for propping up an economy based upon foraging. The social organization that had evolved to accommodate complex foraging was poorly adapted to handle major episodes of resource stress. Social organization in Natufian hamlets principally functioned to intensify and delimit access to a few critical resources, thus both of these tendencies were increased as a response to resource shortages. Hunting and collecting were intensified. Control over resource lands was increased at regional, community, and probably even at household levels. In general, these strategies failed because they were ultimately incapable of elevating the ceiling on those wild resources upon which Natufians depended and even acted to lower this ceiling over time. But, it is interesting to examine the Natufian social organization at a more specific scale to see why it failed, and to look at the archaeological evidence that is used to support this reconstruction.

In contrast to simple foragers, Natufians apparently had a ranked society. Cemeteries are common to Natufian sites. Analysis of the burial patterns in and between the sites has identified a number of attributes commonly related to non-egalitarian societies. In utilizing Binford's (1971) ethnographic survey of mortuary practices, G. Wright (1978) draws upon the different group burials, the presence of grave furniture that cross-cuts sex lines, the recurrence of a specific symbolic artifact (e.g., dentalia shells) in a few burials, and the association of elaborate grave goods with children as evidence for inherited status and subgroup differentiation in Natufian communities. He goes on to propose that social differentiation in the Natufian resulted from a need for the redistribution of storable surpluses and for the maintenance of internal order in a relatively large community (G. Wright, 1978:218–219).

As in other non-egalitarian societies, ranking would have represented a social device that was designed to increase the economic security of Natufian communities. Status differentiation is often manifested in such societies through the development and acquisition of huge resource surpluses. Ranking, then, often provides a social incentive for intensification. It may also broaden the geographic scope of the resource base through trade or ritual exchange. Therefore, when confronted with a decline in resources, tendencies toward ranking in Natufian society were likely to have been heightened. A synchronic parallel to this proposition is seen in the indirect correlation between resource stability and the degree of ranking among complex foragers on the northwest coast of North America. Riches (1979:150) notes that from south to north the stability of resources declines and that this is accompanied by a shift from intra-group prestige to inter-group ranking. Inter-group ranking is more effective in redistributing resources between, rather than within, resource catchments and thus functions to alleviate local scarcity.

Ranking, however, did not reduce the scarcity that threatened Natufian society but exaggerated it instead. The intensified hunting and collection driven by heightened social differentiation would actually have accelerated the depletion of resources. And because the decline of these resources was widespread, a broadening of the exchange network failed as a long-term countermeasure. Intensified hunting and collection would also have accelerated the shift from a high protein to a low protein-high carbohydrate diet that, in turn, would have stimulated population growth, thus worsening a bad situation. Gazelle, wild cereals, and nuts (the foods critical to the Natufians) are associated with high reproductive rates and population densities, but they are not immune to over-exploitation. If these resources are ordered according to their susceptibility to over-exploitation, Natufians would have initially experienced a decline in gazelle followed by a decline in wild cereals and nuts. This trend toward an increasing portion of plant foods in their diet is reflected in the strontium-calcium ratios and dental attrition scores of Natufian skeletal populations. Other dental attributes point to an increasing consumption of sticky carbohydrates through time (Smith, et al., 1985). The irony here is that the social responses of the Natufians to scarcity exaggerated rather than alleviated their problem. The stress on resources was actually heightened through accelerating their depletion and fueling Natufian population growth.

Kinship and postmarital residence patterns may have represented another dimension of Natufian social organization that was related to resources and their control. Kinship among simple foragers is typically oriented bilaterally and lacks corporate descent groups. This pattern reinforces a highly flexible social organization that in turn maximizes the fluidity of group composition and access to neighboring resources (Lee and DeVore, 1978:7—9). Complex foragers, on the other hand, tend to have less flexible social structures characterized by corporate unilineal descent. In criticizing the universal application of a corporate unilineal model to foraging societies, Lee and DeVore (1978:8) point out that such a corporation requires two conditions: some resource around which to incorporate and some means of defining who has rights over the resources. Given the critical importance of certain resource (particularly those providing storable surpluses) to complex foraging societies, it is not surprising that corporate unilineal descent has developed as a mechanism for defining and transmitting ownership. Resource lands are normally inherited by individuals and nested into larger geographic scales that are viewed as being owned by the community. Examples of such a pattern are found among Northwest coast complex foragers, where ownership was exercised over fishing sites, shellfish beds, berrying grounds, and hunting areas (Riches, 1979:149); among the Ainu, where fishing and hunting grounds were owned by local and river groups (Watanabe, 1972); and among the Owens Valley Paiute, where seed plots were held matrilineally (Steward, 1938:57).

Osteological evidence from Natufian skeletal populations is indirectly indicative of community endogamy, a practice strongly associated with matrilocal residence and matriliny (Murdock, 1967). Analysis of the burials recovered from Hayonim Cave revealed that third molar agenesis was present in 47% of the sample (Smith, 1973). Congenital absence of the third molar is a genetically determined trait that is inherited as a Mendelian recessive characteristic. In that it occurs at relatively low frequencies (0–20%) for other populations, significant inbreeding or endogamy is indicated for the Hayonim community. The persistence of abnormally high frequencies of third molar agenesis throughout the five phases of Natufian occupation suggest a duration of the practice on the order of 1,000 years. The continued evidence for endogamy over as many as 50 generations indicates that the practice was a habitual part of the social fabric of the community and not a brief response to a sporadic demographic flux. Furthermore, the geographic scale of endogamy was apparently limited to the community level, for third molar agenesis is found at normal frequencies at other Natufian sites.

Although not conclusive, a cross-cultural comparison of post marital residence patterns shows a strong correlation between matrilocal residence, matriliny, and endogamy (Murdock, 1967). Perhaps the importance of gathered resources (i.e., wild cereals and nuts) to the Natufian subsistence base induced women to maintain and transmit the ownership of resource territories. But the linkage between the economic role of women, matrilocality and matriliny has been questioned. Lancaster (1976) has shown, for example, that for simple horticulturists in Africa there are no direct and simple economic links to matriliny. Others (Ember and Ember, 1971; Divale, 1974) have also questioned the economic basis for matrilocality and, instead, argue that variations in male activities (warfare, hunting, trade) account for differences in postmarital residence patterns and descent. Harris (1980:281), for example, proposes that when warfare, hunting, and trade shift from short-distance forays to protracted long-distance expeditions, matrilocality emerges as a "permanent core of mothers, daughters, and sisters" who oversee the economic and social needs of the family and community. Archaeological evidence suggests that the Natufians were engaged in long-distance expeditions associated with widespread trade and the acquisition of new territory on the edges of their homeland. Dentalium shells, found in Natufian sites and burials by the thousands, are indicative of extensive trade given the distances from their sources on either the Mediterranean or Red Sea coasts.

Whether maintained by the economic role of women or by activities that demanded the males' absence, Natufian matriliny would seem to be at odds with the previously presented evidence for female infanticide. How could selective female infanticide have been tolerated in a society in which women looked after the economic and social needs of the family and community? Divale and Harris (1976:532) furnish a clue to solving this riddle when they hypothesize that

any sudden shift from high-protein to low-protein, high-calorie diets, should produce a spurt of population growth, followed by an increase in female infanticide and the intensification of warfare.

As we have seen, the Natufians did experience a dietary shift toward the greater consumption of carbohydrates. And, when combined with the loss of natural fertility-dampening mechanisms controlled by mobility, the Natufian population grew dramatically. Divale and Harris (1976) argue that such population growth induces scarcity whereupon warfare for the defense and acquisition of resource lands follows. Selective female infanticide or neglect thus confers upon such societies a mechanism for both controlling population and rearing a maximum number of "fierce and aggressive warriors." Therefore, selective female infanticide and a matrilocal residence pattern were both indirectly related to shortages in resources.

System Instability and Adoption of New Strategies

When confronted with a dramatic rise in their numbers and a marked decline in resources, the Natufians responded with attempts to control population growth, intensify production, acquire new resource lands, and secure their existing territory. The specific counterstrategies that they adopted were not new, for they consisted merely of elevating aspects of an existing adaptive strategy that had been in place from the emergence of the Natufian. However, the combined effects of population growth and loss of resources produced the first major test of the system's capacity to adjust to changing conditions. In general, the system failed to make the necessary adjustments because although its elements reinforced the intensified exploitation of resources, the abundance of these resources could not be increased. Natufians as complex foragers, then, had come to rely upon an adaptive system that could not be successful in the context of foraging over the longterm.

Within 500 years after the onset of drier conditions, all but five of the 23 major Natufian hamlets had been abandoned. By this time the Natufian adaptive system had failed and the society was undergoing major changes. The Natufian population replaced complex foraging with divergent strategies: incipient horticulture in what remained of the Mediterranean woodlands and simple foraging in the expanded steppe zone. The evolutionary succession of the Natufian underscores the weakness of complex foraging and highlights the ephemeral, transitional nature of the system.

The basic framework of the Natufian lifestyle could be maintained only by developing a means of elevating the ceiling on resources through horticulture. Although it was an undeniably important economic step, the shift from complex foraging to incipient horticulture was more closely related to the social and demographic patterns that emerged with the Natufian than to any technical discovery associated with plant management. For 2,000 years the Natufians had monitored, harvested, stored, and processed wild cereals. They were likely to have possessed the requisite knowledge for cultivating cereals, but cultivation was not required.

It was only in those localities associated with a predictable water supply in the Mediterranean woodlands that Natufians would have been able to supplement the diminishing wild cereals with cultivated ones. As previously described, Natufian hamlets were located at points where a constellation of critical resources came together. With the onset of drier conditions, year-round water sources became less abundant and cereal stands retreated upslope to higher elevations. Many hamlets were abandoned because of the loss of one or both of these critical resources. Those communities that were located near permanent springs and commanded access to cereal stands at high elevation would still have experienced growing economic hardship as their cereal resources became increasingly remote and less predictable. The moist ground conditions surrounding such hamlets, with their disturbed terrain and rubbish areas, would have provided an ideal setting for wild cereals to volunteer themselves. With limited cultivation, then, these areas could have been expanded with domesticated cereal stands assuming an ever increasing role in augmenting the dwindling wild cereal resources. In support of these ideas, we find that the Natufian sites that reveal continued occupation into the early Neolithic period are all associated with a permanent water supply.

Initial cereal cultivation would have only supplemented an economy still based upon hunting and gathering. Horticulture would have elevated the overall resource ceiling and thus sustained sedentary lifeways, but it would have done nothing to relieve the stress on the high protein part of the diet. Like their Natufian predecessors, early Neolithic (PPNA) communities continued to rely upon gazelle herds as their principal meat source (Bar-Yosef, 1981a). Although we lack direct nutritional information for the early Neolithic interval, the addition of some cultivated cereals to the diet would hardly be expected to have alleviated the nutritional stress common to Late Natufian times. It was not until the late Neolithic (PPNB) period, some 1,000–1,500 years after the first evidence of cultivated cereals, that we see evidence for increasing meat consumption (Smith, et al., 1985) accompanied by a shift from gazelle to caprovine (sheep/goat) exploitation. Although direct morphological evidence pointing to domestication of caprovines does not appear until later, indirect evidence has prompted several scholars to argue for some level of herd management during the PPNB (Hecker, 1982).

For approximately 1,000 years following the collapse of the Natufian and the emergence of horticulture, the Mediterranean woodlands appear to have been sparsely inhabited. Famine, migration, or the concentration of the population may account for the marked decline in sites when compared to the Late Natufian. In the absence of evidence for a rise in site numbers in regions peripheral to the southern Levant at this time, a migration hypothesis lacks serious support. The PPNA town of Jericho with its moat, wall, and watchtower certainly points to a new scale of community size and adds weight to the idea that the region's population was concentrated rather than reduced. But Jericho is extraordinarily large when compared to the other PPNA sites that resemble Natufian hamlets in size. My guess is that there was a concentration of the population in settings where large tracts of arable land, suitable for hoe cultivation, adjoined year-round water sources. Overall, however, I suspect that the population density of the PPNA period was well below that of the Natufian. It was not until the PPNB period that we have evidence that the population density of the region swelled past that of the Natufian. This was probably induced by a combination of factors including horticulture based upon a wide range of cultigens, incipient domestication of caprovines, and a climatic amelioration that induced an expansion of the Mediterranean woodlands.

Discussion thus far has focused upon the evolution of the Natufians who inhabited the core of the Mediterranean woodlands. What evidence is available to trace the trajectory of the Natufians living on the very edge of the Mediterranean zone when it began to shrink? Most of our knowledge of this region has come about only in the last decade. We know that Natufian hamlets were occupied about 11,000 years ago in the Negev highlands (Henry, 1973a, 1976; Marks and Larson, 1977), on the edge of the Jordanian Plateau (Henry, et al., 1985) and in Black Desert of northeast Jordan (Betts, 1985). Though there is no clear record in the two Jordanian study areas of the replacement of the Natufian, an archaeological industry known as the Harifian succeeds the Late Natufian in the highland Negev and neighboring areas by about 10,500 years ago (Scott, 1977). What is important about the Harifian is that it can be directly tied to the Natufian through shared artifact inventories, yet it reveals a mobile pattern of settlement common to a simple foraging strategy. The Harifians apparently occupied large base camps during the winter wet season at high elevations, with a dispersal of the population into smaller, more mobile units during the dry season (Scott, 1977). It is interesting to note that, unlike the PPNA sites, none of the Harifian sites overlies a former Natufian hamlet. While the PPNA adaptive strategy followed that of the Natufian in being based upon intensified exploitation and strategic placement of settlements, Harifians returned to a simple foraging strategy in which mobility provided for their security.

Summary

In this chapter I have presented a model that accounts for the origin, growth, and collapse of the Natufian culture. The model essentially holds that the Natufian emerged from a simple foraging base because of the intensive exploitation of cereal and nut resources of the Mediterranean woodlands. This first transition was triggered by the worldwide elevation of temperature about 12,500 years ago and the attendant expansion of the Mediterranean woodlands into the uplands of the Levant. With the shift from mobility and conservation to sedentism and intensification, the Natufian adaptive strategy sacrificed a number of natural mechanisms that assisted in controlling population and responding to scarcity. Under the combined weight of a sharp rise in population and dwindling resources, the Natufians' complex foraging system collapsed, initiating a second transition. Along the margin of the shrinking Mediterranean woodlands, Natufians returned to a simple foraging pattern characterized by the Harifian. In the Mediterranean woodlands many sites were also abandoned, but in localities adjacent to year-round water and upland resources, continued settlement was sustained through incipient cultivation of cereals.

In presenting the model, I have furnished a sketch of the supportive evidence. In the following chapters, the evidence will be described in greater detail and its interpretation developed more fully. These chapters provide a comprehensive background for paleoenvironmental reconstructions (Chapter 3) and an overview of the cultural historic framework (Chapter 4) for the Levant at the end of the Ice Age. Additional chapters are devoted to describing each of the archaeological complexes, Geometric Kebaran, Mushabian, and Natufian (Chapters 5, 6, and 7), that together form the cultural mosaic of the region at this time. The final chapter presents an integrated picture of the evolution and interaction of different societies, following different adaptive strategies in an environmentally complex region of the world during an interval of dramatic climatic-environmental change.

3
Present and Past Environments

An understanding of those factors that create the contemporary environmental mosaic of the Levant is a key to defining the distribution of environmental zones in the past and identifying the critical resources associated with these zones. A knowledge of the seasonal and spatial distribution of these resources is basic to the reconstruction of prehistoric ecologies. Similarly, such knowledge is necessary to full appreciation of the impact that the changes in climate, and concomitant environmental adjustments, had on the distribution of critical resources.

The environmental diversity of the Levant is derived in part from its pivotal geographic position. In bridging Africa, Asia and Europe, the coastal corridor that skirts the eastern Mediterranean basin has at various times been colonized by biotic communities indigenous to each of the continents. The marked topographic and meteorologic variation of the region has also acted to create environmental refuges for plant and animal relics of earlier periods. As a consequence of these geographic, topographic, and meteorologic factors, the Levant presently enjoys a remarkably complex mosaic of environmental settings, particularly for such a small area dominated by a generally arid climate. Not only are forest, steppe, and desert zones found in relatively close proximity, but the distributions of these major biotic communities are easily altered by slight changes in precipitation and temperature patterns. The Levant would also appear to have been a region of considerable environmental diversity and sensitivity to changes in climate throughout the Pleistocene.

Physiographic Units

In general, the major physiographic features of the Levant tend to parallel the Mediterranean coastline and include: the coastal plain, the hill zone, the Rift

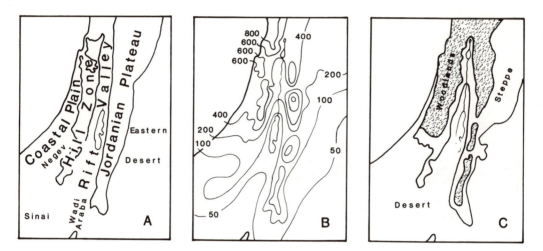

Figure 3.1. *Maps of the Levant showing the relationships between (A) physiography, (B) rainfall in mm, and (C) vegetation communities.*

Valley, and the Jordanian Plateau (Figure 3.1). Although the modern geomorphic settings and shoreline features often differ from those of the terminal Pleistocene, the overall topography of the region has changed little over the last 10,000 to 13,000 years.

COASTAL PLAIN

The Mediterranean coastal plain of the Levant is restricted to narrow beaches and coves in the north along the coasts of Syria, Lebanon, and northern Israel, but opens to a relatively wide plain south of the Carmel promontory. In this southern section of coastal Israel three continuous sandstone ridges, separated by only a few kilometers, run parallel to the coast. The ridges, locally termed "kurkur" ridges, represent consolidated dunes that formed adjacent to the coastline during the Pleistocene. The ridges have acted to retard the migration of shoreline dunes to more inland areas but also block the direct flow of streams that seek the coast from the Mediterranean hill zone. Swamps that form around the mouths of streams choked by the influx of Mediterranean sands are also checked in their inland expansion by the kurkur ridges.

The coastline of the Levant has been built through the deposition of local alluvial sediments in conjunction with vast quantities of coarse sand derived from the Ethiopian highlands and introduced from the Nile by the eastward flowing Mediterranean Longshore Current. These different sources of sand for the coastal deposits have resulted in significant differences in edaphic conditions for the coastal plain. In addition to the quantity of sand relative to other sediments decreasing on the Levant coast from south to north, the coast south of the

Carmel promontory is formed primarily from siliceous sands, while north of this point local sands rich in carbonates form the principal sediment.

Because of their higher carbonate content and clay fraction the coastal sediments of the north (which are derived from the chalks and limestones of the Mediterranean hill zone) are more suitable for supporting cereal grasses than are the sands that dominate the coast of the southern Levant. The topography of the northern Levant coast, however, is not conducive to the development of cereal grasses. North of the Carmel promontory, the coastal plain narrows to little more than the width of a narrow beach and is often interrupted by headlands and cliffs. Cereal stands along this section of the coast would be restricted primarily to the outlets of valleys. Edaphic conditions also differ between the eastern and western belts of the coastal plain. Whereas the western portion of the plain is dominated by red sands, the eastern section has clayey, carbonate rich sediments derived from the *terra rossa* soils that are swept down from the nearby Mediterranean hills.

MEDITERRANEAN HILLS

During the last major mountain-building phase, the Alpine Orogeny, the hills and mountains of the Levant began to form through folding along an S-shaped path stretching from Sinai to western Syria. Subsequent episodes of faulting, upwarping, and erosion, however, have provided the regional variation of the hill zone.

The folding reflected by the Levantine Fold Belt took place between early Mesozoic and early Cenozoic times. Subsequent faulting, often running perpendicular to this belt, began in the early Pliocene and did much to form the local topography. Lineated upwarping, running parallel to the Jordan Rift Valley, however, is viewed as perhaps the most significant factor in shaping the structure of the hill zone (Horowitz, 1979:54–55). The upwarping, apparently of Pleistocene age, affected all of the preceding tectonic structures and produced the relief that characterizes the hilly and mountainous spine of the Levant today.

A near-continuous hilly to mountainous ridge extends throughout the Levant from near Hatay in southeastern Turkey to the central Negev of Israel. From north to south this zone of hills and mountains includes the Ansaryie Mountains, the Lebanon Mountains, the Galilee Mountains, the Samarian Hills, the Judean Hills, and the Central Negev Highlands (Figure 3.1). Although less well defined, the line of hills continues into Sinai as evidenced by the jebels of Hillal, Yelek, and Maghara. Those sections of the hill zone south of the Galilee rarely exceed elevations of 1,000m. The highest reaches of the Ansaryie and Galilee Mountains attain just over 1,300m and 1,200m, respectively; the Lebanon Mountains reach elevations of over 3,000m.

The hill zone is composed principally of Cretaceous limestones and dolomites that are separated by less resistant layers of chalky marl. Although not extensive in their coverage, volcanic rocks primarily in the form of basalts are found in various parts of the hill zone, most notably in the Lower Galilee. The limestones and chalks are rich in flints and thus provided for an ubiquitous distribution of fine quality raw material for the production of stone tools.

The weathering of the limestones of the hill zone has resulted in the development of the distinctive red, clayey, *terra rossa* soil, while rendsina soils have formed on the chalks and "soft" limestone. Rendsina soils are richer in carbonates than *terra rossa* but contain a smaller clay fraction. The smaller clay fraction makes rendsina soils more friable and easily cultivated but also increases their susceptibility to erosion. Although much less extensive in coverage than *terra rossa* and rendsina soils, basalt soils are important in that they are particularly good for the growth of cereal grasses. Even though the parent material of *terra rossa* and basalt soils are quite different, the color, texture, and chemical composition of the two soils are remarkably similar.

LEVANTINE RIFT SYSTEM

The northernmost section of the great Syrian-East African Rift divides the hill zone of the Levant from the Arabian Plateau. The Jordan Rift Valley forms the southern part of this section and stretches from the Gulf of Aqaba to the Hula Basin. To the north, the Litani, Beqaa, and Ghab valleys follow the rift to its northern terminus at the base of Mount Amanous near Hatay, in southern Turkey.

Four successive, superimposed fault-systems have been noted by Horowitz (1974, 1979) in the Jordan Rift Valley. An early Pliocene or late Miocene episode of faulting that resulted in the opening of the Red Sea was followed by a "Preglacial to Glacial Pleistocene" phase that created the Gulf of Aqaba and the Jordan Rift Valley with the Dead Sea Basin as its center. This second phase of faulting, synchronous with the upwarping of the Levantine hill zone, separated the Jordan Rift Valley and Mediterranean drainage systems. The third Middle Pleistocene phase was of only local significance and confined to the central and northern Jordan Rift Valley. Although apparently of only moderate intensity, the fourth phase of faulting produced the present morphology of the Jordan Valley and took place only some 18,000 years ago (Neev and Emery, 1967; Horowitz, 1979). At this time the Dead Sea assumed its modern morphology, the late Pleistocene Lisan Lake disappeared, Lake Galilee was formed, and the Hula Valley was significantly deepened.

The Jordan Rift Valley encompasses the Wadi Araba, the Dead Sea, the Lower Jordan Valley between Lake Galilee and the Dead Sea, the Lake Galilee area, and the Upper Jordan Valley (i.e., the Jordan River north of Lake Galilee and the Hula Basin). The Dead Sea represents not only the lowest part of the Rift Valley but also the lowest terrestrial point on earth with an elevation of approximately 398m below sea level. South of the Dead Sea, the floor of the Wadi Araba only rises to a little over 200m above sea level before falling to the Gulf of Aqaba. To the north, the floor of the Rift Valley stays below sea level until reaching the Upper Jordan Valley, where elevations of approximately 200m above sea level are recorded in the Hula Basin.

Although the Jordan Rift Valley contains alluvium that has been recorded to depths of 7,000m, only that part of the rift north of the Dead Sea has sufficient water to utilize these rich alluvial soils for agriculture. Also, much of the central part of the Jordan Rift Valley is dominated by soils with high salinity, while the Wadi Araba consists principally of poor sandy soils (Zohary, 1962:8–15). Wild cereals, therefore, were likely to have been restricted to the northern reaches of the Rift Valley during glacial times.

In Lebanon and Syria, the Rift is occupied by the Litani, Beqaa, and Ghab valleys. These valleys divide the Lebanon and Anti-Lebanon (Jebel el Sharqi) ranges as well as the Ansaryie Mountains and the Zawayie Hills.

JORDANIAN PLATEAU

The area east of the Levantine Rift, the Transjordanian Block, began to be up-lifted during Oligocene-Miocene times. The most pronounced movement occurred along the edge of the Rift Valley, inducing the block that forms the Jordanian Plateau to tilt gently to the east. Most mountains formed along the edge of the plateau accentuate the elevational differences between the broken highlands bordering the rift and the lower, relatively flat expanses of the Syrian Desert to the east.

The Jordanian Plateau is stratigraphically similar to the Levantine Hill Zone, consisting mainly of Cretaceous limestones, dolomites, and sandstones. Older strata represented by Pre-Cambrian and Cambrian rocks are also exposed along the eastern edge of the Jordan Rift Valley because of the pronounced tilting of the Transjordanian Block. Extensive Pleistocene age basalt covers relatively large areas of northern Jordan and the Golan Plateau.

Although *terra rossa*, rendsina, and basalt soils are found in the highlands bordering the rift, rocky desert soils and sands characterize the plateau as it merges with the Syrian Desert.

Climate

In general, the Levant enjoys a Mediterranean climate characterized by marked seasonal differences in precipitation patterns and relatively moderate temperatures. Differences in topography, latitude, and proximity to the Mediterranean Sea, however, induce considerable local variations in climate in the region.

ATMOSPHERIC CIRCULATION

The Levant lies in a transition zone between the subtropical and cyclonic circulation belts. In the winter, the Levant is predominantly in the cyclonic belt; in the summer the system is displaced to higher latitudes and the region comes under the influence of the subtropical zone. This change from cyclonic to tropical systems is responsible for the marked seasonality in precipitation, with 70–80% of annual precipitation occurring between November and February.

In the subtropics the predominant air movement is subsident. Descending air compresses, heats up, and becomes drier, thus reducing the possibility of rain. Although in the summer the frequent development of a barometric low over the Persian Gulf draws moisture-bearing winds off the Mediterranean across the Levant, temperature gradients are insufficient to produce rain. Drops in nighttime temperature, however, often result in considerable quantities of dewfall.

With the onset of winter and the return of the cyclonic belt to the Levant, air off the Mediterranean is frequently subjected to cooling and gaining moisture. Air ascending over barometric lows, passing along warm and cold fronts, or along the Polar Front of converging air masses, is likely to gain moisture and produce rain or snow in the Levant. The paths of cyclones crossing the eastern Mediterranean and cold air masses coming from eastern Europe and the Balkans determine the length and intensity of winter precipitation in the region.

REGIONAL CLIMATIC PATTERNS

Precipitation generally increases from south to north and west to east in the Levant as a result of atmospheric circulation patterns and proximity to the Mediterranean Sea (Figure 3.1). In that the rain-bearing cyclonic belt returns to the Levant from north to south in the autumn and leaves the Levant from south to north in the spring, a cline of increasing precipitation occurs to the north, i.e., a "northern directional factor" (Orni and Efrat, 1966). The prevailing tracks of rain-bearing winter storms enhance the northern directional factor by most often travelling over the Syrian and Lebanese coasts. A "western directional factor" is created by the Mediterranean, which provides moisture that dissipates inland to the east.

In conjunction with the northern and western directional factors, topography plays an important role in determining regional rainfall patterns. Orographic precipitation is particularly significant in the southern Levant, where greater precipitation at higher elevations will tend to compensate for the overall greater aridity of the area. Not only do these higher elevations result in greater precipitation, but the attendant lower temperatures reduce transpiro-evaporation rates. As a consequence of greater precipitation and reduced transpiro-evaporation rates, mesic biotic communities indigenous to the northern Levant are able to survive at high elevations in the relatively arid southern Levant. A comparison of precipitation, temperature, and elevation contours of the southern Levant shows the strong correlation that exists between the three variables (Figure 3.1).

Environments

Although few members of the biotic community have gone unaffected by some form of human activity, the plant community remains the most accurate expression of the diversity and distribution of pristine environments in the Levant. Considering the small size and the generally arid character of the region, the Levant contains a remarkably high diversity of plant species. Zohary (1962:39) reports 718 genera and about 2,250 species of vascular plants for Palestine and 2,865 species for Syria and Lebanon. In comparing these figures to those reported by Good (1947) for the British Isles (1,750 species), Denmark (1,600 species), Germany (2,680 species), and Poland (2,000 species), it is clear that the Levant fails to show the low diversity of species that characterizes most arid regions. The diversity of species derives, in part, from the geographic position of the region and the corresponding overlap of phytogeographic zones indigenous to Africa, Asia, and Europe.

In fact, the three major phytogeographic zones of the Levant are representative of southern European (Mediterranean), western Asian (Irano-Turanian), and African (Saharo-Sindian) plant communities (Figure 3.1). Located in Israel, and probably representative of the Levant as a whole, these three zones account for over 97% of the plant species that show a definite environmental preference. The Mediterranean zone accounts for 57%, the Irano-Turanian zone 20%, and the Saharo-Sindian zone 20% of the species (Horowitz, 1979:129). As might be expected from their different continental associations, the three zones have quite different moisture and temperature requirements as reflected in their distributions.

MEDITERRANEAN ENVIRONMENT

The Mediterranean environment receives between 350mm and 1,200mm of precipitation annually and is generally confined to areas that experience temperatures with moderate seasonal extremes; i.e., short, mild, wet winters and long, warm, dry summers. Although generally characterized by a climax vegetation of evergreen forest and maquis, the Mediterranean environment consists of quite distinct upland and lowland zones.

Above elevations of 300m, the vegetation community is grouped around the evergreen Palestinian oak (*Quercus calliprinos*) with local associations including the Palestinian terebinth (*Pistacia palaestina*), juniper (*Juniperus phoenicea*), Jerusalem pine (*Pinus halepensis*), laurel (*Laurus nobilis*), Judas tree (*Cercis siliquastrum*), Syrian maple (*Acer syriacum*), and cedar (*Cedrus libani*).

At lower elevations, the Palestinian oak is replaced by the deciduous Tabor oak (*Quercus ithaburensis*) in well watered parts of the coastal plain that front the hill zone and in interior valleys. In drier areas with chalky bedrock, the Palestinian oaks give way to carob trees (*Ceratonia siliqua*) as the dominant climax vegetation. Atlantic terebinth (*Pistacia atlantica*) demarks the transition zone between the driest parts of the Mediterranean environment and the steppic Irano-Turanian environment.

IRANO-TURANIAN ENVIRONMENT

The Irano-Turanian zone receives from 200mm to about 350mm of precipitation annually, accompanied by low winter and high summer temperatures. Because precipitation occurs in the winter, heavy snowfall is common.

The plant community is composed mainly of low brush or dwarf bushes with large expanses of ground surface exposed between plants. Sagebrush (*Artemisia herbae-alba*) is the most characteristic plant of the zone. Where the Irano-Turanian steppe grades into the Mediterranean zone, ground cover of grasses and herbs becomes denser, with trees and shrubs also becoming more common. Atlantic terebinth (*Pistacia atlantica*), the principal tree of the Irano-Turanian zone, is generally confined to high elevations where it receives sufficient moisture. *Zizyphus lotus*, a large shrub with dense foliage, also demarks better watered parts of the Irano-Turanian environment, but, unlike the Atlantic terebinth, it is restricted to those elevations beneath 300m above sea level.

SAHARO-SINDIAN ENVIRONMENT

In receiving less than 200mm of rainfall annually, the Saharo-Sindian zone represents the driest of environments in the Levant and also covers the greatest area. For the most part, the zone falls above the 21°C isotherm and thus experiences extremely high transpiro-evaporation rates. Desert vegetation, consisting mainly of dwarf bushes, characterizes the plant community. Plants are sparsely distributed, with bare ground of rock or sand covering large expanses often hundreds of square meters in area. Wadi beds, however, normally support a much denser and more diverse plant assemblage that includes low shrubs and some desert-adapted trees.

The most common plants are low shrubs including bean caper (*Zygophyllum dumosi*) and *Anabasis articulata*. Areas of drift sand often support forests of Ghada trees, *Haloxylum persicum*, which are in fact only tall shrubs. Trees are restricted to thorny acacias (*Acacia albida*, *A. tortilis*, and *A. laeta*) that are most often found along the beds of wadis.

Paleoclimates and Environments

A reconstruction of past environments and climates requires that paleoenvironmental evidence be interpreted in the light of those factors that govern the modern zonal distribution of environments in the region. While the extent of forest, steppe, and desert zones in the Levant appears to have fluctuated greatly toward the end of the Pleistocene, the meteorologic parameters, edaphic requirements,

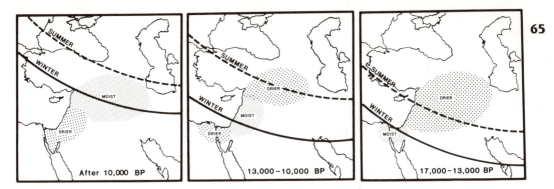

Figure 3.2. *A reconstruction of the latitudinal shifts in storm tracks and the related climatic changes in the Levant between 17,000 and 10,000 years ago.*

and biotic composition of these environments probably differed little from those of their contemporary counterparts. It is further assumed that, as with the modern environments, the distribution of paleoenvironments was determined by the interplay of latitudinal, marine, and elevational influences on climate.

ATMOSPHERIC CIRCULATION AND PALEOCLIMATES

Although recent paleoenvironmental syntheses for the Levant have noted significant climatic-environmental fluctuations for the terminal Pleistocene (Butzer, 1975; Leroi-Gourhan, 1978; Farrand, 1979; Bottema and Van Zeist, 1981; Goldberg, 1981; Henry, 1981, 1983; Bintliff, 1982), they have also confirmed separate climatic-environmental successions for the northern and southern Levant, an idea initially advanced by Butzer (1975:551; 1978:7–11). Given the importance of latitude in the modern relationship between atmospheric circulation and precipitation patterns, it is not surprising that latitudinal shifts in circulation belts would have had different climatic expressions in the northern and southern parts of the region. With the depression of circulation belts to lower latitudes during the late Last Glacial episode, moisture-bearing winter storms would have been displaced from the northern Levant to travel more often across the southern Levant.

Field evidence suggests that between 17,000 and 13,000 years ago the prevailing winter storm path was positioned in the extreme southern Levant at a latitude 30°–31°N (Figure 3.2a). With the worldwide elevation of temperature some 13,000 B.P., atmospheric circulation belts and the predominant paths of winter storms appear to have migrated to the north (Figure 3.2b). Continued elevation of surface temperature and the attendant retreat of continental glacial masses would have resulted in the winter storm tracks of the Levant assuming their modern positions (i.e., 35°–36°N) by about 11,000 years ago (Figure 3.2c). Not only is this model of climatic change for the Levant consistent with the differences observed in paleoenvironmental successions between the northern and southern parts of the region, but the model is also supported by the temporal and geographic clines in environments as displayed by field data from intervening areas.

A shift in atmospheric circulation belts to lower latitudes during the Pleistocene has long been a popular notion (Childe, 1929; Zeuner, 1959). The early ideas of a migration of storm tracks south of the Alps in Europe and across the Mediterranean basin, however, also assumed increased summer rainfall and the development of pluvial conditions for the circum-Mediterranean area. Although retaining the idea of a latitudinal shift in storm paths, H. E. Wright (1977) has suggested that during late Last Glacial times winter storm tracks would have moved over North Africa and thus denied the northern Mediterranean basin its characteristic winter rainfall. He goes on to argue that the Levant would have experienced similar aridity until the emergence of a Mediterranean climate at the end of the Pleistocene (H. E. Wright 1977:293). Though the field evidence, drawn mainly from pollen diagrams, supports the model advanced by Wright for the northern Mediterranean basin and the northern Levant, data from the southern Levant actually indicate greater available moisture during the late Last Glacial.

In a recent review of the paleoclimatic evidence for the region, Bintliff (1982) integrates several models to accommodate the evidence for terminal Pleistocene moist phases in the Levant. Relying heavily upon Lamb's (1975a, 1975b) ideas concerning the relationship between atmospheric circulation patterns and climate, Bintliff (1982:500) suggests that strong pressure gradients would have been produced at the Mediterranean latitude because of a combination of global warming and a North Atlantic chilled from glacial melt-water. He argues that these conditions would have created the humid phases of the southern Levant.

In an overview of terminal Pleistocene regional conditions of the Near East, Butzer (1975, 1978) noted four major zones falling roughly along a north to

Figure 3.3. *Comparison of pollen diagrams from localities in the Levant and the Northern Highlands. Note that the periods of maximum forest expansion, indicated by peaks in arboreal pollen, occur first in the southern Levant (Lake Hula and Hayonim Terrace) followed at progressively later times in areas to the north.*

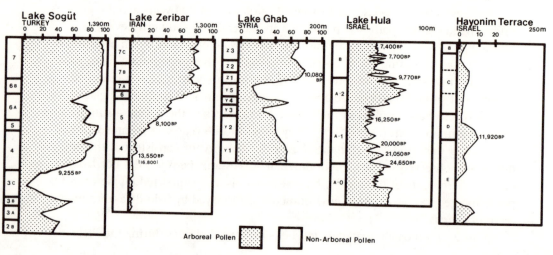

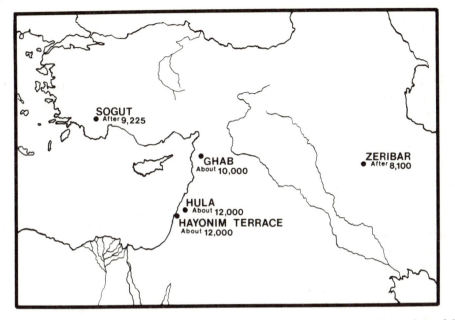

Figure 3.4. *Map showing the locations of the pollen diagrams and the approximate dates of the peaks in arboreal pollen. All dates are given in years* B.P.

south axis. The zones consist of the Northern Highlands, the northern Levant, the southern Levant, and the Desert Belt. In Butzer's reconstruction the southern Levant was associated with "cool and relatively moist conditions," but drier conditions are noted both to the north and south of this zone. The pattern of regional conditions in the Near East, as presented in Butzer's synthesis, is consistent with the proposed depression of storm tracks during the late Last Glacial, but the subsequent northward migration of storm paths in the Levant was not noted in his studies. Although the emergence of warmer and moister conditions has been recognized for the Northern Highlands at the beginning of the Holocene, the northward shift of a zone of moister conditions in the Levant has been obscured by the paucity of well dated paleoenvironmental evidence from the southern Levant.

With the completion of large-scale archaeological investigations accompanied by paleoenvironmental studies in the Negev (Marks, 1976, 1977a) and Sinai (Bar-Yosef and Phillips, 1977), in conjunction with the development of well dated pollen diagrams from northern Israel (Henry, et al., 1981; Tsukada diagram in Bottema and Van Zeist, 1981), a clearer picture of the temporal and spatial patterning of terminal Pleistocene climatic conditions has emerged for the region. A comparison of episodes of high arboreal pollen frequencies, which are indicated in several important diagrams from the Near East (Farrand, 1979:387) reveals a pattern in concert with the proposed northward migration of storm paths beginning about 13,000 years ago. A terminal Pleistocene arboreal peak in the Hayonim Terrace diagram is followed by a sequence of similar peaks in the Hula, Ghab, Sogüt, and Zeribar diagrams (Figure 3.3). The arboreal peaks, however, occurred at progressively later times to the north and northeast of the southern Levant (Figure 3.4). Whereas the peaks at Hayonim Terrace and Lake

Hula appeared about 12,000 B.P., the maximum forest expansion at Lake Ghab is noted about 2,000 years later. Similarly, forest expansion was delayed until the early and mid-Holocene at Lake Sogüt and Lake Zeribar.

A comprehensive review of palynologic, zoologic, and geomorphic evidence from terminal Pleistocene deposits in the Levant provides an even more detailed reconstruction of the changes in climatic conditions (Henry, 1983). By synthesizing paleoenvironmental evidence obtained from archaeological sites, as well as natural deposits, greater chronological precision and geographic coverage is provided in the review. While the temporal and spatial patterns for a wide array of field data point to a continued northward shift of the moisture bearing winter storm track beginning some 13,000 years ago, a reconstruction of the environmental consequences of these changes in atmospheric circulation must also take into account local marine and orographic influences on climate.

Even with the maximum depression of winter storm paths to the south over the Negev and Sinai during the late Last Glacial, that section of the Levant north of about 31°30' would not have experienced a dramatic reduction in winter precipitation by the moderating influences of marine and orographic rainfall. At this latitude (31°30'N), the hilly spine of the Levant emerges parallel to the coastline and is separated from the Mediterranean by less than 50km. With increased elevation and reduced distance to the sea, conditions for locally generated winter rains improve north of this point within the hill zone of the Levant. The principal environmental effects of a southern shift in storm tracks on the distribution of the Mediterranean environment in the Levant, therefore, would have been along the zone's eastern margins. In the rain shadows along the western edge of the rift and the western margin of the Syrian desert, the Mediterranean forests would have receded at the expense of an expanding Irano-Turanian steppe. West of the rift and in the higher elevations east of the rift changes in the biotic composition of the Mediterranean environment may have occurred, but these areas probably remained forested.

Local geography would also have played an important role in determining the environmental impact of the shifts in storm paths over the extreme southern Levant, i.e., south of approximately 31°N latitude. Although the routing of the storms over Sinai and the Negev would have increased winter rainfall in these areas, the configuration of the Sinai coastline and the absence of a massive hill zone fronting the coast would not have allowed these areas to benefit optimally from the shift in winter storm paths. Given the west to east circulation, the storms crossing Sinai and the Negev would not have collected large quantities of Mediterranean moisture but would have been relatively dry from passing over North Africa. Although the isolated mountains in Sinai, the Negev Highlands, and the Edom Plateau certainly would have enjoyed increased precipitation, the amount of orographic rainfall characteristic of the northern Levant could never have been realized in the south because of the absence of massive uplands along the coast. Furthermore, the orientation of the Sinai coastline along an east-west axis does not allow storms to move inland as does the roughly north-south oriented coastline of the Levant north of approximately 31°N latitude. Though a marginal Mediterranean environment may have developed along the coast in northern Sinai and the Negev, the higher and presumably better watered inland areas of Sinai and the Negev were apparently unable to support Mediterranean forests during late Last Glacial times (Schmida, 1977; Horowitz, 1976).

Local factors, therefore, are more likely to have enhanced the moisture production of winter storms in the northern than in the southern Levant as atmospheric circulation belts moved northward some 13,000 years ago. A marked increment in precipitation would be expected to have occurred when the prevailing storm paths reached approximately 31°N latitude because of the change in orientation of the Levant coastline and the emergence of a nearby hill zone parallel to the shore.

PALEOENVIRONMENTAL FIELD EVIDENCE

An evaluation of paleoenvironmental field evidence by broad latitudinal zones, approximating the subregions of the Near East defined by Butzer (1978), confirms a diachronic shift of storm paths to the north in the Levant during the terminal Pleistocene.

Northern Highlands In resting on the northern periphery of the Levant, the Northern Highlands began to experience the increased available moisture associated with the northward migrating winter storm track only at the beginning of the Holocene. The principal evidence of terminal Pleistocene environments for this region comes from pollen diagrams of deep sediment cores that have been taken from Lake Zeribar in northwestern Iran (Van Zeist, 1967; Van Zeist and Bottema, 1977) and Lake Sogüt of southwestern Turkey (Bottema and Van Zeist, 1981) (Figure 3.3).

Both of the diagrams indicate that the late Last Glacial period (i.e., from about 16,000 B.P. to 11,000 B.P.) of the Northern Highlands was relatively dry (Bottema and Van Zeist, 1981: 130). Following this interval, both diagrams reflect a more humid setting as expressed in the rise of arboreal pollen frequencies. It should be noted, however, that El-Moslimany (1986) suggests that the apparent forest expansion was triggered by a decline in snowfall and a shift to greater summer rainfall rather than a rise in overall precipitation. She bases her argument on the ecology of oak and pistachio trees, which are tolerant of aridity and low temperatures but sensitive to heavy snowfall.

The diagrams are characterized by steppe indicators, principally in the form of *Artemisia*, for their late Last Glacial intervals. An increase in *Quercus* and *Pistacia* pollen in zone 5 of the Zeribar diagram denotes the emergence of an oak-pistachio forest at about 10,500 B.P. (Van Zeist and Bottema, 1977); rises in

Juniperus, Quercus, and *Pinus* in zone 4 of the Sogüt diagram are dated to about 9,200 B.P. (Van Zeist, et al., 1975; Bottema and Van Zeist, 1981).

Palynological investigations of terminal Pleistocene archaeological sites in the Northern Highlands have furnished evidence in agreement with the Zeribar and Sogüt diagrams. Pollen studies are confined to the sites of Zarzi (Leroi-Gourhan, 1976), Shanidar Cave (Leroi-Gourhan, 1969), and Zawi Chemi Shanidar (Leroi-Gourhan, 1981b). The pollen evidence from Zarzi, dated to between 14,000 B.P. and 12,000 B.P. on typologic grounds, indicates a cold, dry setting. In contrast, the pollen diagrams developed from the Shanidar cave and Zawi Chemi Shanidar deposits (radiocarbon dated to ca. 10,600 B.P. and 10,000 B.P., respectively) reveal more humid conditions (Leroi-Gourhan, 1981:79).

Faunal remains recovered from the terminal Pleistocene archaeological deposits of Palegawra Cave (Turnbull and Reed, 1974), Ali Tappeh (McBurney, 1968); and Belt and Hotu Caves (Coon, 1957) provide for unusually well dated paleoenvironmental reconstructions that support the sequence on the basis of pollen evidence. The deposit of Palegawra Cave, located in the Zagros Mountains of Iraq, has yielded a stratigraphic series of radiocarbon dates that range from about 14,500 B.P. to 12,000 B.P. (Braidwood and Howe, 1960; Turnbull and Reed, 1974; Henry and Servello, 1974). The caves of Ali Tappeh, Belt, and Hotu are situated near the southern shore of the Caspian Sea and provide a younger stratigraphic sequence that spans late Last Glacial and early Holocene times; i.e., from about 12,400 B.P. to 10,000 B.P. (McBurney, 1968:395–396,408). The prominence of gazelle and paucity of deer remains in late Last Glacial deposits of these sites indicate a steppe setting for the Northern Highlands prior to about 11,000 years ago. Similarly, the higher frequencies of deer remains in the early Holocene layers (i.e., after 11,000 B.P.) of Ali Tappeh and Hotu Caves may be attributed to the expansion of forests associated with the onset of moister conditions and lower temperatures at the end of the Pleistocene.

Northern Levant A pollen diagram from sediment cores taken from the Ghab Valley in northwestern Syria furnishes the principal evidence for terminal Pleistocene environments of the northern Levant (Figure 3.3). In following the Levantine Rift on a north-south axis, the Ghab Valley holds the Orontes River and acts as a rough divide between forest covered mountains to the west and predominantly open steppe to the east. Given such an environmental boundary position, one would suspect that a vegetational history of the valley would accurately reflect past changes in available moisture.

A diagram of the upper section of the 11m–long Ghab log core indicates that during the terminal Pleistocene the area was covered by steppe until some 11,000 to 12,000 years ago, when there was a rapid expansion of forest (Niklewsky and Van Zeist, 1970; Bottema and Van Zeist, 1981:118). During an interval within the late Last Glacial, the diagram shows very low arboreal frequencies associated with high *Artemisia,* chenopodiaceae, and gramineae values.

Following this interval, there is a marked rise in arboreal pollen frequencies with a radiocarbon date of ca. 10,000 B.P. near the peak. Based upon these data, Bottema and Van Zeist (1981:118) argue that greater available moisture induced an expansion of forest in northwestern Syria some 11,000 to 12,000 years ago, with the most humid conditions occurring between 8,000 B.P. and 10,000 B.P.

The Ghab diagram, then, suggests that a remarkably similar climatic and vegetational history prevailed during the terminal Pleistocene for the Northern Highlands and the northern Levant. The only exception to the correspondence in climatic successions between the two regions may rest in the moist interval occurring somewhat earlier in the northern Levant.

Southern Levant The quantity and variety of paleoenvironmental evidence for the southern Levant (that part of the Levant falling between 31° and 34°N) greatly exceed those of similar data for the northern part of the region. Perhaps as an expression of this greater temporal precision and geographic coverage of terminal Pleistocene environmental data, the southern Levant reveals the greatest variability in paleoenvironmental sequences in the region. Although paleoenvironmental successions for the area lack synchroneity, they do support the proposed northward migration of storm tracks beginning about 13,000 years ago.

Pollen Evidence Palynological studies of the Lake Hula sediments furnish the best-dated sequence for the terminal Pleistocene of the southern Levant and thus provide a useful reference diagram. Horowitz (1971, 1979) and Tsukada have recently analyzed and interpreted separate series of sediment cores from Lake Hula with quite different results. Although Tsukada's study has yet to be published in detail, it is included in the regional synthesis of Bottema and Van Zeist (1981:113–16). The Tsukada diagram is much better dated than the diagram of the K-Jam core developed by Horowitz. Whereas the Horowitz diagram, drawn from a 120m core, furnished a single radiocarbon date, the Tsukada core of 54m yielded eleven radiocarbon determinations.

With respect to terminal Pleistocene environments, zones A-1, A-2, and B of the Tsukada diagram are important (Figure 3.3). Zone A-1 corresponds to a very dry interval represented by a forest-steppe environment between approximately 24,000 and an inferred date of 14,000 B.P. This zone shows declining arboreal pollen and a concomitant increase in steppe indicators, such as *Artemisia* and chenopodiaceae, prompting Bottema and Van Zeist (1981:116) to suggest that the climate of the Hula area "must have been drier than during any other period covered by this diagram."

In contrast to the Tsukada diagram, Horowitz (1971, 1979) interprets the 25–18m interval (or zone 6) of his K-Jam diagram as reflecting a cool and humid "Late Würm Pluvial" between 16,000 B.P. and 12,000 B.P. This interval is characterized by a marked rise in arboreal pollen, dominated by *Quercus*, with a concurrent decline in grasses (gramineae) and sedges (cyperaceae). The climatic interpretation is certainly consistent with the vegetational composition of this interval, but the chronology may be in error. Although this interval immediately follows a radiocarbon date of $18,000 \pm 195$ B.P., the interval is not bracketed by a younger date as is zone A-1 of the Tsukada diagram. The "Late Würm" arboreal peak in the Horowitz diagram most likely corresponds to the marked rise in arboreal pollen associated with zone A-2 of the Tsukada diagram. The moist interval identified in the Tsukada diagram is also expressed in other lines of evidence (e.g., faunal studies, geomorphic investigations) in addition to other pollen diagrams (Henry and Leroi-Gourhan, 1976; Leroi-Gourhan, 1978; Henry, et al., 1981; Henry, 1982), from numerous deposits that are dated between 12,500 and 11,000 years ago. The absence of a moist interval during this age in the reconstruction by Horowitz strongly suggests that he is incorrect in the chronologic assignment of the interval.

Additional confirmation of dry conditions at this time for the northern reaches of the southern Levant comes from the deposit of Hayonim Terrace located in the western Galilee of northern Israel (Figure 3.4). Layer E, containing a Geometric Kebaran assemblage, can be indirectly dated to between 13,000 and 14,000 years ago on the basis of 20 radiocarbon dates for the complex and a date of $11,920 \pm 90$ B.P. (SMU-231) for lower Layer D (Henry and Leroi-Gourhan, 1976). The near absence of arboreal pollen (restricted mostly to conifers) from the middle of Layer E prompted Leroi-Gourhan to suggest that this interval represented an exceptionally dry and cold episode of late Last Glacial times (Henry, et al., 1981:44).

During this period conditions for the southern part of the southern Levant appear to have been less severe, with available moisture actually exceeding modern levels. In the Lower Jordan Valley, alluvium that contains a Kebaran occupation (Fazael VII) and thus probably dates to between 14,000 and 17,000 B.P. has a pollen diagram characterized by a relatively high percentage (28%) of arboreal pollen (Alon, 1976; Goldberg, 1981; Goring-Morris, 1980). Although the area is dominated by steppe vegetation today and receives around 200–300mm of precipitation annually, climax Mediterranean forest is found within a few kilometers beginning at elevations receiving over 350mm to 400mm rainfall. Only a slight increment in annual precipitation over modern conditions, therefore, would have been sufficient to support a Mediterranean forest in the environs of Wadi Fazael. Further to the south, pollen data from the late Upper Paleolithic site of Ain Agev (Horowitz, 1976: 65; Marks, 1976:230), located in the Central Negev and dated to between 18,000 and 17,000 B.P., points to a vegetational community similar to the northwestern Negev of today; i.e., an open landscape dominated by herbs with isolated stands of trees. This reconstruction suggests slightly greater available moisture, perhaps on the order of 100mm to 200mm annually, for the Central Negev highlands.

Beginning about 13,000 years ago, an episode of greater available moisture and elevated temperature was associated with Early Natufian occurrences throughout the southern Levant (Henry and Leroi-Gourhan, 1976; Leroi-Gourhan, 1978; Henry, et al., 1981; Henry, 1981). This warm, moist episode is reflected in the marked rise of arboreal pollen in zone A-2 of the Tsukada diagram and also finds expression in dated diagrams from archaeological deposits at Hayonim Terrace Layer D (Henry, et al., 1981), Ein Mallaha IV (Leroi-Gourhan, 1978; Davis and Valla, 1978), and Wadi Judayid Layer C (Henry, 1982; Henry, et al., 1985). The diagram from Hayonim Terrace shows a significant rise in pollen of trees and aquatic plants in the upper part of Layer E with a corresponding peak in these pollen frequencies during the deposition of Layer D, dated to 11,920 ± 90 B.P. (SMU-231). The diagram from Ein Mallaha, in the Upper Jordan Valley, indicates a similar moist interval associated with a radiocarbon date of 11,590 ± 90 B.P. (LY-1660) for Layer IV. A preliminary palynological investigation of the Early Natufian site of Wadi Judayid, located on the southern edge of the Jordanian Plateau, also reveals a moist episode characterized by typical Mediterranean flora that includes oak, elm, olive, chaste tree, and cereal grasses. The diagram is associated with three radiocarbon dates that range from 12,000 to 12,750 B.P.

Pollen recovered from Late Natufian and Harifian deposits indicate that drier conditions began to replace the Early Natufian moist phase by about 11,000 B.P. and prevailed until after 10,000 B.P. (Henry, 1981, 1983). The onset of an arid episode during this period is also reflected in the upper part of subzone A-2 of the Tsukada diagram where arboreal pollen, composed mainly of oak, declines precipitously. Widespread palynological evidence from the Late Natufian deposits of Hayonim Terrace Layer B (Henry and Leroi-Gourhan, 1976; Henry, et al., 1981), Tel Mureybet (Leroi-Gourhan, 1978), Fazael IV (Bar-Yosef, et al., 1974), Rosh Zin (Horowitz, 1976), and Rosh Horesha (Horowitz, 1977, 1979) indicates considerably drier conditions for the region than those of Early Natufian times. Radiocarbon dates associated with the Late Natufian horizons at Tel Mureybet and Rosh Horesha also fix this interval to between ca. 11,000 and 10,000 years ago. Further evidence for this dry episode comes from the well dated Harifian site of Abu Salem, located in the Central Negev. The site, which furnishes a pollen assemblage resembling that of the nearby Late Natufian of Rosh Horesha (Horowitz, 1977:324−325), has been dated to ca. 10,150 B.P.

Faunal Studies Initial attempts to trace terminal Pleistocene climatic changes through faunal successions in the Levant stressed the proportionate representation of Persian fallow deer (*Dama mesopotamica*) and gazelle remains (Garrod and Bate, 1937; Bate, 1932). In that *Dama* are associated with wooded areas and a more moist biotic setting than steppe-desert-adapted gazelle, the relative frequencies of *Dama* and *Gazella* from archaeological contexts were presumed to be accurate indicators of past climatic settings. As reflected in the often cited *Dama-Gazella* curve of the Carmel Caves (Garrod and Bate, 1937), the shift to greater proportions of gazelle in the Natufian deposits of the site of El Wad suggested an onset of drier conditions. The climatic reconstruction based upon the *Dama-Gazella* curve, however, failed to find support in subsequent investigations that employed faunal data (Hooijer, 1961) and other lines of evidence for building paleoclimatic sequences (Henry, 1975). Given these data, the *Dama-Gazella* curve appears to have been incorrectly interpreted because of the lack of consideration given to the preferential hunting patterns of Natufian groups (Henry, 1975), i.e., a "cultural filter" (Reed, 1963).

Studies of microfaunal remains, clearly less sensitive to cultural bias than megafauna, recovered from the terminal Pleistocene deposits of Hayonim Cave (Bar-Yosef and Tchernov, 1966) and the adjoining terrace (Henry, et al., 1981), point to climatic oscillations that parallel those changes reflected in the recent pollen studies. The Early Natufian deposits of Hayonim Cave are associated with a rodent fauna that comprises 21% woodland forms and a mesic land snail (*Sphincterochila cariosa*) that is intolerant of habitats receiving less than 500mm of precipitation annually (Bar-Yosef and Tchernov, 1966). The Hayonim Terrace faunal assemblage also reveals diachronic trends, in the successions of squirrel and freshwater mollusc remains, that follow the pollen fluctuations. Squirrel (*Sciurus*) remains, indicative of forest cover, accounted for over one-half of the medium and small animals in the Early Natufian Layer D, but declined consistently through Layer C to account for only 28% of the category by Late Natufian times in Layer B (Henry and Leroi-Gourhan, 1976).

A recent study of shells from the site shows a similar shift as the frequencies of freshwater molluscs rise sharply in Layer D, peak in Layer C, and decline abruptly in Layer B (Reese, 1982). The changes in the frequencies of freshwater molluscs thus clearly parallel the trends for pollen of aquatic plants and presumably reflect shifts in the availability of standing water near the site (Henry, et al., 1981).

The presence of typical Mediterranean megafauna in Early Natufian deposits in modern steppe-desert environments also points to greater available moisture and a greater extension of the Mediterranean park-forests during Early Natufian times. Fauna characteristic of the well watered Mediterranean zone, such as cattle (*Bos*), pigs (*Sus*), red deer (*Cervus elephus*), and roe deer (*Capreolus capreolus*), have been recovered from the Early Natufian horizon (A-2) of Erq el Ahmar in the Judean Hills (Vaufrey, 1951). The remains of wild cattle and sheep (*Ovis orientalis*) have recently been identified at the Early Natufian site of Wadi Judayid on the southern slopes of the Jordanian Plateau (Henry, et al., 1985). And, even with the onset of drier conditions during Late Natufian times, the environment remained more lush than the modern setting as evidenced by *Dama* remains from the Late Natufian site of Rosh Zin in the Negev (Henry, 1976).

While changes in the composition of faunal assemblages generally have been viewed as indirect expressions of shifts in available moisture, a recent examination of the changes in the body size of terminal Pleistocene mammals provides a measure of changes in the region's surface temperature as well. Analysis of gazelle (*Gazella gazella*), fallow deer (*Dama dama*), wild cattle (*Bos primigenius*), wild goat (*Capra aegagrus*), wild boar (*Sus scrofa*), wolf (*Canis lupus*), and fox (*Vulpes vulpes*) remains from Pleistocene and Holocene archaeological deposits shows a clear diminution of body size synchronous with the Early Natufian (Davis, 1981). The reduction in body size of Late Pleistocene mammals is thought to have been associated with the temperature elevation of some 12,500 years ago in much the same manner as body size is related to temperature today by "Bergmann's rule" (Davis, 1981). Davis's study furthermore attempted to estimate the magnitude of the Pleistocene-Holocene temperature elevation for the region on the basis of modern size-temperature relationships among mammals. With tooth length used as a size variable for fox, wolf, and boar, near-identical results of approximately 15°C were obtained for the three species (Davis, 1981). Although a temperature elevation of this magnitude is considerably higher than other generally accepted estimates ranging from 4−8°C, it would tend to support the upper extreme of this range.

In summarizing the environmental implications of the faunal evidence recovered from Natufian sites, Tchernov (Bar-Yosef and Tchernov, 1966; Tchernov, 1981) describes the Mediterranean woodland as having been more widespread than today, but he also observes that there was a steady encroachment of the desert boundary throughout the Holocene. This expansion of the steppe-desert zone at the expense of Mediterranean woodland may well account for the remarkably high rates of extinction, immigration, and speciation recorded for rodent groups of the southern Levant following the terminal Pleistocene transition (Tchernov, 1981:90). Rates of faunal succession during this interval take on an even greater significance when it is noted that they markedly exceeded any other interval during the Pleistocene.

Geological Studies Recent geologic studies of archaeologic deposits and natural localities in the Negev (Goldberg, 1976) Sinai (Goldberg, 1977), southern Jordan (Henry, et al., 1981), and the lower Jordan Valley (Bar-Yosef, et al., 1974; Goldberg, 1981; Noy, et al., 1980) have produced a sequence of major geomorphic events of the terminal Pleistocene which can be compared to palynological and faunal successions. Goldberg (1981:64−65) has recently presented a climatic reconstruction based on a synthesis and interpretation of several stratigraphic sequences from the region. Goldberg's (1981:64) reconstruction presents a climatic sequence, for the period of 10,000−20,000 B.P., that consists of three intervals: (1) a "dry" interval, 20,000−16,000 B.P.; (2) a "moist" interval, 16,000−12,000 B.P.; and (3) a "drier" interval, 12,000−10,000 B.P. The reconstruction, however, is not in full accord with the climatic sequence based upon palynological and faunal evidence.

The first "dry" interval is in partial chronological agreement with Tsukada's subzone A-1 (ca. 24,000−14,000 B.P.), which is also associated with drier conditions. Goldberg suggests that climatic amelioration began by 16,000 B.P., but

Bottema and Van Zeist (1981) estimate that climatic improvement did not begin before 14,000 B.P. The lack of chronological agreement between the two sequences, however, supports the postulated northward migration of storm tracks within the southern Levant. Goldberg's geomorphic evidence for a moist interval that began ca. 16,000 B.P. is derived mainly from the southern part of the southern Levant (Sinai, Negev, Lower Jordan Valley); evidence for such a moist phase in the northern part of the region (Western Galilee, Upper Jordan Valley) does not appear until ca. 13,000 B.P.

Goldberg (1981:60) observes that a red, clayey paleosol is widespread over the Gebel Maghara area of northwestern Sinai and apparently developed for the most part prior to 14,000 years ago. A single Geometric Kebaran occupation (LN VII), recorded within the upper part of the paleosol, indicates that the final stages of pedogenesis occurred as late as 14,000 B.P. Assuming some 3,000–4,000 years for development of the paleosol (an estimate consistent with the thickness, clay content, and size of carbonate concretions), relatively moist conditions and a stable surface must have prevailed between ca. 17,000 and 14,000 years ago. Such a proposal is consistent with the deposition of a red clayey alluvium, containing Kebaran artifacts and high frequencies of arboreal pollen, in the Wadi Fazael of the Lower Jordan Valley.

Although the period from 14,000 to 13,000 B.P. is also included in Goldberg's "moist" interval, the geomorphic evidence for this conclusion is unclear. In the Gebel Maghara area, the red paleosol is overlaid by up to 2m of well sorted, crossbedded aeolian sands that contain numerous Geometric Kebaran and Mushabian occupations dated for the most part between 13,000 and 14,000 B.P. Although localized occurrences of quasi-lacustrine, interbedded sands, silts, and clays are reported within this interval, these deposits are possibly attributed to the localized damming of drainages by migrating dunes and not widespread lake development (Goldberg, 1981:60–61).

A contemporary Geometric Kebaran site (QB-8), in the Qadesh Barnea area of eastern Sinai, is associated with fluviatile sands that have been strongly bleached and gleyed, presumably as a result of high water table (Goldberg, 1981:59). Goldberg (1981:59) notes, however, "It is not yet clear whether the sands are essentially ones reworked from the Upper Paleolithic or instead represent a renewed period of dune accumulation." From the same period in the central Negev, the Mushabian site of D101B (Marks, 1977b:10) rests within a thin veneer of colluvial silts. The colluvium is viewed as denoting a slight change to moister conditions but of insufficient magnitude to promote a protective vegetative cover (Goldberg, 1981:58).

Additional geomorphic evidence for this interval comes from the Wadi Fazael, where Geometric Kebaran sites are associated with a yellow-red stoney colluvium (Bar-Yosef, et al., 1974; Goldberg, 1981). Although the colluvium is interpreted as representing a "generally wetter episode," this inference is based principally upon the high arboreal pollen frequency obtained from the deposit and not on geomorphic evidence. In fact, Goldberg (1981:62) questions the compatibility of the two lines of evidence in noting that the frequency (30%) of arboreal pollen is "somewhat higher than might be expected, considering the colluvial nature of the site." The integrity of the pollen data is also compromised by the reworked nature of the sediments and the potential contamination of the pollen samples (Goring-Morris, 1980:22, 89). In summary, one might suggest that the episode between 13,000 and 14,000 B.P. was dominated by a slightly moister climate than the modern regime yet was essentially dry in character.

Detailed geomorphic investigations for the period between 10,000 and 13,000 B.P., equivalent with the Natufian, are principally limited to the areas of Wadi Fazael and Wadi Salibiya (Bar-Yosef, et al., 1974; Noy, et al., 1980; Goldberg, 1981). Goldberg (1981) includes most of this period in his "drier" interval (12,000–10,000 B.P.) and associates both Early and Late Natufian occupations with these dry conditions.

Although his climatic reconstruction for the later part of this interval (11,000–10,000 B.P.; Late Natufian) is in agreement with pollen and faunal evidence from elsewhere in the region, the earlier part of the period between 13,000 and 11,000 B.P. is clearly not in accord with the quite moist conditions that are identified throughout the southern Levant. There are, in fact, no clear geomorphic or palynologic data that would indicate "drier" conditions for the Early Natufian occupations of the Wadi Fazael or Wadi Salibiya areas. The Early Natufian site of Fazael VI is contained within a "dark grey brown stoney colluvial clay" that cannot be related to the depositional history of the area (Goldberg, 1981:61).

The absence of pre-Natufian sites in the Wadi Salibiya area is viewed as denoting the maximum extent of Lake Lisan at ca. 13,500 B.P., and the subsequent shrinkage of the lake is attributed to increasing aridity (Goldberg, 1981:62–65). An alternative explanation for the retreat of the Lisan Lake rests in the worldwide elevation of surface temperature (ca. 6–8°C) that took place about 12,500 years ago. Even with an increment in precipitation during Early Natufian times, the increased evaporation associated with such a rise in temperature may well have resulted in a net reduction of the Lisan Lake.

This scenario may well explain the "problematical" tufas that underlie the Late Natufian site of Salibiya I (Goldberg, 1981:65). Stratigraphically, the tufas and associated "gray brown silty clays" are positioned between the eroded Lisan formation and overlying Natufian marsh clays (Noy, et al., 1980:70–71; Goldberg, 1981:62). If the Lisan Lake began its retreat during Early Natufian times, as suggested by Goldberg (1981), then the clays and tufas must be Early Natufian in age. The spring activity related to an elevated water table, resulting in the tufas, would then be in agreement with the Early Natufian moist interval even though the Lisan Lake was shrinking. The overlying Late Natufian marsh clays, rich in carbonates and gypsum, indicate drier conditions (Noy, et al., 1980:72) and mesh well with the regional patterns drawn from other lines of evidence (Henry, 1981).

Other stratigraphic sequences representing an Early Natufian moist phase replaced by drier conditions are found at Beidha (Kirkbride, 1966; Mortensen, 1970) and Wadi Judayid (Henry, 1982) in southern Jordan. At both sites, Early Natufian occupations are overlain by 2–3m of crossbedded drift sand (Mortensen, 1970:4 Henry, et al., 1985).

Summary

The position of the Levant as a land bridge between Europe, Africa, and Asia has created a diverse environmental mosaic. The configuration of the mosaic is sensitive and predictably related to certain subtle changes in temperature and precipitation patterns, and these same relationships are presumed to have prevailed throughout the Pleistocene.

Field evidence drawn from palynological, faunal, and geologic studies allows for the reconstruction of environments throughout the Levant during the terminal Pleistocene. Attempts at pan-Levantine climatic-environmental syntheses are made difficult, however, by the lack of synchroneity in events throughout the region. Although the climatic successions of these various areas are not synchronous, they do reveal a pattern that suggests a northward migration of moisture-bearing winter storm tracks beginning about 13,000 years ago, coincident with a major worldwide elevation of surface temperature.

These changes in climate and their environmental consequences acted to twice alter the distribution of cereal and nut resources at the end of the Ice Age. Beginning around 13,000 years ago, a worldwide elevation in temperature triggered an expansion of the Mediterranean woodlands into the Levantine uplands synchronous with the onset of moister conditions. And with the continued northward migration of these moisture bearing storm tracks, the Mediterranean zone progressively retreated from the southern Levant to the northwest and to higher elevations before an expanding steppe and desert.

4
Archaeological Complexes of the Levant: An Overview

Research over the last decade has revealed a complicated cultural history for the Levant at the end of the Ice Age. Most earlier studies attributed the variability in material culture of this period to chronological developments, but it is now clear that much of the archaeological diversity is a reflection of the differing adaptive strategies that were employed by contemporary groups. In order to understand the diverse ecologies of these terminal Pleistocene populations, archaeological data need to be correlated with specific socioeconomic units. Linkages between artifact assemblages, ethnic entities, and economic patterns need to be established. This process entails the definition of archaeological units, based upon the patterned variation in artifacts, and the subsequent integration of these units with economic, demographic, and environmental evidence. A successful completion of these tasks, however, first necessitates addressing several difficult and cumbersome questions regarding terminology and classification of artifacts.

The general reader not specializing in Near Eastern prehistory or lithic analysis may find the central section of this chapter to be of little interest and may want to move on to the conclusions.

Terminology and Systems of Classification

Regardless of theoretical approach, prehistorians by necessity organize their evidence according to material culture units, temporal-spatial units, and ultimately social and economic units. Cultural historians as well as processualists either formally or informally structure their evidence along these lines in order to describe or explain human behavior of the past. Although the synthesis and integration of these lines of evidence is prerequisite to constructing cultural histories and identifying cultural processes, the initial development of independent classificatory systems for each of these lines of evidence is needed to avoid circular reasoning and terminological ambiguities. Although an initial informal system of classification and attendant terminology has emerged for the material culture and the temporal-spatial phenomena of the terminal Pleistocene Levant, a corresponding classification of the related social and economic phenomena is lacking. Such terms as "industry," "complex," "culture," "population," "groups," "people," and "economy" are often used indiscriminately with no real attempt to distinguish between material culture and socioeconomic classifications.

In an effort to introduce a classification of social phenomena in this study, I have adopted the classificatory hierarchy developed by Clarke (1968), but with modification. Clarke's system of organizing archaeological phenomena into hierarchical scales reflective of social entities (i.e.,culture, culture group, and technocomplex) implicitly incorporated environmental, economic, demographic, temporal and spatial variables (Clarke, 1968, 1979). Although he presented a highly detailed procedure for defining these scales through variation among artifacts, Clarke was much less specific concerning the patterned variability in the other lines of evidence (i.e., environment, economy, demography) and concerning how such variability could be used to assist in the definition of cultures, culture groups, and technocomplexes. In applying Clarke's system of classification to the terminal Pleistocene Levant, I have made two general modifications. First, I have employed independent classificatory systems for the material culture and for prehistoric socioeconomic data (Table 4.1). In this manner the definitions of different hierarchical scales (complex, industry, phase/facies) for material culture data are based only upon similarities and differences in ar-

TABLE 4.1
The sequence proposed for classifying material culture, temporal-spatial, and social phenomena that are associated with archaeological inquiry.

| | Sequence of Classification | | |
	Step 1	Step 2	Step 3
Field	Classification of material culture based on affinities of artifact assemblages	Ordering of material culture units into time-space scales	Classification of social field based on material culture and ancillary data
Evidence drawn from	Material culture data field (e.g., lithic artifacts)	Stratigraphic, chronometric, archaeostratigraphic, and biostratigraphic units	Environmental, economic, demographic, material culture units
Scales of classification	Into scales of increasing specificity: Complex industry phase/facies	Into decreasing time-space scales	Into scales of technocomplex, culture group, culture

tifact inventories and not upon a priori assumptions concerning the correlations that existed between cultural behavior and its material residue.

Secondly, I have employed specific environmental, economic, demographic, spatial, and temporal evidence in conjunction with the already developed material culture units for the definition of the socioeconomic scales (i.e., culture, culture group, and technocomplex). Through the explicit incorporation of these ancillary lines of evidence into the definition of prehistoric social scales, a realistic correspondence is maintained between the detail of the scale and the resolution of our socioeconomic inferences. Clarke (1979:164), in fact, was especially critical of the lack of a realistic correspondence between archaeological evidence and the degree of social inference drawn from such data in noting that

It seems more probable that the uncertainty about the grosser archaeological entities stems from their real complexity . . . and above all from the wholesale use of the term "culture" for every category of assemblage population whatever their structure or time and space dimensions.

The use of a discrete classificatory system for organizing the social inferences drawn from archaeological phenomena obligates archaeologists to recognize the existence of more than one social scale (i.e., culture, culture group, and technocomplex) and to recognize the importance of ancillary data (e.g., demographic, environmental, and economic evidence) in conjunction with artifactual data for defining such social scales. The use of such a system demands a much more sophisticated and realistic social classification of archaeological phenomena. Although Clarke's system of classification of social phenomena has not been comprehensively employed in the Levant, several studies have utilized certain aspects of his system of classification (Henry, 1973a, 1975; Bar-Yosef, 1981a; Marks and Friedel, 1977), and this study builds upon these.

MATERIAL CULTURE CLASSIFICATION: THEORY

As in all classificatory systems, the classification of material culture requires an arbitrary selection of the field, the scales, the attributes, and the criteria from an infinite array of material culture phenomena (Dunnell, 1971). Clearly, in order to identify the various patterns that material culture may assume, numerous classifications may be developed. But in developing any material culture classificatory system, at least two conditions need to be met:

1 The range of selected attributes and criteria should be consistent within scales.
2 The attributes selected for classification should have a high probability of occurrence within the field of phenomena under classification.

Although both of these conditions appear to be common sense requirements for a classification, all too often they are not satisfied. For example, in Near Eastern prehistory the attributes and criteria that traditionally have been used in identifying the units in the largest scale of artifact assemblage groups (i.e., complex) vary through time. Whereas attributes and criteria are based upon lithic technology and typology for the definition of material culture units for most of Near Eastern prehistory, attributes and criteria are based upon different material culture fields, including lithic typology, architecture, and burial patterns and even an economic field (e.g., food production) for the definition of certain Epipaleolithic and Neolithic complexes. The attributes and criteria are clearly not consistent within the same scale in such classifications. This observation is not intended to challenge the importance of a wide range of attributes and criteria being employed in classification, but it does argue for consistency in their application once they have been selected.

The second condition is primarily related to sampling procedures. The attributes and criteria chosen for classification should have a high probability of being present within the field of phenomena selected for classification; i.e., such attributes should be consistently present in adequate numbers in the inventory of recovered evidence. As a general rule in satisfying this condition, the specificity of the attributes and criteria used in the classification will be inversely related to the magnitude of the temporal and spatial dimensions of the field. For example, more detailed and hence more discriminating attributes will be needed for the definition of an industry than of a complex.

Lithic assemblages perhaps represent the best basis for classification of the material culture phenomena in the prehistory of the Levant at the end of the Ice Age, given the two conditions listed above. Lithic assemblages not only represent a field of data common to all terminal Pleistocene archaeological sites, but they also provide large data sets that are amenable to quantification and detailed attribute analysis. Within this field the scales of complex, industry, and phase/facies furnish a hierarchical arrangement that defines increasing affinities between lithic assemblages as determined by the increasing number and specificity of the attributes and criteria within these scales. It is important to note that although they are not formally considered in the classification, the temporal and spatial scopes of the various scales are inversely related to the levels of affinity displayed by the assemblages belonging to those scales (Figure 4.1).

An artifact *assemblage* represents the only unit common to material cultural, temporal-spatial, and social classifications; thus the definition of an assemblage is quite important. In order for an assemblage to serve as a strong vehicle for correlation, it should consist of some part of the material culture residue of a spatially limited and temporally brief occupation by a group that was representative of a discrete culture.

The largest and most loosely bound scale in the classification is that of *complex*. Lithic artifact assemblages belonging to a complex should have a high level of general technological affinity and a low level of typological affinity as determined by their sharing of a polythetic set of attributes related to blank produc-

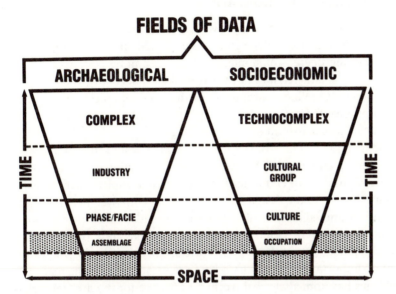

Figure 4.1. *Diagram of the relationship between archaeological and prehistoric socioeconomic classifications, with their respective scales, and the dimensions of time and space. Note that both the temporal and spatial dimensions increase from lower to higher scales.*

tion and tool manufacture. The criteria established for satisfying membership in a complex should designate a range for the frequencies of certain technological characteristics (e.g., bladelet production, microburin technique) and tool classes (e.g., geometric microliths, backed bladelets).

An intermediate scale in the classificatory hierarchy is that of *industry*. Lithic assemblages classified to the scale of industry should have a high level of affinity in sharing specific technological attributes (reflective of both method and technique of production) in conjunction with certain typological attributes at the class and type levels. Classification schemes similar to that proposed for this scale are commonly employed in Near Eastern prehistoric studies (Bar-Yosef, 1970; Marks, 1976, 1977a). The criteria used in the identification of the technological and typological parameters for industry affiliation should include specific quantitative boundaries (e.g., bladelet widths) as well as frequency ranges.

The lowest and most internally homogeneous scale is that of *phase/facies*. Those lithic assemblages comprising a phase/facies should have a very high level of affinity. Such assemblages should share the specific technological and typological attributes indicative of industry affiliation in addition to specific stylistic attributes. Stylistic attributes should include those attributes shown to be unrelated to function. Specific modes of retouch (Henry, 1973a, 1977), the positions and orientations of retouch on certain tool types (Close, 1978), and specific applications of the microburin technique (Marks and Simmons, 1977) are examples of such stylistic attributes.

MATERIAL CULTURE CLASSIFICATION: APPLIED

The classification, as presented here, has two important ramifications. First, a hierarchical arrangement of assemblage groups is proposed and made explicit on the basis of the varying degrees of similarity observed among certain techno-logical and typological characteristics of the assemblages. Secondly, the classification provides precisely defined parameters of these taxonomic units on the basis of the quantitative variability observed within certain technological and typological characteristics across all of the assemblages.

Prior to discussing the details of the classification, I would like to address some areas of potential criticism. All too often the quantification of archaeologi-cal phenomena is viewed as an end in itself and in many instances merely reaf-firms the obvious. This is not the case with the procedure employed here because the classification has immediate practical as well as broader theoretical impor-tance. As previously argued, this kind of material culture classification is prereq-uisite to the development of a realistic prehistoric socioeconomic classification, but, perhaps more important, an explicit and precise means of ordering material culture assemblages has immediate real world significance for the archaeologist confronted with the ordering of a large number of assemblages with varying degrees of similarity.

QUESTIONS OF SCALE

With the dramatic increase in Paleolithic research in the Levant, we are now finding that even within the relatively brief episode of the terminal Pleistocene the traditional taxonomic labels and limited scales are inadequate to accommo-date the newly discovered diversity in material culture (Henry, 1982, 1987a; Bar-Yosef, 1981). The increasing recognition of greater diversity in material cul-ture for this period is derived, in part, from more detailed and thus more dis-criminating analytic procedures, but the enlarged geographic arena of research has also played a significant role. Over the last decade the expansion of research into the arid zone of the Levant has led to the discovery of assemblage groups that previously were unknown (e.g., the Mushabian and Harifian).

Using the traditional organizational framework, one is confronted with the dilemma of where to place newly discovered assemblages that fail to fall within the parameters of existing taxa. Whereas such assemblages can be placed under existing taxonomic labels that offer the "best fit," this acts to expand the tech-nological and typological definitions of taxa and thereby reduces their integrity. Alternatively, entirely new taxonomic labels can be generated, but this proce-dure lacks a means of denoting the more general levels of techno-typological similarity that may be present between newly discovered and existing taxa. Clearly, what is required to resolve this problem is a hierarchical taxonomic framework whereby differences and similarities between assemblages can be ex-pressed at different scales.

Although a hierarchical taxonomy has not been employed for the classification of the Levantine Epipaleolithic in a comprehensive manner, an implicit two-tiered classification was introduced by Bar-Yosef (1970, 1975, 1981a) for the ordering of the archaeologically and geographically diverse Geometric Kebaran into the scales of "complex" and "group." As a result of this initial effort, the scale of complex has come to be recognized as representing a higher order and more general level than the scales of industry or group. The relationship of the units of industry and group, however, has not been defined. Furthermore, explicit boundaries (in real techno-typological terms) between these scales have not been developed for any Epipaleolithic taxon, nor has a classificatory system incorporating multiple scales been employed comprehensively across other Epipaleolithic complexes. Several techno-typological studies have been employed to classify Geometric Kebaran (Bar-Yosef, 1970), Natufian (Bar-Yosef, 1970; Henry, 1973a, 1976), Mushabian (Bar-Yosef and Phillips, 1977), Negev Kebaran (Marks and Simmons, 1977), Harifian (Marks, 1973; Marks and Scott, 1976; Phillips, 1977; Scott, 1977) and Hamran (Henry, 1982; Jones, 1983) assemblages, but a single classificatory scheme utilizing the same set of attributes has not been applied across these diverse assemblage groups.

QUESTIONS OF QUANTIFICATION

In order to develop the classification system as described, the "vertical" boundaries between scales and the "horizontal" boundaries between taxa, at the same scale, must be defined by differences in degree rather than differences in kind. The comparative procedure used for assessing the differences among artifact assemblages therefore depends upon quantifying certain assemblage characteristics as opposed to identifying *fossiles directeurs* or guide fossils.

Aside from not serving the classificatory objectives outlined in the study, guide fossils, as far as I can determine, are limited to only one taxonomic unit, the Harifian, within the late Levantine Epipaleolithic. Whereas various studies have either directly or indirectly attributed guide fossils to the Natufian (e.g., Helwan lunate) and the Geometric Kebaran (e.g., trapeze-rectangle), a detailed examination of Levantine Epipaleolithic assemblages shows that these artifact varieties are useful taxonomic indicators only in degree and not in kind. The futility of the guide fossil or "presence-absence" approach to the formation of material culture units is underlined by the fact that almost all assemblage characteristics appear to some degree in all Geometric Epipaleolithic assemblages.

The quantitative profiles evinced by the frequencies of certain attributes must thus be relied upon for the discovery and definition of taxonomic units. These profiles can be determined by the ranges, means, and standard deviations for attribute frequencies and metrics of assemblage groups at various scales. Although means and standard deviations are descriptors that allow for the statistical validation of these various groupings *post facto*, ranges in the frequencies of certain attributes prove more useful for determining the initial placement of an assemblage. Similarly, non-overlapping ranges for the attribute frequencies of two or more assemblage groups are the fundamental criteria used in this study for defining the quantitative parameters of such groups.

CATEGORIES OF DATA

Five categories of data, related to various chipped stone assemblage characteristics, were used in the classification. The assemblage characteristics include: (1) major tool classes, (2) varieties of geometric microliths, (3) varieties of backed bladelets, (4) bladelet dimensions, and (5) microburin indices. These categories of assemblage characteristics were selected because they have proved to be useful in discriminating between assemblages (Bar-Yosef, 1970; Henry, 1973a; Marks, 1976; Marks and Simmons, 1977; Bar-Yosef and Goring-Morris, 1977) and are also commonly presented in publications of Epipaleolithic research. Data sets for each of the assemblages included in the study are presented in Appendices A, B, and C and are summarized in various tables and figures for each taxon. These data were obtained from the published results of other studies, as indicated in the Appendices, and from my primary analysis.

The category of *major tool classes* includes those tool forms that constitute the majority of Epipaleolithic tool-kits. Scrapers, burins, notches-denticulates, backed bladelets, and geometric microliths represent the principal tool classes in most Epipaleolithic assemblages. The various detailed tool type lists that have been generated for the Levantine Epipaleolithic (Bar-Yosef, 1970; Henry, 1973a; Marks, 1976; Marks and Simmons, 1977; Hours, 1974) and that form the basis for these classes represent subtle modifications of a morphological typology that was initially developed by Tixier (1963) for the Epipaleolithic of North Africa.

In each of the major tool classes there are various types of tools, with most

Figure 4.2. *Schematic illustration of representative tools from the major tool classes.*

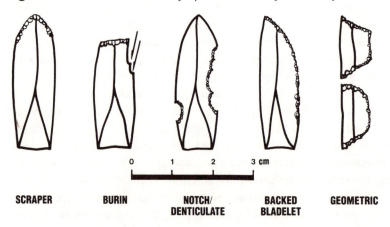

SCRAPER	BURIN	NOTCH/ DENTICULATE	BACKED BLADELET	GEOMETRIC

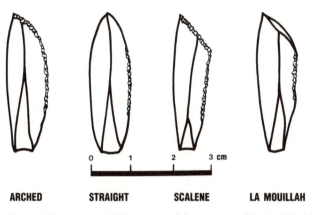

ARCHED STRAIGHT SCALENE LA MOUILLAH

Figure 4.3. *Schematic illustration of the varieties of backed bladelets.*

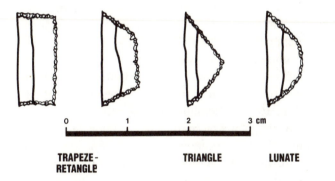

TRAPEZE-
RETANGLE   TRIANGLE   LUNATE

Figure 4.4. *Schematic illustration of the varieties of geometric microliths.*

of the classes being dominated by tool types fashioned from blade or bladelet blanks (Figure 4.2). Simple end-scapers, angle burins, and notches and denticulates manufactured from blades and bladelets constitute the majority of the scaper, burin, notch, and denticulate classes. The microlithic component of the assemblages not only represents the majority of the Epipaleolithic tool-kits but also generally proves to be the most useful component for defining certain assemblage groups. Therefore, the backed bladelet and geometric microlith classes, constituting the greatest part of the microlith component, are dealt with in greater detail than other classes of tools.

Although a number of *backed bladelet varieties* are present in the assemblages of the Levantine Epipaleolithic, four forms are the most important for the definition of assemblages (Figure 4.3). These forms include arched backed bladelets, straight backed bladelets, *lamelles scalene*, and La Mouillah points.

The *varieties of geometric microliths* found in the Levantine Epipaleolithic primarily included trapeze-rectangles, triangles, and lunates (Figure 4.4). In that the angles of truncations displayed by trapezes and rectangles tend to grade between the two types, these types have been combined to form a single geometric variety, a trapeze-rectangle. Also, it should be noted that those microliths classified as "proto-trapezes," "proto-rectangles," and "proto-lunates" in Bar-Yosef's (1970) type list are not considered as incomplete geometric microliths, but as backed and truncated bladelets. The presence of a mastic substance still visible on such specimens recovered from sites in Sinai (Bar-Yosef and Goring-Morris, 1977:199, 121) and traces of wear on similar artifacts excavated from sites in southern Jordan (Jones, 1983) argues that at least some, if not all, of the backed and truncated bladelets were finished tools.

The *dimensions of bladelets* were determined by measuring the maximum length of a specimen along its striking axis and measuring its maximum width perpendicular to this axis (Figure 4.5). Measurements were taken on samples of unbroken blanks that displayed lengths greater than twice their widths; i.e., that were lamellar in form. Whereas this procedure does not make an arbitrary distinction between bladelets (i.e. blanks that are less than 50mm in length) in the computation of the dimensional profiles of assemblages, it does provide an overall description of the lamellar component of the debitage.

The *microburin indices* of the assemblages were calculated through traditional procedures (Tixier, 1963) and revised procedures (Bar-Yosef, 1970; Henry, 1973a, 1974; Marks and Larson, 1977). Microburins appear in assemblages as by-products of the process of dividing blank pieces of debitage, most often bladelets, through controlled single-blow truncations delivered on notched or abruptly retouched edges (Figure 4.6). The division of a blank by the microburin technique generates a proximal or distal microburin that only in rare instances is modified into a tool (Marks, 1973). Under most circumstances, the portion of the blank opposite the end of the microburin was subsequently manufactured

Figure 4.5. *Bladelet dimensions.*

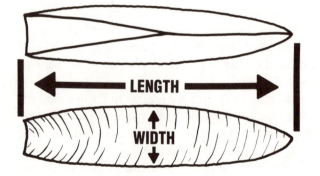

into a tool such as a truncated bladelet (e.g., arched backed bladelet) or geometric (e.g., lunate).

The traditional statistic used in comparing the frequencies of microburins between assemblages is the microburin index (IMbt); however, this computational method has come under criticism because it lacks sensitivity to the degree of utilization of the technique (Bar-Yosef, 1970:165; Henry, 1973a, 1974; Marks and Larson, 1977). In order to increase the sensitivity of the statistic to the actual intensity by which the technique was employed, Bar-Yosef (1970:165) proposed that the index be restricted to retouched microliths and Henry (1973a:78–79; 1974) suggested that calculations be somewhat more delimited to include only those tools that resulted from the microburin technique.

MATERIAL CULTURE CLASSIFICATION: RESULTS

The material culture classification, as previously described in theory and application, allows for the segregation of 87 Epipaleolithic assemblages (recovered from Jordan, Syria, Israel, and Egyptian Sinai) into three major complexes, each

Figure 4.6. *Diagram of the elements associated with the microburin technique. Note that microburins are defined by the microburin facet or scar appearing on the inverse surface of a blank, while* piquant triedres *and La Mouillah points are identified by a microburin scar on the obverse surface. Also note that a La Mouillah point is formed predominantly by abrupt retouch (backing), whereas a small retouched concavity (notch) creates the* piquant triedre *(modified after Henry, 1974).*

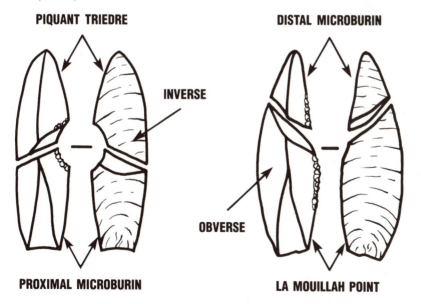

PIQUANT TRIEDRE DISTAL MICROBURIN

INVERSE

OBVERSE

PROXIMAL MICROBURIN LA MOUILLAH POINT

TABLE 4.2
The various units of the material culture classifications at the scales of complex, industry, and phase.

Complex	Industry	Phase
Mushabian	Sinai Mushabian Negev Mushabian Madamaghan	Helwan Harif Late Early
Geometric Kebaran	Group I Group II Group III Group IV	
Natufian	Natufian Harifian	Early Late

Figure 4.7. *Percentage profiles of major tool classes for the Mushabian, Geometric Kebaran, and Natufian complexes. For the assemblages within each complex, ranges of percentages are indicated by bars and means by closed circles.*

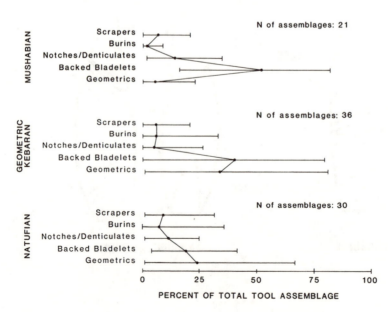

with their constituent industries and phases (Table 4.2). The complexes consist of the Mushabian, Geometric Kebaran, and Natufian.

These assemblages have previously been included under a variety of traditional taxonomic labels that comprise the Mushabian, Kebaran, Geometric Kebaran A, Geometric Kebaran B, Natufian, Harifian, Negev Kebaran, and Hamran (Bar-Yosef, 1981a; Henry, 1983). The assemblages share to varying degrees a geometric microlithic component in the form of trapeze-rectangles, triangles, and lunates; this characteristic distinguishes them from earlier nongeometric Epipaleolithic assemblages and is generally associated with assemblages that date from around 14,000 to 10,000 years ago in the Levant.

MUSHABIAN COMPLEX

The 21 assemblages included in the Mushabian Complex are characterized by high frequencies of backed bladelets that are principally in the form of arched backed bladelets, *lamelles scalene*, and La Mouillah points (Appendix A; Figures 4.7 and 4.9). Although geometric microliths are present, they appear in low frequencies and show considerable variation in form (Figure 4.8). The microlithic tools were fabricated from relatively short ($\bar{x} = 31$mm), wide ($\bar{x} = 13$mm) bladelets with a length:width ratio that averages 2.5:1 (Appendix A, Figure 4.10).

Figure 4.8. *Percentage profiles of the varieties of geometric microliths for the Mushabian, Geometric Kebaran, and Natufian complexes. For the assemblages within each complex, ranges of percentages are indicated by bars and means by closed circles.*

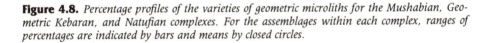

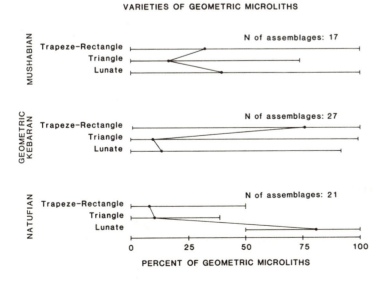

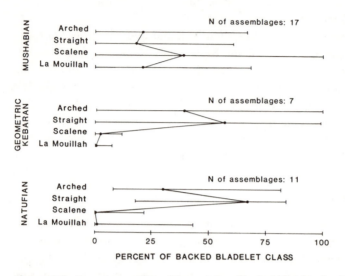

Figure 4.9. *Percentage profiles of the varieties of backed bladelets for the Mushabian, Geometric Kebaran, and Natufian complexes. For the assemblages within each complex, ranges of percentages are indicated by bars and means by closed circles.*

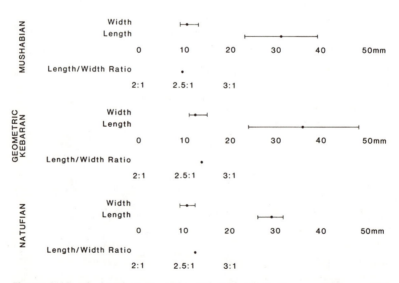

Figure 4.10. *The lengths and widths of bladelet samples from assemblages within each complex expressed in means (closed circles) and standard deviations (bars). Length: width ratios are based on the ratios of mean values.*

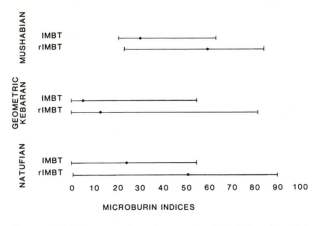

Figure 4.11. *A comparison of conventional (IMbt) and restricted (rIMbt) microburin indices for the Mushabian, Geometric Kebaran, and Natufian complexes. Ranges of microburin indices are indicated by bars and means by closed circles.*

The manufacturing process habitually employed the microburin technique, as evidenced by high microburin indices (Figure 4.11), for the controlled truncation of bladelets prior to their final fabrication into arched backed or scalene forms. The relatively high frequencies of La Mouillah "points" are likely to be a reflection of those bladelets in an intermediate stage of manufacture; that is, after sectioning by the microburin technique but prior to final retouching into finished backed and truncated bladelets. The microburin technique also may have been utilized for the fabrication of geometric microliths, but these tools represent only a minor part of Mushabian Complex assemblages.

GEOMETRIC KEBARAN COMPLEX

The assemblages of the Geometric Kebaran Complex are characterized by high frequencies of both backed bladelets and geometric microliths (Appendix B; Figure 4.7). Unlike the Mushabian, the backed bladelets are dominated by straight backed forms, and the geometric microliths are composed primarily of trapeze-rectangles (Figures 4.8 and 4.9). Whereas the bladelet blanks from which the backed bladelets and geometrics were fashioned are only slightly wider ($\bar{x} = 13.7$mm) than those of the Mushabian, they are much longer ($\bar{x} = 35.8$mm), with a 2.6:1 length:width ratio. There is considerable variability in the microburin indices for Geometric Kebaran Complex assemblages. The assemblages of the Group III and Group IV industries exhibit restricted microburin indices above 25, the remainder of the complex evinces indices under 20 (Appendix B).

It should also be noted that outside of Group III and Group IV assemblages the microburins found in Geometric Kebaran Complex assemblages are dominated by Krukowski microburins (Bar-Yosef and Goring-Morris, 1977:125), a form that is often accidentally produced in the fabrication of abruptly retouched bladelets (Bordes, 1957). The production of trapeze-rectangles in the Geometric Kebaran Complex assemblages apparently involved, for the most part, snapping bladelets without the use of the microburin technique. It is interesting to note that when used, the microburin technique in the Geometric Kebaran Complex was more strongly tied to the production of lunates and triangles than to the production of trapeze-rectangles. This is seen in the high frequencies of lunates in Group IV assemblages (Henry, 1982:433) and the production of triangles in Group III assemblages.

NATUFIAN COMPLEX

In many ways the assemblages of the Natufian Complex are the most difficult to characterize because they display the least specialized tool-kits (i.e., the major tool classes are relatively well balanced) in conjunction with the greatest range of variation about each tool class (Appendix C, Figure 4.7). With respect to the average frequencies of major tool classes, the Natufian Complex differs from both the Geometric Kebaran and Mushabian in displaying higher frequencies of geometric microliths than backed bladelets (Figure 4.7), but several important assemblages (e.g., Hayonim Terrace B1-D, Ein Mallaha Ib-Iv, and Abu Salem) represent exceptions to this general pattern.

An examination of the varieties of backed bladelets and geometric microliths contained in Natufian Complex assemblages, however, provides a clear means of identifying the complex. First, in contrast to the assemblages of the Mushabian Complex, the backed bladelet component of Natufian Complex assemblages is almost exclusively composed of arched and straight backed varieties and rarely contains *lamelles scalene* or La Mouillah points (Figure 4.9). Secondly, the geometric component of Natufian Complex assemblages differs from the Geometric Kebaran Complex in always being dominated by lunates (Figure 4.8).

Technologically, Natufian Complex assemblages were based upon the production of relatively short ($\bar{x}=29$mm), wide ($\bar{x}=11$mm) bladelets with an average length:width ratio of 2.6:1 (Figure 4.10). Interestingly, in contrast to the considerable range of variation exhibited in the tool classes, Natufian Complex assemblages display a remarkable homogeneity with respect to blank production (Henry, 1973a, 1977). For example, one can note the limited parameters of bladelet dimensions for Natufian Complex assemblages relative to those for the Geometric Kebaran and Mushabian complexes (Figure 4.10).

The utilization of the microburin technique appears to have been a habitual part of the technology of the Natufian Complex, although the degree by which the technique was employed varies both spatially and temporally. As initially recognized in the early work of Garrod (1958) and Neuville (1934, 1951), and subsequently confirmed by a more comprehensive seriation associated with radiocarbon dates, the microburin technique became more intensively utilized during the course of the Natufian. The technique also appears to have been employed to a greater degree in the southern than the northern Levant (Henry, 1973a, 1977).

Assemblages of the Natufian Complex also display a specific mode of application of the microburin technique in sectioning bladelets during the process of fabricating geometric microliths (Henry, 1974). This mode of application entailed partially completing a lunate through an arched truncation of a bladelet and then sectioning the bladelet through the microburin technique (Figure 4.12). The procedure resulted in an element that required only minimal retouch along the thin beveled edge, resulting from the microburin scar, for fabrication into a finished lunate. The Natufian microburin technique, enabling knappers to fabricate exceedingly small lunates, may well be reflected in the general trend of progessive diminution of lunates through time within the Natufian (Neuville, 1951; Henry, 1973a; Bar-Yosef, 1981a). This mode of application enjoyed a wide geographic distribution, for it has been recorded in assemblages from sites of Hayonim Terrace in the western Galilee (Henry and Leroi-Gourhan, 1976), Rosh Zin in the highland Negev (Henry, 1974), Wadi Judayid in southern Jordan (Henry, et al., 1985), and Khallat A'naza in northeastern Jordan (Betts, 1982).

Another unique application of the microburin technique has been observed for the production of a point variety in the Harifian Industry, a constituent unit of the Natufian Complex as proposed in this study. The fabrication of Harif points (Marks, 1973) entailed retouching bladelets into distal oblique truncations and then removing their proximal ends with the microburin technique (Figure 4.12). Although the variation in the basal modification of Harif points indicates that

Figure 4.12. *The specific modes employed in application of the microburin technique in the Mushabian, Natufian, and Harifian industries.*

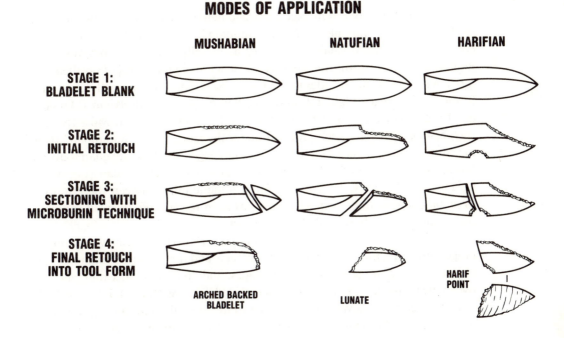

the microburin technique was not applied in all cases, the mode of application as described was the most common way by which the points were produced.

A comparison of the modes of application of the microburin technique reveals fundamental differences between the Mushabian Complex and the industries (i.e., Natufian and Harifian) of the Natufian Complex (Figure 4.12). As used in the Mushabian Complex, the application of the technique preceded most of the retouching of a blank into its finished form, whereas in the production of lunates and Harif points in the Natufian Complex most of the retouching of a specimen preceded the application of the microburin technique and left only minor retouching for finishing the tool.

SCALES OF INDUSTRIES AND PHASES

The Mushabian, Geometric Kebaran, and Natufian complexes can each be divided into two or more constituent industries by using the same five categories of assemblage characteristics that were used for the initial definition of the complexes. The Mushabian Complex can be segregated into three industries (the Sinai and Negev Mushabian and the Madamaghan), the Geometric Kebaran Complex comprises four industries (Group I, Group II, Group III, and Group IV), and the Natufian Complex includes two industries (the Natufian and the Harifian).

INDUSTRIES OF THE MUSHABIAN COMPLEX

Three major groups of assemblages, labelled here as industries, can be identified in the Mushabian Complex. In using traditional taxonomic labels, one group corresponds to the Mushabian Industry as initially defined by Bar-Yosef and Phillips (1977:257–58) from sites in the Gebel Maghara region of northeastern Sinai. A second group includes those assemblages that were originally discovered in the central Negev highlands and classified as the Negev Kebaran (Marks, et al., 1972; Marks, 1977a, 1977b; Marks and Simmons, 1977). Most recently, such assemblages have been grouped under the label of the "Ramonian" (Goring-Morris, 1987). And a third group of assemblages, the Madamaghan Industry, has recently been described for the mountains of southern Jordan (Henry and Garrard, 1988; Henry, 1987a). Although some affinity between the groups of assemblages from the Negev and Sinai has been recognized, detailed comparative studies have only recently been conducted.

The *major tool classes* of the Sinai and Negev Mushabian display overlapping ranges; however, mean frequencies for scrapers and notches/denticulates are significantly higher for the Negev assemblages, and an even greater difference between the industries is noted in the backed bladelet class (Table 4.3, Figure 4.13). The Madamaghan shows closer affinities to the Sinai than to the Negev Mushabian in all but the scraper class. The three industries display near identical frequencies for the burin and geometric classes.

TABLE 4.3
The percentages of major tool classes, varieties of backed bladelets, and varieties of geometrics for the Sinai and Negev Mushabian industries. Ranges (r) in percentages of the assemblages within each industry, mean (x̄) percentages for the industries.

	Sinai Mushabian		Negev Mushabian		Madamaghan	
	r	x̄	r	x̄	r	x̄
Major tool classes						
Scrapers	0 – 21	6.9	2 – 17	7.5	7 – 8	7.5
Burins	0 – 9	2.8	0 – 4	1.6	5 – 6	1.0
Notch-denticulates	2 – 26	10.7	6 – 35	19.6	5 – 6	5.5
Backed bladelets	16 – 82	57.3	24 – 76	45.2	52 – 69	60.5
Geometrics	1 – 11	8.6	0 – 9	2.4	1 – 8	4.5
Varieties of backed bladelets						
Arched	14 – 67	31.8	0 – 22	7.75	41 – 44	42.5
Straight	0 – 6	2.1	0 – 61	31.5	12 – 39	25.5
Scalene	9 – 58	25.7	14 – 100	60.3	0 – 2	1.0
La Mouillah	13 – 67	43.6	0 – 3	.4	20 – 42	31.0
Varieties of geometric microliths						
Trapeze-rectangles	0 – 94	34.7	0 – 100	19.6	40 – 100	70.0
Triangles	0 – 74	25.9	0 – 33	9.0	0 – 27	13.5
Lunates	0 – 100	39.3	0 – 100	46.4	0 – 33	16.5

Figure 4.13. *Percentage profiles of major tool classes for the Sinai and Negev Mushabian industries. Ranges of percentages are indicated by bars and means by closed circles.*

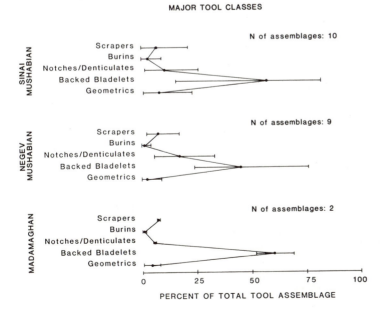

TABLE 4.4
**Conventional (lMbt) and restricted (rlMbt) microburin indices for the industries
of the Mushabian Complex. (r = range, $\bar{x}$ = mean)**

| | Sinai Mushabian | | Negev Mushabian | | Madamaghan | |
	r	$\bar{x}$	r	$\bar{x}$	r	$\bar{x}$
IMbt	24–63	57.8	19–25	21.1	20–51	35.5
rIMbt	40–75	52.7	23–84	68.3	49–66	57.5

The greatest differences between the industries are found in the *backed blade-let class* (Table 4.3, Figure 4.14). Where the Sinai Mushabian and the Mada-maghan consistently contain La Mouillah points (23–33% of the class), such points are absent from Negev Mushabian assemblages. Scalene and straight backed bladelets dominate the Negev Mushabian; arched backed bladelets fur-nish the highest average frequencies for the class in the Sinai Mushabian. Sca-lene bladelets are rare in the Madamaghan, while arched and straight backed bladelets are found in high frequencies.

Varieties of geometric microliths found in each of the Mushabian Industries display considerable variation as indicated by wide ranges for each variety (Table 4.3, Figure 4.15). This variability among assemblages is induced in part by the low frequencies of geometric microliths for the assemblages of the Mushabian Complex. Although the ranges in frequencies for the varieties of geometric mi-

Figure 4.14. *Percentage profiles of varieties of backed bladelets for Sinai and Negev Mushabian industries. Ranges of percentages are indicated by bars and means by closed circles.*

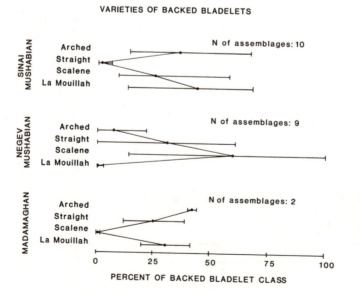

VARIETIES OF BACKED BLADELETS

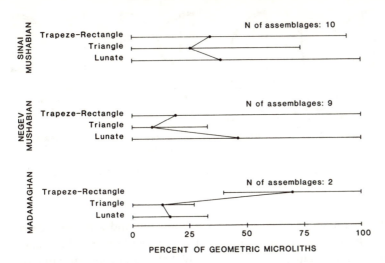

Figure 4.15. *Percentage profiles of varieties of geometric microliths for Sinai and Negev Mushabian industries. Ranges of percentages are indicated by bars and means by closed circles.*

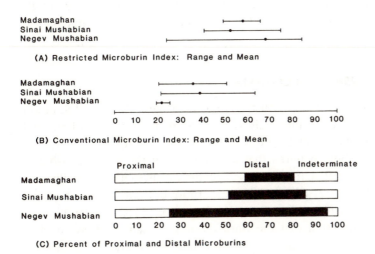

Figure 4.16. *A comparison of the Madamaghan, Sinai, and Negev Mushabian industries based on (A) restricted microburin indices, (B) conventional microburin indices, and (C) the types of microburins.*

croliths overlap among the three industries, the average frequencies for the varieties of geometrics reveal different patterns. Trapeze-rectangles, on the average, dominate the Sinai Mushabian and the Madamaghan, but lunates are the dominant variety within the Negev Mushabian.

An examination of the *microburin technique* shows that the Negev Mushabian stands apart from the Sinai Mushabian and Madamaghan with respect to both the degree and mode of utilization (Table 4.4, Figure 4.16). The Sinai Mushabian and Madamaghan assemblages display significantly higher conventional microburin indices (IMbt) than the Negev Mushabian. However, restricted microburin

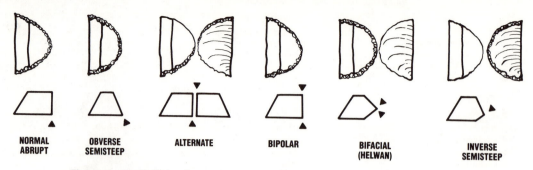

| NORMAL ABRUPT | OBVERSE SEMISTEEP | ALTERNATE | BIPOLAR | BIFACIAL (HELWAN) | INVERSE SEMISTEEP |

Figure 4.17. *Varieties of retouch that occur on backed tools, within the Levantine Epipaleolithic (modified after Henry, 1973a).*

indices (rIMbt) show a slight reversal of this relationship and a much greater overlap between the ranges for the indices of the three industries. These data would imply that in the production of truncated bladelets and geometric microliths, the microburin technique was utilized to a greater extent in the Negev Mushabian. Differences among the industries are also found in the frequencies for the types of microburins. While the Sinai Mushabian and Madamaghan exhibit higher frequencies of proximal microburins, the assemblages of the Negev Mushabian evince markedly higher frequencies of distal microburins (Figure 4.16).

PHASES OF THE MUSHABIAN COMPLEX

In their analysis of seven Negev Mushabian assemblages, Marks and Simmons (1977:263) proposed a two-phase division of the industry (i.e., Harif and Helwan Phases) based upon a series of typologic, stylistic, and technological attributes. Two basic attribute patterns that are manifest in the Negev Mushabian seriation include the relative frequencies of geometric microliths (Harif Phase = 0–1%; Helwan Phase = 2–6%) and the proportions of Helwan retouch (Figure 4.17) in the geometric microlith class (Harif Phase = 0–33%; Helwan Phase = 53–78%). It was suggested that the Harif Phase preceded the Helwan Phase because of the stylistic similarities between the latter phase and the Early Natufian, but this observation initially lacked either radiometric or stratigraphic evidence for support. Such a suggested chronology would place the Helwan Phase from approximately 12,500 to 11,000 B.P., given Early Natufian cross-reference dates, and the Harif Phase sometime before 12,500 B.P. Recently a radiocardon date of $13,530 \pm 144$ (SMU-1268) was obtained from D101B (Kaufman, 1983), a Harif Phase Negev Mushabian site, which provides additional support to the seriation.

The Sinai Mushabian assemblages would appear to be chronologically sensitive to the same attributes (i.e., frequencies of geometrics and Helwan retouch). Additionally, trends in the proportionate frequency of La Mouillah points provide another avenue for seriating Sinai Mushabian assemblages. If the Sinai Mushabian assemblages are ordered chronologically on the basis of the proportions of geometric microliths in the tool-kits, a series is created that begins with Mushabi I and terminates with Nahal Lavan IV (Table 4.5). This ordering is in close harmony with the radiometric and stratigraphic evidence available for the industry. Not only do those assemblages with the lowest frequencies of geometric

TABLE 4.5
**Seriation of Sinai Mushabian Industry based on percentages of geometric micro-
liths. Note that seriation is in agreement with available radiocarbon dates and
stratigraphic sequence. ($\overline{x}$ = mean)**

Assemblages	Percent Geometrics	Percent Denticulates	C14 Dates (B.P.)
Nahal Lavan IV	23	26	
Mushabi IV	19	19	
Mushabi XIX	11	12	
Mushabi V, surface	11	11	
Mushabi V, excavated	8	4	12,700 ± 90
			990 ± 110
Mushabi XIV, surface	4	8	
Nahal Hadera II	3	10	
Nahal Hadera I	3	17	
Mushabi XIV, level 1	2	5	13,450 ± 500
$\overline{x}$ of 5 dates			13,532 ± 224
Mushabi I	1	5	13,310 ± 110

microliths yield the oldest radiometric dates, but where stratigraphic relationships can be defined (i.e., at Mushabi XIV, Mushabi V, and Mushabi XIX), the
lower assemblages always display the lower frequencies of geometrics.

In examining the frequencies of geometric microliths in the series, a marked
increment can be noted between Mushabi XIX (11%) and Mushabi IV (19%).
Helwan retouch is rare or absent in those assemblages grouped before this increment yet represents a significant portion of the backed bladelets and geometrics
of both Mushabi IV and Nahal Lavan IV. In recalling the increased frequency of
denticulates in the Helwan Phase of the Negev Mushabian, it is noteworthy that
both Mushabi IV and Nahal Lavan IV show a marked rise in denticulates (19%
and 26%, respectively) when compared to the earlier Sinai Mushabian assemblages (range 2–17%).

On the basis of these typological and stylistic observations, it seems reasonable to divide the Sinai Mushabian into early and late phases using as a
boundary the point where marked changes occur in typologic and stylistic
trends. Mushabi I, Mushabi XIV, Mushabi V, and Mushabi XIX would then fall
within an Early Phase, whereas Mushabi IV and Nahal Lavan IV would correspond to a Late Phase. Again, as with the Helwan Phase of the Negev Mushabian, the high frequencies of Helwan retouched microliths in the Late Phase of
the Sinai Mushabian suggest contemporaneity with the Early Natufian (i.e. after
12,500 B.P.). The two dates from the Early Phase Sinai Mushabian site of Mushabi V (average of 12,893 ± 100 B.P.) would certainly support this view.

The Madamaghan Industry, as evidenced by the stratigraphic sequence at
Tor Hamar, appears to parallel the trends observed in the Negev and Sinai Mushabian Industries (Table 4.6). The transition from Layers C-B to A at Tor Hamar
shows changes in the proportionate frequencies of geometric microliths, Helwan
retouch, and notches/denticulates quite similar to those observed between the
Harif and Helwan Phases of the Negev Mushabian. Parallels between the Mada-

TABLE 4.6
Comparison of temporal sensitive attributes and C14 dates for the three Mushabian Complex industries.

	Sinai Mushabian		Negev Mushabian		Madamaghan (Tor Hamar)	
	Early	Late	Harif Early	Helwan Late	C-B	A
Geometrics	0–11	19–23	0–1	2–6	0–1	2.4
Helwan retouch	rare	common	0–33	53–78	0–33	44
La Mouillah	5–58	9	0–1	0–1	17–19	27
Notch-denticulates	5–10	5–17	0–6	5–10	1–6	10
C14 dates (B.P.)	13,310–12,700	—	13,530	—	12,700	

maghan and Sinai Mushabian with regard to temporal trends in La Mouillah point frequencies are more complex. In the Early Phase of the Sinai Mushabian, La Mouillah points increase in relative frequency through time but then decline markedly in the Late Phase. In the Tor Hamar sequence, La Mouillah points increase in abundance through time. Comparison of these sequences may indicate that the Tor Hamar occupation (encompassed by Layers C, B, and A) is roughly synchronous with the final part of the Early Phase of the Sinai Mushabian. Radiocarbon dates from Mushabi V (12,700 ± 90) and Tor Hamar (12,683 ± 323) are, in fact, quite similar. The Tor Hamar sequence also shares certain trends with the Negev Mushabian succession. When compared to this sequence, the Tor Hamar occupation would appear to be roughly synchronous with the last of the Harif Phase (Tor Hamar Layers B, C) and the early part of the Helwan Phase (Tor Hamar Layer A).

In summary, a synthesis of the seriation schemes, radiometric dates, and stratigraphic successions for the Sinai and Negev Mushabian and the Mada-maghan would suggest a parallel and probably synchronous development in three subregions of the southern Levant. The earlier phases of the industries share an emphasis on backed bladelet varieties, whereas the later phases of the industries show a marked rise in geometric microliths (particularly lunates), denticulates, and Helwan retouch. The emphasis upon lunates and Helwan retouch is believed to reflect the synchroneity between later phases of the Mushabian and the Early Natufian.

INDUSTRIES OF THE GEOMETRIC KEBARAN

At least four industries can be identified in the Geometric Kebaran Complex. In using traditional taxonomic labels, these industries generally correspond to three "groups" of Geometric Kebaran assemblages that have been defined by Bar-Yosef (1981a: 396–98) and to the recently defined Hamran Industry of southern Jordan (Henry, 1981, 1982; Jones, 1983). The salient characteristics of these

TABLE 4.7
The ranges (r) and means (x̄) for the percentages of the major tool classes for the industries of the Geometric Kebaran Complex.

Major Tool Class	Group I r	Group I x̄	Group II r	Group II x̄	Group III r	Group III x̄	Group IV r	Group IV x̄
Scrapers	0–17	5.0	0–15	4.6	8–21	15.8	3–10	5.8
Burins	0–33	11.5	0–11	1.6	3–16	9.2	0–28	10.2
Notch dents.	0–17	4.0	1–10	4.2	0–17	7.6	2–27	8.3
Backed bladelets	25–79	49.8	11–78	43.5	15–35	25.3	3–59	19.0
Geometrics	1–48	18.3	5–81	33.5	7–27	17.9	6–48	26.0

industries are reflected in the patterned variation of geometric microliths, the dimensions of bladelets and geometrics, and microburin indices.

Although the frequency profiles of the major tool classes of the industries exhibit considerable overlap in the ranges of various tool classes, the mean frequencies displayed by the profiles point to some of the general differences between the industries (Table 4.7, Figure 4.18). Whereas the frequencies of the

Figure 4.18. *Percentage profiles of the major tool classes for the four industries of the Geometric Kebaran. Ranges of percentages are indicated by bars and means by closed circles.*

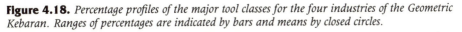

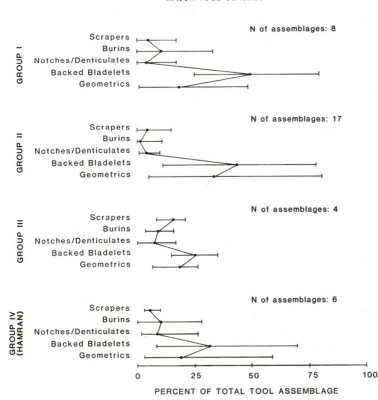

PERCENT OF TOTAL TOOL ASSEMBLAGE

TABLE 4.8
The ranges (r) and means (x̄) of the percentages of the varieties of geometric microliths for each of the Geometric Kebaran industries. The percentages are tabulated within the geometric microlith class for each assemblage.

Tool Type	Group I		Group II		Group III		Group IV	
	r	x̄	r	x̄	r	x̄	r	x̄
Trapeze-rectangles	86–100	92.3	99–100	99.9	1–16	8.0	7–81	48.7
Triangles	0– 10	3.8	0– 1	0.0	59–99	73.7	0–21	3.7
Lunates	0– 10	6.3	0	0.0	0–34	18.0	15–92	47.5

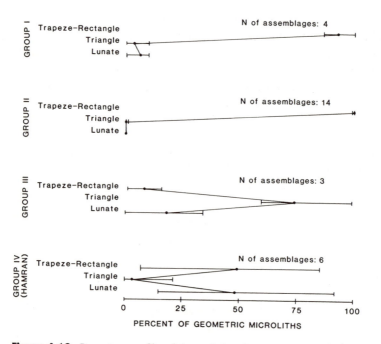

Figure 4.19. *Percentage profiles of the varieties of geometric microliths for the four industries of the Geometric Kebaran. Ranges of percentages are indicated by bars and means by closed circles.*

backed bladelet and geometric classes of Group III industries are roughly balanced, the backed bladelet class clearly dominates the tool assemblages of Groups I, II, and IV (Hamran) industries.

The geometric microlith class, however, proves to be the most important class for defining the constituent industries of the Geometric Kebaran Complex (Table 4.8, Figure 4.19). The patterned variation in the frequencies of trapeze-rectangles, triangles, and lunates produces discrete profiles for each of the industries. Group I and Group II industries have similar frequency profiles in that they share high frequencies of trapeze-rectangles. Group II assemblages, however, are composed almost entirely of trapeze-rectangles; Group I assemblages have lower trapeze-rectangle frequencies accompanied by low frequencies of triangles and lunates. Group III assemblages can be readily distinguished by their high frequencies of triangles. In contrast, the Group IV assemblages display markedly higher lunate frequencies than found in any of the other Geometric Kebaran industries.

The variation in the widths of bladelets and geometric microliths has been used as a criterion for distinguishing between the assemblages that are included within the Group I and Group II industries (Bar-Yosef, 1981a). Although data are not available for comparing the widths of geometrics and bladelets across all of the Geometric Kebaran industries, a comparison of the metric data that are available point to relatively wide bladelet production in Group II and Group III assemblages but to more narrow bladelet production for the Group IV and Group I assemblages (Table 4.9). Data on the mean maximum length of bladelets denote the production of shorter bladelets in Group III than Group II assemblages and even shorter bladelets in Group IV. Similar data are unavailable from the Group I Industry. The length:width ratios of bladelet samples perhaps pro-

TABLE 4.9
A comparison of the dimensional data for bladelet samples from the industries of the Geometric Kebaran. (r = range, $\bar{x}$ = mean, S.D. = standard deviation)

	r	$\bar{x}$	S.D.
Maximum width of geometrics[a]			
Group I	4.5–6.4	5.6	—
Group II	6.6–8.6	7.9	—
Group III	—	—	—
Group IV	—	—	—
Maximum width of bladelets[b]			
Group I	—	—	—
Group II	9.8–15.5	13.2	—
Group III	—	12.4	4.9
Group IV	8.4–9.5	8.9	2.8
Maximum length of bladelets[b]			
Group I	—	—	—
Group II	36.7–44.1	41.5	14.4
Group III	—	36.1	12.6
Group IV	—	24.7	5.0
Length:width ratio of bladelets			
Group I	—	—	—
Group II	—	3.1	—
Group III	—	2.9	—
Group IV	—	2.8	—

[a]Geometric widths taken from Bar-Yosef (1981a), Fujimoto (1979:55), Jones (1983).
[b]Bladelet dimensions taken from Marks (1976), Marks and Simmons (1977:121), Fujimoto (1979), Henry (1973a), Henry (1982), Jones (1983).

vide a better overall impression of the dimensions and morphologies of blanks that were produced in the industries of the Geometric Kebaran. Group II assemblages reveal the longest bladelets relative to their widths, whereas Group III and Group IV assemblages exhibit lower and more similar length: width ratios (Table 4.9).

Data associated with the microburin technique furnish some additional assistance in identifying the industries of the Geometric Kebaran, but patterned variation is not as clear as in other data sets. In general, the conventional and restricted microburin indices (Table 4.10) show that although the microburin technique was employed to some extent in all the industries the technique was used habitually only in the Group IV Industry. For example, in Group III the Ein Gev IV assemblage with its high indices (i.e., IMbt of 56 and rIMbt of 83) reflects the intensive, habitual utilization of the technique, but similar data from assemblages of Nahal Oren, layer VII imply that the technique was not consistently employed. A clear and consistent industry-wide utilization of the microburin technique can only, in fact, be supported by the indices associated with the Group IV assemblages.

PHASES OF THE GROUP IV (HAMRAN) INDUSTRY: CLARIFICATION

General technological and typological trends, which have temporal and spatial significance, have been identified in the Geometric Kebaran Complex (Bar-Yosef, 1981a). It is only in Group IV, however, that specific diachronic patterns can be defined at the scale of an industry.

TABLE 4.10
A comparison of microburin indices for the industries of the Geometric Kebaran. (r = range, $\bar{x}$ = mean)

	Group I		Group II		Group III		Group IV	
	r	$\bar{x}$	r	$\bar{x}$	r	$\bar{x}$	r	$\bar{x}$
IMbt	0–6.5	1.6	0–12	3.3	0–55.8	15.0	0–23	9.7
rIMbt	0–0	0.0	1–22	6.9	0–82.5	30.3	0–48	25.8

TABLE 4.11
A comparison of the original and revised classifications of Hamran assemblages.

Complex	Original Industry	Phase	Complex	Revised Industry	Phase
		Final	Geometric	Group IV	II
	Hamran	Late	Kebaran		I
		Middle		Group II	
		Early	Kebaran	Early Hamran	

A series of stratified rockshelters in southern Jordan have recently revealed an unbroken sequence that spans the Geometric Epipaleolithic. Although the sequence is best defined by developments in the backed bladelet and geometric classes, certain technological trends with respect to bladelet dimensions and microburin technique are also apparent.

The typological succession of the microlithic component follows the general trends of the Epipaleolithic of the Levant in that backed bladelets come to be replaced by trapeze-rectangles, which are in turn succeeded by lunates as the most common microliths. With one exception, however, the assemblage groups that form the sequential stages of this developmental sequence do not have counterparts elsewhere in the Levant. That is to say, they fall outside the published technological and typological parameters for the Kebaran, Mushabian, Natufian, and Geometric Kebaran (as previously defined). For this reason, I suggested a few years ago that a new Epipaleolithic taxon, the Hamran, be introduced to accommodate these assemblages and that the stages of development be correlated with four Hamran phases (Henry, 1982:430–36). Although such a proposal seemed a reasonable means of identifying these distinct assemblage groups at the time, such a classification is inconsistent with that proposed in this study for two reasons. First, the technological and typological differences between the four assemblage groups that represent the Hamran phases are of the magnitude that "industrial," as opposed to "phase," distinctions should be applied to three of these groups. Secondly, the assemblage group that represents the Middle Hamran Phase cannot be distinguished on technological and typological grounds from the Group II Industry of the Geometric Kebaran Complex as defined in this study. Therefore, in order to bring the Hamran assemblages into correspondance with the classificatory system as proposed here, I suggest the following modifications to the initial classification (Table 4.11).

The nongeometric Early Hamran Phase, although not directly encompassed by this study, should be considered as the Early Hamran Industry, most probably a constituent unit of the Kebaran Complex. As mentioned, the Middle Hamran Phase assemblages fall within the parameters of the Group II Industry of the Geometric Kebaran Complex and should be labeled as such. The Late and Final Hamran assemblages should be combined under the label of the Group IV Industry with two phases (I and II) that correspond to the original Late and Final Phases, respectively.

The two phases of the Group IV Industry are distinguished on the basis of differences in frequencies of geometric microliths and microburins in conjunction with differences in bladelet dimensions (Table 4.12). Phase I assemblages are dominated by trapeze-rectangles (72%) within the geometric class, display relatively low microburin indices, and contain bladelets with length:width ratios of 2.9:1. In contrast, Phase II assemblages exhibit high frequencies of lunates (77%), moderate to high microburin indices, and wider bladelets, with length:width ratios averaging about 2.6:1. It should also be noted that Helwan

TABLE 4.12
Comparative data for Phase I and Phase II of Group IV. (r = range, $\bar{x}$ = mean, S.D. = standard deviation)

	Late Hamran Industry	
	Phase I	*Phase II*
Trapeze-rectangles[a]	72	23
Lunates[a]	28	77
IMbt	12	23
rIMbt	16	31
Maximum width bladelets		
$\bar{x}$	24.7	24.7
S.D.	4.9	5.0
Length:width ratio	2.9:1	2.6:1

[a]Percentage of geometric microliths.

TABLE 4.13
Comparative data for Natufian and Harifian industries. (r = range, $\bar{x}$ = mean, S.D. = standard deviation)

	Natufian		Harifian	
	r	$\bar{x}$	*r*	$\bar{x}$
Major tool classes				
Scrapers	1–32	11.7	3–32	13.0
Burins	1–36	12.8	0–3	0.9
Notch-dents.	1–25	9.7	2–18	10.7
Backed bladelets	4–38	16.2	6–23	5.9
Geometrics	2–62	33.5	1–22	5.9
Varieties of backed bladelets				
Arched	16–33	24.7	8–82	49.8
Straight	67–84	75.3	18–64	40.1
Scalene	0	0.0	0	0.0
La Mouillah	0–3	1.0	0–43	6.9
Varieties of Geometrics				
Trapeze-rectangles	0–28	10.3	4–37	11.9
Triangles	2–20	14.7	5–36	24.9
Lunates	60–98	79.0	50–90	63.1
Microburin technique				
IMbt	0–47	13.74	18–45	32.6
rIMbt	0–80	27.00	47–72	61.1
Bladelet Dimensions	$\bar{x}$	S.D.	$\bar{x}$	S.D.
Maximum width	10.7	2.5	12.2	3.7
Maximum length	28.1	4.9	32.25	8.9
Length:width ratio	2.62:1		2.64:1	
Point types	*r*	$\bar{x}$	*r*	$\bar{x}$
Harif and Mushabi types	0–0	0.0	2–54	22.0

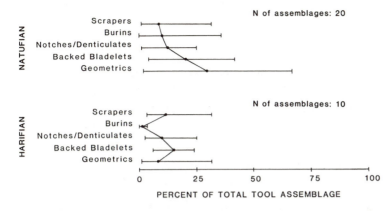

Figure 4.20. *Percentage profiles of the major tool classes from Natufian and Harifian industries. Ranges of percentages are indicated by bars and means by closed circles.*

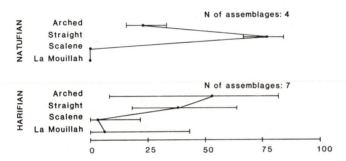

Figure 4.21. *Percentage profiles of varieties of backed bladelets for Natufian and Harifian industries. Ranges of percentages are indicated by bars and means by closed circles.*

lunates, absent from Phase I, make their appearance as a minor element in Phase II assemblages of Group IV.

INDUSTRIES OF THE NATUFIAN COMPLEX

The Natufian Complex consists of the Harifian and Natufian industries with the latter divisible into Early and Late phases. In comparing the assemblages of the two industries, the most obvious difference rests in the presence of Harif and Mushabi points in the Harifian and their absence from the Natufian (Table 4.13). Although Harif and Mushabi points serve as useful *fossiles directeurs*, a comparison of the industries, based upon the five standard assemblage characteristics that are used in this study, denotes other significant differences between the industries. But perhaps more importantly, such a comparison underlines the considerable similarities that exist between Natufian and Harifian assemblages, thus justifying their joint inclusion within the Natufian Complex.

An examination of the major tool classes reveals significantly higher frequencies of burins and geometrics in the Natufian, but the ranges in the frequencies for these classes show some overlap (Table 4.13, Figure 4.20). The lower geometric frequencies in the Harifian may be an expression of Harif and Mushabi points having come to partially replace geometrics as arrow tips. Within the backed bladelet classes, straight backed bladelets show clear differences in the means and ranges of frequencies between the two industries (Table 4.13, Figure 4.21). Geometric microliths, on the other hand, display similar frequency profiles for the two industries, although triangles tend to be more common in the Harifian. Microburin indices have overlapping ranges for the industries, but the Harifian shows less variation in microburin frequencies and higher mean scores (Table 4.13). The dimensional data for bladelets indicate that while Natufian samples are shorter and wider than those of the Harifian, their length:width ratios are nearly identical (Table 4.13).

In summary, assemblages of the Natufian and Harifian industries have remarkably similar basic technologies and general typologic profiles. Whereas the principal difference between the industries rests in the presence of point types in the Harifian, other subtle typological differences can also be defined.

PHASES OF THE NATUFIAN INDUSTRY

The Natufian Industry displays relatively little technological variability with exception to the microburin technique (Henry, 1973a, 1977), but significant typological variation has been noted since the early studies of Garrod (1958; Garrod and Bate, 1937) and Neuville (1934, 1951). Such variation has been attributed to functional requirements of the tool assemblages, as induced by activity differences both within and between sites (Bar-Yosef and Tchernov, 1966; Henry, 1973a, 1976), and to diachronic trends. Some patterned variation in tool classes of the Natufian has been shown to correspond to differences in biotic zones and settlement types (Henry, 1973a, 1973b, 1976), while variation in retouch varieties is clearly diachronic in nature. Recent suggestions have been made for the recognition of various geographic facies within the industry (M.-C. Cauvin, 1981), but at present the techno-typological parameters of such facies have not been defined.

The patterned typologic variation that has been defined is reflected in the diachronic trends in the styles of retouch and the dimensions of geometric microliths. The general stratigraphic trends of the diminution of geometric microliths (particularly lunates) and the shift from bifacial (Helwan) to normal abrupt retouch were initially noted by both Garrod and Neuville. More precise excavation and analytic techniques, increased sample sizes, and associated radiocarbon dates have allowed for considerable refinement to these early seriation schemes.

An examination of the retouch varieties from stratified and radiocarbon-dated assemblages points to a decline in the frequency of bifacial (Helwan) lunates in favor of normal abrupt retouch varieties from earlier to later deposits (Figure 4.22). The radiocarbon dates associated with the deposits indicate that abrupt retouch had come to replace bifacial retouch as the predominant form by around 11,000 years ago. Although this replacement would appear to have been

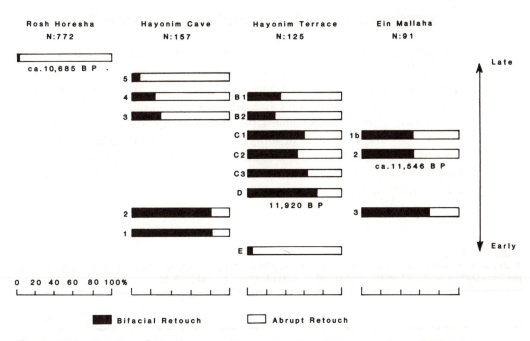

Figure 4.22. *Seriation of Natufian assemblages using the relative proportions of bifacial (Helwan) and abrupt retouch as illustrated by bar graphs (after Henry, 1982). Note the order of stratified assemblages.*

a smooth, gradual transition, it seems reasonable to identify those assemblages dating from about 12,500–11,000 B.P. and dominated by bifacial retouch as Early Natufian, while referring to assemblages dating after 11,000 B.P. and exhibiting principally abrupt retouch as Late Natufian.

An alternative seriation scheme that relies upon trends in the average length of lunates has also been proposed (Bar-Yosef and Valla, 1979; Bar-Yosef, 1981a). The general reduction in the average lengths of lunates through time in the Natufian is an indirect expression of the shift in frequency from bifacial to abrupt backed lunates, for as originally observed by Neuville (1951:130), bifacial lunates are longer on the average than abrupt retouched varieties. Perhaps as a consequence of other temporally unrelated factors, however, the dimensional seriation scheme appears less reliable than the seriation based upon variations in retouch. For example, the assemblage from Rosh Horesha is firmly assigned to the Late Natufian on the basis of radiocarbon determinations and almost exclusively abrupt retouch, yet the mean lengths of the lunates from Rosh Horesha match or exceed mean lunate lengths from Early Natufian assemblages (Figure 4.23).

Stratigraphic Evidence and Radiocarbon Dates

In ordering the Mushabian, Geometric Kebaran, and Natufian Complexes chronologically, radiocarbon dates become the primary source of evidence because of the paucity of stratigraphic sequences. Stratigraphic successions that bridge complexes are known from only five sites, whereas 44 radiocarbon dates have been obtained from 20 sites (Table 4.14). The stratigraphic and radiometric data, however, are in agreement in defining the chronologic relationships of the three complexes. These data confirm that the Geometric Kebaran preceded the Natufian and that the Mushabian was generally coeval with the Geometric Kebaran and the Early Natufian.

TABLE 4.14
A list of the radiocarbon dates for the Mushabian, Geometric Kebaran, and Natufian Complexes. Dates with asterisks not used in calculations of Table 4.15.

Site	Level	Radiocarbon Years B.P. [a]	Lab no.	Mat. [b]
Geometric Kebaran				
Mushabi XIV	Level 2	13,690 ± 740	MC-992	C
		13,750 ± 285	QC-201	C
		13,830 ± 490	RT-447d	C
		14,200 ± 100	RT-473b	C
		14,330 ± 120	SMU-226	C
Mushabi XVI		13,060 ± 220	RT-447c	C
Mushabi XVII		14,170 ± 480	SMU-661	C
Mushabi XVIII		13,930 ± 110	SMU-217	C
Qadesh Barnea 8	Level D/E	13,930 ± 120	Pta-2159	C
	Level G	14,130 ± 160	Pta-2158	C
Site D5 (Nahal Zin)	Bottom fire pit	15,820 ± 1,730	Tx-1121	C*
	Rodent hole	13,170 ± 230	I-5497	C
	Rodent hole	18,840 ± 680	SMU-7	C*
Nahal Oren	VII	15,800 ± 300	UCLA 1776A	B*
Neve David		12,610 ± 130	OxA-892	B
		13,400 ± 180	OxA-859	B
Mushabian				
Mushabi I		13,310 ± 110	SMU-117	O
Mushabi V		12,990 ± 110	SMU-171	C
		12,700 ± 90	Pta-2175	C
Tor Hamar	Layer C	12,680 ± 320	SMU-1399	C
Mushabi XIV	Level 1	12,900 ± 235	QC-202	C
		13,260 ± 200	MC-993	C
		13,800 ± 130	SMU-225	C
		13,800 ± 150	RT-473a	C
		13,900 ± 400	RT-417	C
Mushabi XVII		14,170 ± 480	SMU-661	C
Site D 101 B (Nahal Zin)		13,530 ± 144	SMU-268	C
Shunera IV		11,000 ± 140	Pta-3690	C*
		11,700 ± 140	Pta-3690	C
Natufian: Early				
El Wad Cave	Layer B2	11,920 ± 650	UCLA	B
Terrace	Layer B2	11,475 ± 650	UCLA	B
Kebara Cave	Layer B	11,150 ± 400	UCLA	B

continued

TABLE 4.14 cont.

Site	Level	Radiocarbon Years B.P.[a]	Lab no.	Mat.[b]
Hayonim Terrace	Layer D	11,920 ± 90	SMU-231	C
Hayonim Cave Loc 4/7		12,360 ± 160	OxA-742	S
Loc 4/5		12,010 ± 180	OxA-743	S
Ein Mallaha	III	11,740 ± 570	LY-1661	C
	III	11,310 ± 880	LY-1662	C
	IV soil b	11,590 ± 540	LY-1660	C
Jericho	Basal	9,750 ± 240	F-69(GL-69)	C*
	Hut at Base	9,800 ± 247	F-72(GL-72)	C*
	Base	11,155 ± 107	P-376	C
Wadi Judayid	Layer C	12,090 ± 800	SMU-805	C
	Layer C	12,750 ± 1,000	SMU-806	C
	Layer C	12,784 ± 650	SMU-803	C
Wadi Hama 27		11,920 ± 150	OXA-393	S
		12,200 ± 160	OXA-394	S
		11,950 ± 160	OXA-507	S
Beidha	C-01-24:4	12,910 ± 250	AA-1463	C
	C-00-16:4	12,450 ± 170	AA-1465	C
	C-01-23:4, H2	12,130 ± 190	AA-1464	C
	C-01-24:2	10,910 ± 520	AA-1462	C
Natufian: Late				
Rosh Horesha	45 cm	13,990 ± 200	I-5496	C*
	45 cm	10,880 ± 280	SMU-10	C
	45 cm	10,490 ± 430	SMU-9	C
Sefunim	V top	7,730 ± 115	HV-2597	C*
	V top	9,395 ± 130	HV-3368	C*
El Wad Terrace	B1	9,795 ± 600	UCLA	B
Nahal Oren	V	10,046 ± 318	BM-764	B
Mureybet	Phase I	10,590 ± 140	LV-608	C
	I-B	10,590 ± 140	LV-607	C
	I-A	10,030 ± 150	MC-733	C
	I-A	10,170 ± 200	MC-635	C
	I-A	10,090 ± 170	MC-674	C
	I-A	10,230 ± 170	MC-731	C
	I-A	10,230 ± 170	MC-732	C
	I-A	10,350 ± 150	MC-675	C
Tell Abu Hureyra	"Meso."E	10,792 ± 82	BM-1121	C
		11,160 ± 110	BM-1718	
		10,600 ± 200	OxA-170	S
		10,600 ± 200	OxA-171	S
		10,900 ± 200	OXA-172	S
		10,800 ± 160	OxA-386	S
		10,420 ± 140	OxA-397	S
		11,450 ± 300	OxA-883	S
	Trench E	10,700 ± 500	BM-1723	
		10,970 ± 160	OxA-387	B
		11,090 ± 150	OxA-468	B
		10,920 ± 140	OxA-469	B
		10,820 ± 160	OxA-470	B
		10,750 ± 170	OxA-472	B
		10,000 ± 170	OXA-473	B
		10,050 ± 180	OxA-407	B
		10,620 ± 150	OxA-471	B
		10,250 ± 160	OxA-408	B
		11,020 ± 150	OxA-430	B
		10,580 ± 150	OxA-431	B
		10,490 ± 150	OxA-434	B
		10,450 ± 180	OxA-435	B

continued

TABLE 4.14 cont.

Site	Level	Radiocarbon Years B.P. [a]	Lab no.	Mat.[b]
Rakefet		10,980 ± 260	I-7032	B
		10,580 ± 140	I-7030	B
(Salibiya I (Marsh))		11,530 ± 1,550	RT-505A	C
Harifian				
Abu Salem	15–20 cm	9,970 ± 150	I-5498	C
	25–30 cm	10,230 ± 150	I-5499	C
	45–55 cm	10,230 ± 150	I-5500	C
	L22/180–190	10,550 ± 90	Pta-3292	C
	L24/190–200	10,420 ± 100	Pta-3293	C
	L22/120–130	10,140 ± 80	Pta-3291	C
	L21/120–130	10,340 ± 90	Pta-3290	C
	L1/155–160	10,300 ± 100	Pta-3289	C
Ramat Harif	L3/280	10,500 ± 100	Pta-3009	C
	L3/275–280	10,380 ± 100	Pta-3284	C
	L3/220–225	10,300 ± 100	Pta-3001	C
	L3/210–220	10,390 ± 100	Pta-3285	C
	L7/220–225	10,250 ± 100	Pta-3288	C
	L7/180–185	10,100 ± 100	Pta-3286	C
Maaleh Ramon	L1/30–35	10,530 ± 100	Pta-3371	C
East	L1/25–30	10,430 ± 80	Pta-3483	C
Maaleh Ramon		10,400 ± 100	Pta-3483	C
West		10,000 ± 200	RT-1068N	C

[a] Radiocarbon dates are based upon the Libby half-life of 5,570 ± 30 years.
[b] Dated material: B = bone, C = charcoal, O = Ostrich eggshell, S = seed.

MUSHABIAN COMPLEX

The only recorded stratigraphic setting where a Mushabian occupation is related to an assemblage of another complex is found at the Sinai site of Mushabi XIV (Bar-Yosef and Goring-Morris, 1977). At the site, a Mushabian occupation (level 4) was discovered directly overlying a Geometric Kebaran horizon (level 2). Twenty-five radiocarbon determinations indicate, however, that the Mushabian and Geometric Kebaran Complexes were in part coeval. A comparison of the various temporal brackets of the two complexes shows significant overlap in each of the categories examined, although these data also denote a somewhat longer duration for the Mushabian Complex (Table 4.15, Figure 4.23). Within the Mushabian Complex, radiocarbon-dated assemblages are represented mainly by the Sinai Mushabian Industry, with only single dates available for each of the other two industries. Both the Negev Mushabian and the Madamaghan, however are thought to be partially coeval with the Early Natufian based on the cross-reference dating of Helwan retouch (Marks and Simmons, 1977; Henry and Garrard, 1988).

TABLE 4.15
Various data sets that define the temporal sweeps of certain complexes, industries, and phases of the Epipaleolithic.

	N^a	r^b	r^c	r^d	$\bar{x}$	age^e
Mushabian	12	14,650–11,560	14,170–11,700	13,437–13,019	13,228	209
Geometric Kebaran	13	15,330–12,480	14,330–12,610	13,932–13,482	13,707	226
Early Natufian	23	13,160–10,390	12,910–10,910	12,360–11,510	11,935	425
Late Natufian	36	13,080– 9,830	11,530–10,000	10,845–10,389	10,617	228
Harifian	18	10,640– 9,800	10,550–10,000	10,430–10,214	10,332	108

[a] number of radiocarbon dates.
[b] range of point-dates with 1 sigma.
[c] range of point-dates alone.
[d] range of mean of point-dates and mean of sigmas.
[e] mean of point dates and mean of sigmas.

Figure 4.23. *Relative percentages of bifacially retouched lunates and mean lengths of lunates (after Bar-Yosef and Valla, 1982).*

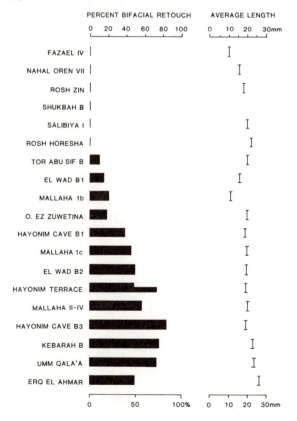

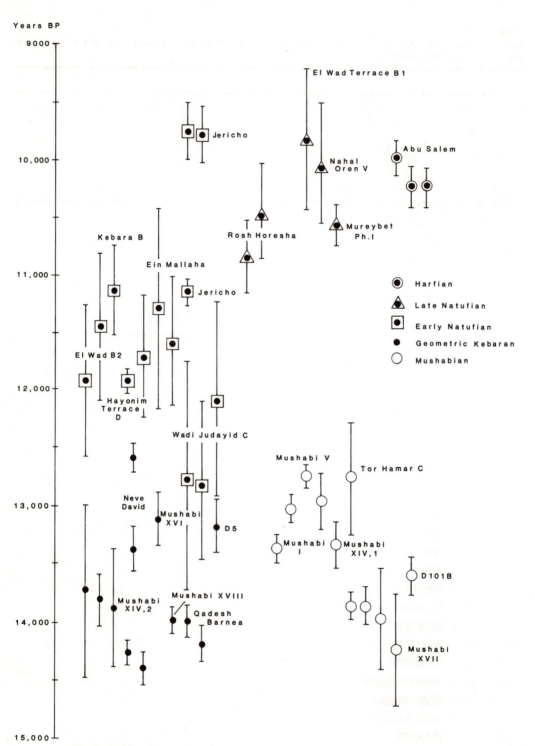

Figure 4.24. *Distribution of radiocarbon point-dates with single sigmas for various Epipaleolithic sites.*

GEOMETRIC KEBARAN AND NATUFIAN COMPLEXES

Geometric Kebaran assemblages are stratigraphically associated with Natufian horizons at four sites: Hayonim Terrace D-E (Henry and Leroi-Gourhan, 1976; Henry et al., 1981), Nahal Oren V–VII (Noy, et al., 1973), El Khiam (Perrot, 1951; Echegaray, 1964, 1966) and Jabrud III (Rust, 1950). In each of these deposits an occupation of the Natufian Industry immediately overlies a horizon of the Geometric Kebaran Complex. Only two of the Natufian assemblages are attributed to the Early Phase of the industry and only one of these (Hayonim Terrace D) is dated by radiocarbon. Of the Geometric Kebaran assemblages, Hayonim Terrace E, El Khiam 8 and 9, and Jabrud III represent the Group I Industry, whereas Nahal Oren VII is a Group III assemblage.

An examination of the radiocarbon dates of the two complexes denotes an overlap in their temporal sweeps only when single standard deviations are considered, and this overlap is mainly caused by the dates from Neve David and Wadi Judayid (Table 4.15, Figures 4.24 and 4.25).

Figure 4.25. *Diagram of the various data sets that define the radiocarbon temporal sweeps of certain Epipaleolithic complexes, industries, and phases (see Table 4.15).*

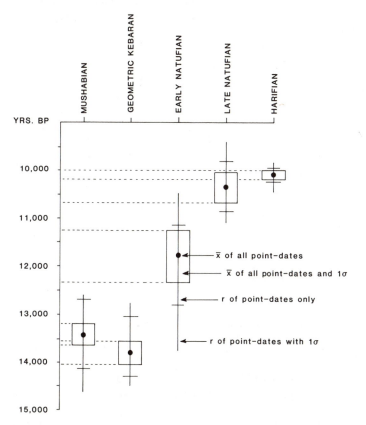

All but three of the radiocarbon determinations for the Geometric Kebaran Complex are related to the Group II Industry, and these come from only two sites, the Group I site of Neve David and the Group III site of Nahal Oren. The Group IV industry remains undated. Although additional dates for these industries are likely to expand the duration of the complex, such revision is unlikely to result in the extension of the complex into appreciably younger time-frames given the many dates associated with the succeeding Early Natufian. On the other hand, it is probable that more dates especially for Group I and Group III assemblages, will better define the beginning of the complex, perhaps on the order of 15,000–16,000 B.P.; this observation rests on the techno-typological continuity that is evident between the Group I Industry and the preceding Kebaran, which is presently dated to no later than 15,700 B.P.

The Natufian, the best dated of the three complexes, is associated with 64 radiocarbon dates from fourteen sites. Of these, however, five dates are quite questionable and should be excluded from the construction of a radiocarbon chronology for the complex. The two young dates (F-69, F-72) from Jericho were determined in the early stages of the development of the radiocarbon dating technique, when the solid carbon method was used, and therefore should be viewed with considerable reservation (Henry and Servello, 1974). The oldest date (I-5496) of the Rosh Horesha series also appears to be inaccurate. It is not only internally inconsistent with the other two dates from the same 5cm level but also fails to overlap with other Natufian dates when point-dates with single standard deviations are compared. Finally, the two dates from Sefunim V appear to be too young. The youngest of these is clearly outside the temporal range of the Natufian, and the other only marginally falls within single sigma range of the complex.

A comparison of the dates associated with Early and Late phases of the industry reveals an overlap in temporal sweeps when all point-dates with their single sigmas are considered. When the mean of point dates with their standard deviations are considered, however, a division between the two phases is denoted at around 11,000 B.P. (Figure 4.25).

The duration of the Harifian Industry was relatively brief, lasting only some 300–600 years, and it shows substantial overlap with the Late Natufian.

Geographic Distribution

In synthesizing the chronologic evidence and the spatial distribution of Epipaleolithic assemblages, a general model can be developed for tracing the changes of the geographic coverage of the various taxa for the period between ca. 14,750 and 10,000 B.P. (Figure 4.26).

During the interval from ca. 14,750 to 12,500 B.P., assemblages of the Mushabian Complex are found west of the Rift Valley in Sinai, the Negev, and

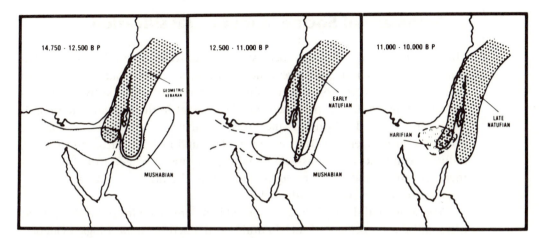

Figure 4.26. *Distribution of the major Epipaleolithic complexes, industries, and phases between 14,750–10,000 B.P. in the Levant.*

along the coastal sands as far north as the Nahal Hadera. East of the Rift, the Mushabian is found in the mountains of southern Jordan and appears to extend along the fringe of the great Syrian desert. Contemporary assemblages of the Geometric Kebaran Complex are distributed throughout the central Levant, south into the Negev and Sinai, and along the Jordanian Plateau east of the Rift Valley.

Beginning around 12,500 B.P., the various industries of the Geometric Kebaran Complex were replaced and consolidated within a single industry, the Early Phase of the Natufian, throughout the core Mediterranean zone (i.e., from the Jordanian Plateau and Judean Hills to the north). At the same time, in the arid zone, only Mushabian assemblages are found for this interval. The proposed contemporaneity of the Early Phase of the Natufian and the Late Phase of the Mushabian is based upon the presence of a unique bifacial retouch in the phases and similar radiocarbon dates for Mushabian and Early Natufian sites in southern Jordan.

In conjunction with the transition from Early to Late Natufian, at around 11,000 B.P., there was an expansion of the Late Natufian into the Negev and other marginal Mediterranean zone settings such as the lava desert of northeast Jordan. Toward the end of this interval, around 10,300 to 10,000 B.P., the Late Natufian of the Negev is succeeded by assemblages of the Harifian Industry that are also found in Sinai. Although the Harifian replaced the Late Natufian in the Negev, the Natufian appears to have persisted in the core Mediterranean zone until around 10,000 B.P., when it was succeeded by early Aceramic Neolithic industries.

Summary of Socioeconomic Classification

The classification of prehistoric social systems into scales of technocomplex, culture group, and culture requires ordering those attributes that are associated with environment, economy, demography, material culture, and the temporal-spatial dimension. In this proposed classification, as in the preceding temporal-spatial and material culture classifications, the artifact assemblages become the primary unit of reference. Thus an assemblage and its larger structures (phase, industry, complex) can be associated with phenomena related to the environment, economy, and demography in addition to the previously discussed temporal-spatial and material culture fields.

The scales and their labels, as proposed here, are taken from Clarke's (1968) hierarchical arrangement of social entities as defined by archaeologic evidence. Although the hierarchical arrangement and the definitions of these scales follow Clarke, the procedure of ordering the diverse phenomema differs slightly from the approach as originally presented. Rather than focusing on the classification of material culture and then informally examining the material culture classificatory units against a background of environmental, economic, settlement, and temporal-spatial patterns, I am suggesting that a single classification be employed in ordering these phenomena. Again it should be stressed that such a classification assists in organizing the phenomena, but it does not explain their relationships.

CULTURE

In the hierarchical scales of the social field, the archaeological culture is defined by the narrowest parameters of variation in environmental, economic, settlement, material culture, and temporal-spatial phenomena. Clarke (1968:285) identified an archaeological culture as follows:

A specific cultural assemblage, an archaeological culture is a polythetic set of specific and comprehensive artifact-types which consistently recur together in assemblages within a limited geographic area.

In the classification of artifact assemblages and their related attributes, it should be possible to recognize the affiliation of assemblages to a specific archaeological culture based on their:

1 *Distribution within a specific environment and/or micro-environments.* Example— sites from which assemblages are derived are predominantly found within the Mediterranean hill zone and associated with the present or former distribution of the Mediterranean biotic community.

2 *Similarities in specific economy.* Example—economic evidence recovered in association with the assemblages indicating an emphasis on cereal collection and gazelle hunting.

3 *Common settlement and demographic patterns.* Example—large permanent or semi-permanent base camps in the form of small hamlets in conjunction with small, non-residential resource exploitation camps. A radial settlement pattern.

4 *Classification as to industry or phase/facies.* Example—assemblages are classified as the Natufian Industry with Early and Late Natufian Phases.

5 *Limited and continuous temporal-spatial distribution.* Example—assemblages are confined to the hill zone of Syro-Palestine and temporally restricted to between 10,000 and 12,500 B.P.: Early Natufian—12,500–11,000 B.P.; Late Natufian—11,000–10,000 B.P.

CULTURE GROUP

The second or middle scale in the social field is the culture group. At the scale of culture group the temporal-spatial dimensions are considerably larger than those of the culture. As a consequence of these enlarged dimensions, the sociocultural dynamics related to change through time and space reduce the homogeneity of those attributes that have been selected for the identification of social units under this scale. Clarke (1968: 320) stressed the dynamic character of a culture group in his definition:

A family of transform cultures; a group of affinally related, collateral cultures characterized by assemblages sharing a polythetic range but differing states of the same specific multistate artifact-types.

As noted by Clarke, the scale of cultural group has both broad theoretical and practical importance in the classification of social entities. The scale allows for enlarging the temporal-spatial scope in the examination of cultural change. Although this larger scope has poorer resolution with respect to specific information content, it provides a better view of the field and thus a greater opportunity for detecting the larger trends in time and space. On a more practical level, the highly specific evidence requisite for classifying an assemblage to an archaeological culture is often not available. On the other hand, assemblages are more likely to contain the more general evidence that is sufficient for classifying an assemblage to a culture group. Clarke (1968:291), in fact, suggested that few, if any, Lower and Middle Paleolithic assemblages should be classified as to the level of culture. He argued that most assemblages from these time-frames were more reasonably classified as to culture group or technocomplex.

Artifact assemblages that are classified to a culture group should share:

1 *A general environmental setting with perhaps minor regional variation.* Example—sites from which assemblages are derived are distributed within the Saharo-Sindian and Irano-Turanian biotic zones.

2 *General economic strategy.* Example—economic evidence recovered in association with the assemblages indicates hunting and gathering strategy focusing on hunting of small megafauna.

3 *A general settlement and demographic pattern.* Example—small transitory encampments and a circulating settlement pattern.

4 *Classification as to industry.* Example—assemblages are classified to the Sinai Mushabian Industry.

5 *Temporal-spatial distribution is large and perhaps discontinuous.* Example—assemblages are found limited to southern Levant and perhaps northeast Africa, and are temporally restricted to between 13,000 and 14,000 B.P.

TECHNOCOMPLEX

The technocomplex represents the largest social scale in the classification. Clarke (1968:322) defined technocomplex as follows:

The technocomplex represents the partly independent arrival of diverse developing cultural systems at the same general equilibrium pattern based on a similar economic strategy, in similar environments with a similar technology and similar past trajectory.

The assemblages included in a technocomplex should share:

1 *Broad macroenvironment settings.* Example—Mediterranean Irano-Turanian and Saharo-Sindian biotic zones.

2 *A generally similar economy.* Example—hunting and gathering economy focusing on small megafauna.

3 *A general settlement and demographic pattern.* Example—small transitory encampments and circular settlement pattern.

4 *Classification as to complex or industry.* Example—Geometric Kebaran complex.

5 *Broad temporal and/or spatial distribution.* Example—assemblages are found throughout the various geographic zones of Syro-Palestine and are temporally limited to between 13,000 and 14,000 B.P.

MATERIAL CULTURE EQUIVALENCES

The classification of the assemblages into complexes, industries, and phases followed by the ordering of these units in time and space provides the foundation for a socioeconomic classification. The socioeconomic classification entails the additional examination of patterns in the environmental, economic, and demographic data that are associated with the assemblages under study. These data will be examined in greater detail in the following chapters (which are devoted specifically to each of the Epipaleolithic complexes) but are summarized at this stage of the study and incorporated into a socioeconomic classification (Table 4.16).

At the largest and most general scale of the socioeconomic classification, a correspondence is indicated between each of the material culture complexes and socioeconomic technocomplexes. Each of the complexes is associated with a

TABLE 4.16
Summary of socioeconomic parameters for the three major Epipaleolithic complexes.

	Mushabian Complex	Geometric Kebaran Complex	Natufian Complex
Habitat	Desert, steppe	Desert, steppe, Mediterranean	Mediterranean
Settlement pattern	Circulating	Circulating	Radiating
Mobility level	High; ephemeral camps	High–moderate; ephemeral, seasonal camps	Low; permanent or semi-permanent hamlets
Economy	Simple foraging	Simple foraging	Complex foraging
Group size	Small	Small–moderate	Moderate–large
Number of constituent industries	3	+4	2
Past trajectory	(?) N.E. African Epipaleolithic	Kebaran Complex of Levant	Geometric Kebaran Complex of Levant

distinct profile with respect to habitat, economy, settlement pattern, mobility level, group size, and numbers of constituent industries. In relying upon Clarke's (1968:322) definition of a technocomplex, the different "past trajectories" or cultural histories of the three complexes are also important. Relative to the Natufian, the Geometric Kebaran and Mushabian complexes show the greatest similarity but nevertheless differ in regard to habitat, mobility levels, group sizes, industrial diversity, and past trajectories. The intermediate socioeconomic scale of culture group can be correlated with the Mushabian and Natufian. The considerable geographic, environmental, demographic, and industrial diversity of the Geometric Kebaran Complex prohibits making a socioeconomic correlation at this more refined scale. Given the large geographic range of the Geometric Kebaran, the accumulation of more evidence for the complex will probably result in culture groups emerging at the scale of industry rather than complex. The Mushabian and Natufian enjoyed a much more limited geographic scope and environmental range that is perhaps reflected in the greater homogeneity in their economic and demographic patterns.

The most detailed socioeconomic scale, that of culture, can presently be applied only to the Natufian and Harifian industries. In both cases, the material culture residue of these prehistoric populations is well defined in time and space. The artifact assemblages of these industries are also associated with a wide range of settlement types (e.g., hamlets, nonresidential exploitation camps) and an abundance of economic evidence. These data allow for the reconstruction of economic and demographic patterns to a degree of resolution not yet attained for industries of the Mushabian and Geometric Kebaran complexes.

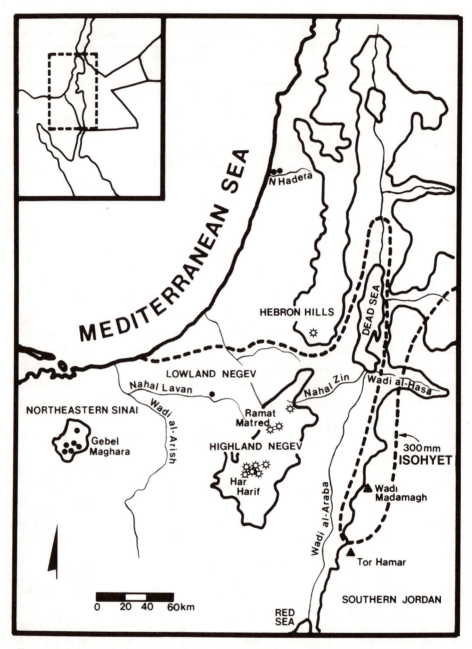

Figure 5.1. *Map showing the distribution of Mushabian Complex sites in the southern Levant. Sites of the Sinai Mushabian Industry are indicated by closed circles (●) and sites of the Negev Mushabian are denoted by open circles (○). The sites of the Madamaghan industry are represented by closed triangles (▲).*

5
The Mushabian Complex

The term "Mushabian" was initially used to describe a series of microlithic assemblages that were discovered in the basin of Wadi Mushabi and neighboring areas of northeastern Sinai in the early 1970s (Phillips and Mintz, 1977:149). At that time, these newly discovered assemblages failed to show parallels with any previously identified taxon in the Levant and thus a new taxonomic unit, the Mushabian Industry, was proposed. On the basis of the similarities in artifact inventories and radiocarbon dates (as outlined in Chapter 4), many more assemblages can now be included in the Mushabian but at the higher-level taxon of "complex." The geographic range of the complex extends over most of the arid zone of the southern Levant, stretching from the Mediterranean coast across the Negev and Sinai into the mountains of southern Jordan (Figure 5.1). There are indications that Mushabian sites may even be present as far north as the Azraq Basin in eastern Jordan.

Temporally, the complex is bracketed by twelve radiocarbon dates to between 14,170 and 11,700 B.P. Although the majority of the dates fall between 13,000 and 13,500 B.P., the presence of Helwan retouch (an attribute common to well dated Early Natufian lithic assemblages) suggests that the complex persisted into a later time-frame—probably on the order of 12,000–11,000 years ago. Conditions generally moister than those of today prevailed during most of the interval between 14,000 and 13,000 B.P., although these conditions were occasionally punctuated by arid episodes. After around 13,000 B.P. the region experienced progressive drying from south to north following the latitudinal shift in winter storm tracks to more northerly positions. By some 11,000 years ago, the environment had deteriorated to such an extent that even the most northern and highest reaches of the Mushabian territory were invaded by the arid zone.

During early Mushabian times, the moist climatic conditions enabled groups intensively to occupy settings in the Sinai, the Negev, and Jordan that today are devoid of surface water and receive under 200mm of precipitation annually. With the progressive drying of the region, accompanied by the expansion of the desert and steppe zones, only the higher and better watered settings along the northern fringes of the Mushabian territory remained available for intensive habitation after around 12,000 years ago.

At this time, Mushabian groups would have come into increasing contact with Natufians as they colonized the margins of the Mediterranean zone as a result of pressure from a growing sedentary population in the core area. In sharing these fringe areas Mushabian groups would have come into competition with Natufian communities, especially over the resources of the uplands. The transhumant cycle of the Mushabians brought them into the uplands only seasonally, but they nevertheless would have felt the progressive loss of food and water sources to Natufian hamlets. Rather than inducing a hostile competition over resources, however, this seasonally overlapping occupation of the uplands appears to have prompted a trading relationship in which Mushabian groups supplied ornamental marine shells to inland Natufian communities in exchange for surplus cereals and nuts. Such a trade arrangement not only enabled Mushabians to maintain their traditional settlement cycle from the coastal lowlands to the uplands, but it also provided Natufian communities with the material symbols of rank and prestige that fueled their intensified economy. This interaction, in conjunction with the continued deterioration of the environment, may have ultimately led to Mushabian groups joining Natufian communities several centuries before these, in turn, failed because of worsening conditions.

Material Culture

The material remains of the Mushabian consist mainly of chipped stone artifacts, although a few specimens of groundstone, worked bone, and ornamental shell have been recorded. This relatively narrow range of behavioral residue can nevertheless be used in reconstructing regional and temporal patterns, defining a settlement system, and examining interaction with neighboring populations.

SINAI MUSHABIAN INDUSTRY

The lithic assemblages that were initially used in the definition of the Mushabian were recovered from four sites in the Mushabi Basin—Mushabi I, Mushabi V, Mushabi XIV, and Mushabi XIX (Phillips and Mintz, 1977). In addition to these, several more assemblages are grouped within the industry in this study on the basis of their similarity across several sets of attributes (see Chapter 4). These include Mushabi IV (Bar-Yosef, 1977:184−93), Nahal Lavan IV (Phillips and Bar-Yosef, 1974), and Nahal Hadera I and II (Kaufman, 1976; Kaufman and

Ronen, 1976). Although these assemblages show some typological differences with those that were originally used in defining the industry, they clearly display closer affinities with the Sinai Mushabian than any other Levantine Epipaleolithic taxon. The Mushabian assemblages recently described by Goring-Morris (1987) were not included within this study.

Tool-kits The primary characteristic of Sinai Mushabian lithic assemblages is the association of the microburin technique with the production of arched backed bladelets, scalene bladelets, and La Mouillah points (Appendix A). Backed bladelets, in fact, account for over 50% of the tool-kit when compared to all other tool classes in Sinai Mushabian assemblages (Table 5.1).

Geometric microliths consisting of trapeze-rectangles, lunates, and triangles follow in importance as a tool class, but at a much lower frequency (i.e., averaging about 12%). Other major tool classes such as scrapers, burins, notches, and denticulates represent a strikingly small proportion of most tool-kits.

Except for the high frequencies of fragments of backed bladelets (i.e., backed bladelets with one or both ends broken), the class is dominated by three types: scalene bladelets, arched backed bladelets, and La Mouillah points (Figure 5.2). In general, the definition of these types in the Mushabian follows that advanced by Tixier (1963) in his description of tools from the North African Epipaleolithic. Although typologically distinct, these three tool types share a general morphology. As bladelets they have been abruptly retouched along one lateral edge and then obliquely truncated into points by retouch (i.e., scalene and arched backed bladelets) or a microburin snap (i.e., La Mouillah points). Not only are these types similar in form, but their dimensional characteristics are nearly identical within the industry as they display an average width of 8mm and an average length of 23mm (Phillips and Mintz, 1977).

Geometrics, ranging from 1−21% of the tool-kit, are composed principally of lunates, triangles, and trapezes. It is interesting, however, that there is no clear pattern of occurrence with these types. Although trapezes furnish the highest mean frequency of the three types, they are absent from two of the assemblages. Trapezes also vary considerably in form and dimensional characteristics, with some clearly being produced by the microburin technique and others apparently

TABLE 5.1
The mean ($\bar{x}$), range (r), and standard deviation (s.d.) of the tool-class percentages for Sinai Mushabian Industry assemblages. Primary data are presented in Appendix A.

Major Tool Classes	$\bar{x}$	r	S.D.
Scrapers	6.8	0−21	8.4
Burins	2.7	0− 9	2.9
Notches and denticulates	10.7	2−26	7.7
Backed bladelets	57.3	16−82	26.3
Geometric microliths	8.5	1−23	7.6
All other tools	14.5	4−40	10.4

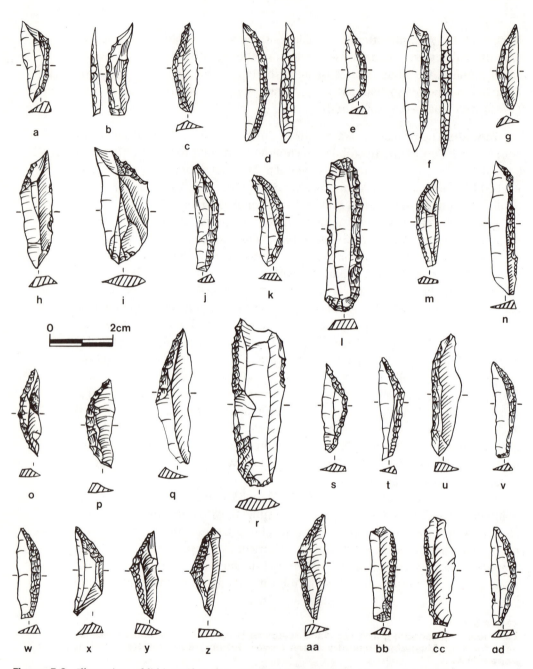

Figure 5.2. *Illustrations of lithic artifacts from Mushabi XIV, Level 1 (redrawn after Phillips and Mintz, 1977). Arched backed bladelets (e,h,j,k,m,o,p,v,w,dd); scalene bladelets (s,t,aa); La Mouillah points (a,b,d,f,j); obtuse bladelets (bb,cc), truncations (q,x), lunates (o,p), triangles (y,z),* piquant triedres (h,i), backed blade (r), endscraper on a backed blade (l).

fabricated from bladelets that were simply retouched to the desired form. Lunates, the dominant geometric type in three assemblages of the industry, consist of both normally backed and Helwan retouched forms (Figure 5.2). Triangles, the least common type of geometric microlith, are rather evenly divided between isosceles/equilateral and scalene forms. As in the case of trapezes, triangles often display the remnants of microburin scars (Figure 5.2).

Lithic Technology In general, the production of relatively short, broad bladelets from single platform cores characterizes the Sinai Mushabian. The bladelets were subsequently sectioned in a controlled fashion through the microburin technique before being fashioned into various tools. Where raw material studies have been conducted, local flint and chert from Cenomanian limestone and dolomite exposures furnished most of the material for tool production. Mushabi IV provides a curious exception to this pattern in displaying a small but noticeable amount of quartz and limestone (Bar-Yosef, 1977:193). The quartz is thought to have come from the conglomerates of the Wadi el-'Arish, minimally some 45km distant, or from southern Sinai.

Our understanding of Sinai Mushabian lithic technology is limited to data drawn from the report of Mushabi IV (Bar-Yosef, 1977) and the attribute study of the Nahal Hadera assemblages (Kaufman, 1976). The proportionate contribution of cores and primary elements (i.e., specimens covered by cortex) indicates that a substantial amount of initial processing was undertaken at Mushabian sites. An examination of the cores shows that single platform types account for about 50% of the class, whereas double platform, 90-degree platform, discoidal, and amorphous types make up the rest. The dominance of single platform cores implies that cores were infrequently rejuvenated, a proposal further supported by the relatively low frequency of core trimming elements. A likely explanation for the apparent lack of interest in extending the use-life of exhausted cores rests in the ready availability of raw material near the sites.

Other Items of Material Culture Beyond the chipped stone assemblages, a few specimens of worked bone, groundstone, and ornamental shell provide a richer picture of the industry's material culture. Two specimens of worked bone, a point and a spatula, were found in association with firepits at Mushabi XIV. Groundstone items were also recovered near hearths at Mushabi XIV and Mushabi V. A mortar and pestle were discovered in the excavation of Mushabi XIV, and limestone slabs were found at Mushabi V. One of the slabs, located in the middle of a concentration of microburins, shows extensive wear thought to have been related to its use as an anvil for sectioning bladelets with the microburin technique (Phillips and Mintz, 1977). The other slab displays a natural basin smeared with traces of red and yellow ochre denoting its use for processing pigment. Mortars and pestles are strongly correlated with the processing of nuts in ethnographic contexts (Kraybill, 1977), but such artifacts appear more closely related to the grinding of pigments during Levantine prehistory prior to the Natufian. Ochre apparently was extensively used in the Mushabian as reflected by the ochre stains noted on many of the flint tools from Mushabi XIV.

Ornamental marine shells in the form of *Dentalium dentale* and *Dentalium elephantisimum* were collected from each of the Sinai Mushabian sites except Mushabi XIX (Phillips and Mintz, 1977; Bar-Yosef, 1977). Dentalium shells are particularly common to Epipaleolithic occupations in the Levant (Reese, 1982). The slender tusk-like shell was apparently used as an ornament without modification in the Sinai Mushabian, although beads were often made from dentalium shells in other Epipaleolithic complexes. The presence of shells from the Red Sea (*D. elephantisimum*) and the Mediterranean (*D. dentale*) points to distant contacts with Sinai Mushabian groups.

NEGEV MUSHABIAN INDUSTRY

The assemblages included in this study of the Negev Mushabian were recovered from seven sites (G1,G3,G9,G14,K6,K7,K9) located in the Har Harif area of the central Negev highlands (Marks and Simmons, 1977), another site (D101B) from the Avdat area of the highlands (Kaufman, 1983), two sites (M141 and M190) described by Yizraeli (1967) from the nearby Ramat Matred, and a site (Ira 23) resting in the southern Hebron Hills of the extreme northern Negev (Valla, et al., 1979). Although assemblages from other sites such as those described from the Halutza Dunes of the western Negev (Noy, 1971) and Tulmeh of the northern Negev (Bar-Yosef, 1970) perhaps should be grouped within the industry, too little information is presently available to be certain of such a placement. Goring-Morris' (1987) "Ramonian" assemblages would also appear to fall within the Negev Mushabian, but his recently published data on the assemblages has not been included in this study.

Tool-kits Negev Mushabian tool-kits are dominated by backed bladelets, principally obliquely truncated and scalene types, in association with moderate frequencies of notches, denticulates, and scrapers (Figure 5.3; Table 5.2). Typo-

TABLE 5.2
The mean ($\bar{x}$), range (r), and standard deviation (S.D.) of the major tool-class percentages for Negev Mushabian Industry assemblages. Primary data are presented in Appendix A.

Major Tool Classes	$\bar{x}$	r	S.D.
Scrapers	7.3	2–17	5.2
Burins	1.6	0– 3	1.1
Notches and denticulates	19.8	6–35	10.5
Backed bladelets	45.3	24–76	15.5
Geometric microliths	2.3	0– 8	2.8
All other tools	23.1	13–35	6.9

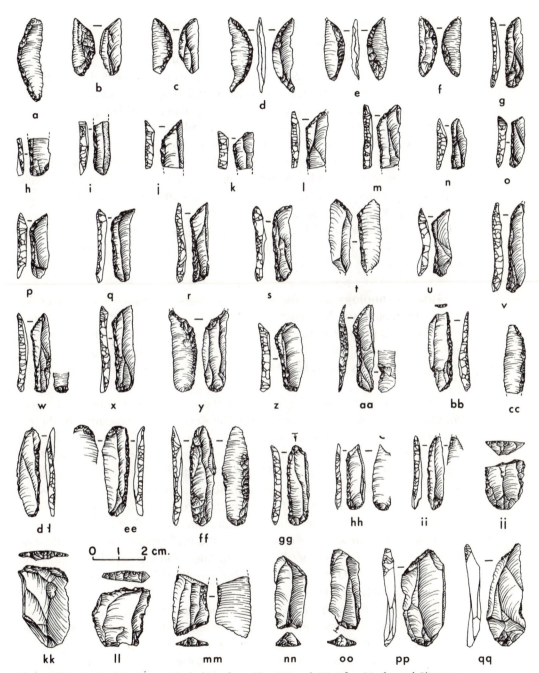

Figure 5.3. *Tools of the Negev Mushabian from Sites K6 and K7 (after Marks and Simmons, 1977). Inversely retouched lunates (a, b); Helwan lunates (e–f); scalene bladelets (g, n–y) (t, Helwan plus inverse retouch); proximal backed bladelet fragments (h, i); fragments of backed and truncated bladelets (j–m); backed and double-truncated bladelets (z–bb); various backed bladelets with modification of one extremity (dd–ii); various truncations (jj–qq).*

logically, the Negev Mushabian differs from the Sinai Mushabian Industry in displaying higher frequencies of notches, denticulates, and scrapers and generally lower frequencies of backed bladelets. Furthermore, within the backed bladelet class, the dominance of obliquely truncated and scalene types in the Negev Mushabian contrasts sharply with the high frequencies of arched backed bladelets and La Mouillah points in Sinai Mushabian assemblages.

The high proportions of straight backed and truncated bladelets opposite snaps furnish another means of distinguishing the two industries. This type conceivably could be interpreted as representing broken tools, such as scalene bladelets, but its abundance and regularity in size suggest that the type more likely reflects "a primitive form of geometric made by backing, a single truncation, and a snap" (Marks and Simmons, 1977:257). If the type was a sort of functional substitute for geometrics, this may explain why geometrics are so poorly represented (0–6%) in the industry. When present, geometrics are normally in the form of lunates and often bear Helwan retouch.

Lithic Technology As in the Sinai Mushabian, the lithic technology of the Negev Mushabian was devoted principally to the production of relatively short, broad bladelets from predominantly single platform cores. These bladelets were subsequently shaped into various tools, mainly pointed bladelets, but the microburin technique was not as intensively employed in this process as it was in the Sinai Mushabian.

The raw material common to the Har Harif assemblages consists of a gray translucent chalcedony that comes from the Cenomanian limestone of the region. The chalcedony, occurring in thin seams and small nodules, is unavailable on the Harif Plateau, but it is widely distributed within the Cenomanian limestones that are exposed less than 5km to the east and south of the plateau. In her examination of the raw material utilization within the Ramat Matred assemblages, Yizraeli (1967) identified a brown chert common to the hammada surfaces of the area and the Cenomanian chalcedony (described by her as a "fine grey flint"). Her study goes on to confirm the preferential use of certain raw materials for production of specific tools. The larger tools, especially scrapers and notches, were manufactured from the brown chert, but the microliths were made mainly from the chalcedony.

The selective use of raw material for the preparation of stone tools was probably caused by a combination of factors. The relative size of the raw material at its source, the suitability of the material for fine retouching, and the durability of the material are all likely to have influenced patterns of use. The brown chert, occurring in larger nodules and being more durable because of its coarse-grain composition, would have made a better material for the larger implements used for scraping and shaft shaving. In contrast, the fine-grained chalcedony present only as small nodules or thin seams would have been more amenable to the fine pressure retouch associated with microliths. What is noteworthy here is that the

TABLE 5.3
The proportionate representation of debitage classes for the Negev Mushabian assemblages.

Debitage Classes	G9	K9	G14	D101B	K6	K5	K7
Cores	5.9	6.1	2.8	1.7	2.8	2.9	4.1
Core trimming element	4.2	4.3	1.2	1.2	4.2	2.5	2.0
Primary elements	15.3	16.4	8.1	4.2	9.6	10.5	12.7
Flakes	42.5	33.7	30.5	26.2	45.9	44.2	37.1
Blades	29.7	33.7	50.6	66.7	32.2	37.2	41.1
Microburins	2.5	5.8	6.7	2.8	5.2	2.6	3.1
(N)	1,199	2,303	2,433	1,635	1,666	2,524	3,200

Natufians, who subsequently colonized the area, adopted an identical pattern of raw material usage (Henry, 1973a).

Studies of debitage provide an understanding of the lithic reduction strategies that were used by Negev Mushabian groups (Marks and Simmons, 1977; Kaufman, 1983). The amount of initial processing associated with the assemblages seems to have been directly tied to the availability of raw material. For example, the frequencies of cores (2.8–6.1%) and primary elements (8.1–15.3%) co-vary directly in the Har Harif assemblages and imply that a significant amount of initial processing (i.e., removal of cortex from raw material and core preparation) was undertaken at the sites (Table 5.3). The lower frequencies of cores (1.7%) and primary elements (4.2%) at D101B mirrors the relative lack of importance of initial processing activities at this site in the Nahal Zin. A survey of the distribution of Cenomanian chalcedony for the region shows that although none of the sites are located on sources of the chalcedony, the Har Harif sites are much closer to extensive deposits of the material. In the absence of quarry sites and evidence for the caching of raw material, the Mushabian reduction strategy would appear to suggest an opportunistic, imbedded procurement system that was tied to a relatively mobile settlement pattern.

The Mushabian reduction strategy was sufficiently flexible to accommodate differences in the availability of raw material, insofar as settlement decisions were unlikely to have been greatly influenced by the distribution of chalcedony. Production efficiency also seems to have been adjusted to balance needs and raw material availability. This is most clearly seen in the differences in core-to-blade ratios for the sites from the two areas. Ratios for the Har Harif assemblages range from 1:5 to 1:18 in comparison to the much higher ratio (1:40) for D101B. These data imply that the reduction strategy enabled the occupants of D101B to extend the productive lives of their cores with a correspondingly greater number of bladelets produced per core in order to compensate for the more distant raw material.

An attribute study of bulb and platform morphologies of debitage samples from the Har Harif assemblages indicates that a shift from hard-hammer percussion to soft-hammer or punch technique took place subsequent to the removal of primary and core trimming elements (after the initial processing of the raw material). Following the initial shaping of cores by hard-hammer percussion, a soft-hammer such as an antler baton or a punch using indirect percussion was apparently used for the removal of bladelets.

After production, bladelets were either fashioned directly into various tools or sectioned through the microburin technique prior to tool fabrication. Micro-burin indices of the Negev Mushabian are considerably lower than those of the Sinai Mushabian but are nevertheless sufficiently high to denote a habitual use of the technique. In the Har Harif assemblages, two applications of the technique were noted—one based upon a single lateral notch and another related to some form of continuous retouch (Marks and Simmons, 1977:240–241). This latter version parallels the application described for the Natufian (Henry, 1974) and is often associated with Helwan retouch, a stylistic attribute also linked to the Natufian.

Other Items of Material Culture Beyond chipped stone artifacts, the Negev Mushabian displays an impoverished material culture confined to specimens of dentalium shell and ochre recovered from the site of D101B.

MADAMAGHAN INDUSTRY

The Mushabian Complex has recently been discovered to have extended east of the Rift Valley into the deserts of southern and eastern Jordan. A survey conducted in the mountains of southern Jordan in 1983–84 revealed two rock-shelter sites (J431 and J436) that contained assemblages pointing to connections with the Mushabian (Henry, 1987a, 1987b; Henry and Garrard, 1988). Sound-ings at these sites produced rich flint assemblages in addition to groundstone items, a worked bone specimen, and numerous faunal remains. Charcoal recov-ered from near the base of Tor Hamar (J431), the largest and deepest site, yielded a radiocarbon date of 12,683 ± 320 B.P. (SMU-1399), thus agreeing nicely with other late Mushabian dates.

The assemblages recovered from Tor Hamar and J431 share several char-acteristics that set them apart from other south Jordan Epipaleolithic indus-tries and, at the same time, point to connections with the Mushabian. These include high microburin indices, moderate frequencies of pointed bladelets (La Mouillah, microgravette, and arched backed varieties), and geometric microliths (trapeze-rectangles, normal and Helwan lunates). A comparison of these assem-blages to that recovered from the nearby Wadi Madamagh rockshelter (Kirk-bride, 1958) reveals several typo-technological similarities sufficiently strong to include all three assemblages in a common taxon—the Madamaghan Industry. Although the Wadi Madamagh assemblage was initially described as a Kebaran occurrence, several of its techno-typological characteristics (e.g., La Mouillah points, geometric microliths, and microburins) fall well outside those of the Kebaran Industry.

A group of assemblages recently recovered from sites in eastern Jordan may also belong to the Madamaghan Industry. The open sites of Wadi Jilat 8 and 6, and Uwenid 14 (Garrard, et al., 1986; B. Byrd, personal communication, 1984) display La Mouillah points, microgravettes, arched backed and pointed bladelets, and high microburin indices. A radiocarbon date of 13,310 ± 120 B.P. (OxA 521) from Wadi Jilat 8 also points to a general synchroneity between these sites and those of southern Jordan.

Tool-kits Madamaghan tool-kits are dominated by backed bladelets and points, with scrapers, notches-denticulates, and geometrics present in much lower frequencies (Table 5.4). Backed bladelets most often occur as straight backed or arched backed types (Figure 5.4). The latter are typically "hook shaped," with the proximal sections displaying straight edges and the distal sections arching strongly past the long axes of the specimens thus forming pointed hooks. Both the straight and arched backed types often show basal truncations.

Points of the La Mouillah and microgravette types are found in moderate numbers. Both types exhibit straight, regularly retouched edges. Many of the microgravettes were initially pointed by use of the microburin technique with the microburin scar subsequently being removed by marginal retouch.

The backed bladelets and points appear to have been used principally to tip projectiles as impact spalls are common to both classes of tools. An analysis of microwear on points and pointed bladelets from Tor Hamar (Henry and Garrard, 1988) indicates that they were mounted obliquely onto wooden shafts, most likely with a natural mastic. Red and yellow ochre was apparently mixed with the mastic as indicated by the numerous backed bladelets and points that show ochre stains along their retouched edges. It is interesting to note that of the 130 specimens from Tor Hamar that show ochre stains, all but four are represented by backed bladelets and points. The almost exclusive use of ochre for the decoration of these tools may reflect the greater role that projectile points played over other tools in advertising ethnic identity among Mushabian groups. In being used as weapons, hunting implements, trading items, and even gaming pieces, points were more likely than other tools to have been present in situations where different social groups were interacting. In such situations, the use of ochre would have brought greater attention to the symbolic messages of social identity that were conveyed by point design and other emblematic characteristics.

Although the points and pointed bladelets appear to have been used to tip shafts, a question emerges as to how these were projected—by throwing stick (atlatl) or bow? The weight of points seems to be the most important factor in answering the question. In his study of several hundred points from North America, Fenenga (1953) concluded that points weighing less than 3.5gm were used as arrowheads, whereas those weighing more than 4.5gm were used as

TABLE 5.4
The mean ($\bar{x}$), range (r), and standard deviation (S.D.) of the tool-class percentages for Madamaghan Industry assemblages. Primary data are given in Appendix A.

Major Tool Classes	$\bar{x}$	r	S.D.
Scrapers	7.9	7.5– 8.3	.4
Burins	1.5	4.0– 6.0	.5
Notches and denticulates	5.7	1.3– 9.6	4.1
Backed bladelets	62.5	51.0–69.0	9.8
Geometric microliths	1.3	.6– 2.4	.9
All other tools	20.8	17.0–28.0	5.6

dart points propelled by an atlatl. The average weight of the points and pointed bladelets from Tor Hamar is 0.49gm, and the heaviest specimen weighs only 2.5gm. These data strongly suggest that the points and pointed bladelets were used as arrowheads. The carbon-14 date from Tor Hamar, and those from other Mushabian Complex sites, would then suggest that the bow and arrow were in use in the Levant as early as some 13,000–14,000 years ago. Whereas the first appearance of the bow and arrow is somewhat uncertain (Wenke, 1984), their presence in the Mushabian would fall among the earliest examples of this technology on a worldwide scale.

Geometric microliths were also likely to have been used to tip arrows or to have served as lateral barbs. Madamaghan assemblages, like the Mushabian Complex as a whole, typically contain low frequencies of geometrics, but various types are represented including triangles, trapeze-rectangles, and lunates with both normal and Helwan retouch.

Scrapers, mainly simple endscrapers and notches-denticulates, occur about equally on flakes and blades (Figure 5.3) and, like other tool classes in the Madamaghan, occur in about the same frequencies as in other Mushabian Complex assemblages.

Lithic Technology The Madamaghan assemblages from southern Jordan are fashioned mainly from a fine, gray Cenomanian chalcedony, thus resembling the Negev Mushabian pattern of raw material usage. Analysis of the bulb and platform attributes of these assemblages also reveals a reduction strategy that parallels that identified for the Negev assemblages (Henry and Garrard, 1988). Both industries shifted from hard-hammer percussion to soft-hammer or punch technique after the initial shaping of the cores. The other major technological characteristic of the Madamaghan was a habitual use of the microburin technique as reflected in indices falling near those of the Sinai and Negev Mushabian.

Other Items of Material Culture The rockshelter deposit of Tor Hamar yielded the richest material culture evidence beyond chipped stone specimens for the industry. Although fragmentary, six specimens of groundstone were recovered from the sounding. Three of the fragments are quite large, coming from

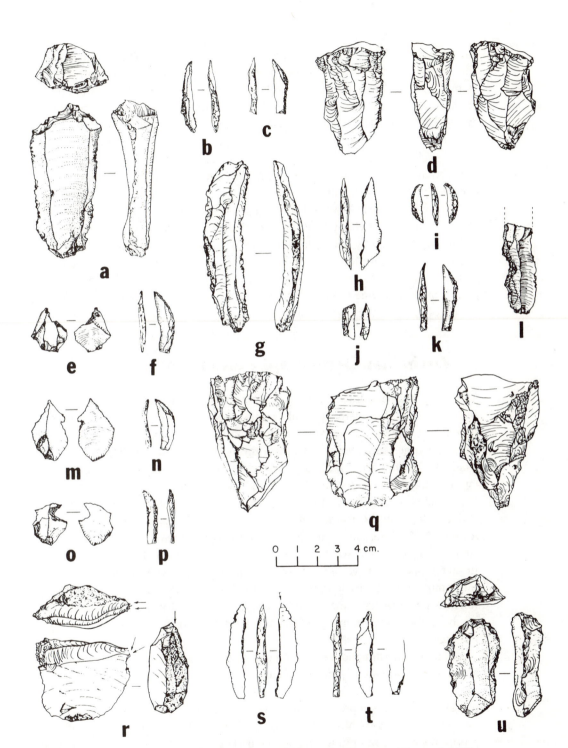

Figure 5.4. *Artifact illustrations of Tor Hamar assemblage (after Henry and Garrard, 1988). Endscrapers (a,u), arched backed bladelets (b,f,k,n,p), La Mouillah points (c,h), cores (d,q), microburins (e,m,o), retouched blade (g), Helwan lunate (i), trapeze (j), notch (l), burin (r), microgravette points (s,t).*

portable bowl shaped mortars fashioned from limestone. The projected rim diameters of the two most complete mortars range from 12–16cm with interior depths of 15–17cm. A small rim section of a finely ground limestone bowl, a handstone, and a large pestle were also recovered. The presence of mortars, a pestle, and a handstone suggests that a wide range of grinding activities were undertaken at the site. Some of the groundstone may have been linked to the processing of ochre, but it seems unlikely that it all would have been devoted to this activity. The large deep mortars, in particular, would appear better associated with the processing of nuts.

The ashy deposit also produced a highly polished bone point and an abundance of marine shells. Of the 268 specimens, dentalium shells are the most common, followed by netrididae and scallops. Many of the shells had been perforated, presumably for stringing as jewelry. Lumps of ochre (red and yellow hematite) were also found throughout the deposit. In her excavation of Wadi Madamagh, Kirkbride (1958) similarly noted a high density of marine shells and lumps of ochre in the shelter's ashy deposit.

Mushabian Demography and Economy

The combined data drawn from Mushabian Complex sites point to their having been generated by relatively small, highly mobile foraging groups, but there is little direct evidence upon which to reconstruct the Mushabian economy. Aside from the large faunal collections from the rockshelters of Tor Hamar and Wadi Madamagh, evidence is limited to a few fragmentary bone elements and ostrich eggshell fragments found at Mushabi V. The sounding of Tor Hamar produced the remains of gazelle, wild goat, equids, wild cattle, hares, tortoises, and partridges (Henry and Garrard, 1988). Gazelle and wild goat, together accounting for over 77% of the fauna, are about equally represented. Although the specialized hunting of gazelle was common to most of the Epipaleolithic, the Tor Hamar hunters appear to have been equally adept at taking wild goats in the craggy mountains of southern Jordan. The near balance between gazelle and wild goat remains suggests that the cliffs and steep canyons near Tor Hamar were exploited at about the same intensity as the flat land located a few kilometers east of the site.

In that lower limb bones are well represented for both gazelle and goat, these animals were apparently not butchered in the field, at least to the extent that uneconomical parts of the carcasses were discarded at the kill site. About half of the gazelle remains represent immature animals. Whereas a high proportion of immature animals within a faunal assemblage has been interpreted as an indication of some form of herd management (Legge, 1972; Perkins, 1966; Hecker, 1982), it has been shown that juveniles typically account for over one-half of "natural" gazelle herds (Henry, 1975; Henry and Garrard, 1988). The rough balance between juvenile and adult remains indicate that there was little hunting preference for either old or young animals and that the age profiles fairly well reflect those of an entire living herd. These data suggest that the herds suffered a catastrophic mortality such as would be associated with their having been hunted by ambush or surround.

SETTLEMENT PATTERNS: RANGE AND SEASONALITY

Questions related to the seasonality and geographic range of Mushabian settlement strategy can be only partially addressed at present, with the most complete evidence coming from sites of the Sinai Mushabian.

Seasonality The sites in the basin of Wadi Mushabi have been interpreted as expressions of winter and summer encampments (Phillips and Mintz, 1977). These interpretations are based upon the seasonal shifts in prevailing winds and the differences in the local exposures of the sites. The seasonal availability of water in different parts of the basin furnishes additional evidence for determining seasonality.

The sites of Mushabi I, IV, and V are located about 1–1.5km from the remnants of an ancient seasonal freshwater lake found in the eastern part of the basin, whereas the sites of Mushabi XIV and Mushabi XIX are situated on the old shoreline of the lake (Figure 5.5). During the Mushabian occupation of the

Figure 5.5. *Map of the Mushabi Basin, northeastern Sinai showing the distribution of Sinai Mushabian sites. Note that the sites of Mushabi I, IV, and V are located some 1–2 km southwest of the ancient lake, whereas Mushabi XIV and XIX occupy lakeshore settings (modified after Bar-Yosef and Phillips, 1977).*

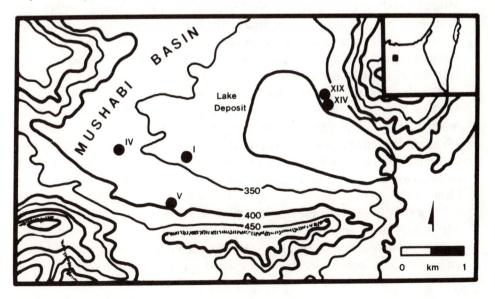

basin the annual moisture budget would have been greater than that of today, but the prevailing Mediterranean climate nevertheless would have induced marked wet and dry seasons. Settlement away from the lake would have been more likely during the winter wet seasons when minor tributaries, such as those near Mushabi I, IV, and V, were charged. On the other hand, the lake shore would have become an attractive camp setting in the spring and early summer. At this time of the year the surrounding area would have lacked surface water while the lake still held runoff from the winter rains.

The seasonal shifts in prevailing wind also provide a clue to the time of year when the sites were occupied. During the excavation of Mushabi V it was discovered that ash and charcoal flecks were dispersed in a northeasterly direction away from several hearths, thus suggesting a southwestern wind during or shortly after the occupation of the site. In that today's prevailing winds blow from the southwest or west during the winter and from the north or northwest in summer (Goldberg, 1977:13), the ash distributions indicate winter encampments at the site. Artifact plots at Mushabi V are also consistent with wind from the southwest, as the major concentration of material would indicate activities upwind of the hearths (Figure 5.6). Such a setting would have enabled the inhabitants of the site to conduct their activities near the heat of the fires without the annoyance of smoke and wind-born cinders.

The topographic settings of Mushabi V and the nearby site of Mushabi I are also consistent with the proposed winter occupations. These site locations are afforded protection from the prevailing winter winds by limestone ridges that flank the basin on the south and southwest. Phillips and Mintz (1977:164), in fact, mention that contemporary Bedouin groups inhabiting the area establish their winter camps in the lee of these ridges for wind protection.

In contrast to Mushabi I, IV, and V, the lakeshore sites of Mushabi XIV and Mushabi XIX are located on the northern edge of the basin and attributed to summer camps. Excavation of Mushabi XIV exposed three hearths displaying charcoal dispersals trending to the south and southeast. Given the previously noted seasonal shifts in wind patterns, the north-to-northwest wind direction indicated by the ash distribution would signify a summer occupation. Unlike the artifact distributions and ash dispersion at winter camps, however, those at Mushabi XIV imply that activities were being conducted downwind from the hearths, presumably within the range of their smoke (Figure 5.7). Over two kilograms of charred material, recovered from the largest of the hearths, contained branches and fruits of juniper (*Juniperus phoenicea*), a fuel prized by local Bedouin for its pleasant aroma and its usefulness in smoking meat (Phillips and Mintz, 1977:170).

Since activities at the site may well have centered on meat or hide smoking, why would these activities have been undertaken downwind from the large hearth? A likely answer is that this may have been done to avoid the swarms of gnats, flies, and mosquitoes that would have plagued such a lakeshore setting during the warm season.

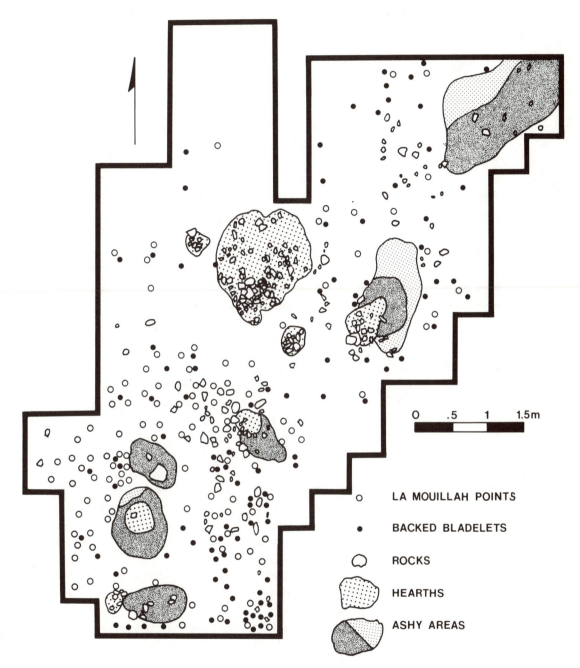

Figure 5.6. *Site map of Mushabi V. Note the predominant distribution of ash to the northeast of the hearths and artifact scatters to the southwest (modified after Phillips and Mintz, 1977).*

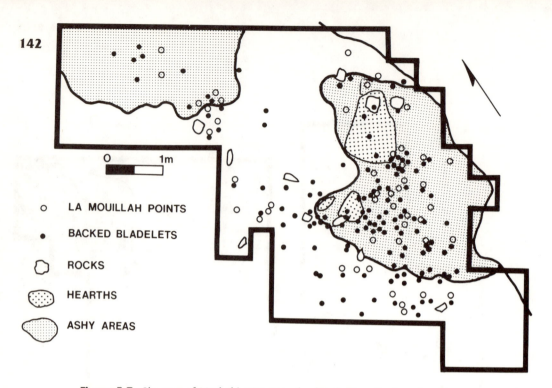

O   1m

○   LA MOUILLAH POINTS

●   BACKED BLADELETS

⬡   ROCKS

▦   HEARTHS

▨   ASHY AREAS

Figure 5.7. *Site map of Mushabi XIV. Note the distribution of ash and artifact scatters to the south of the hearths (modified after Phillips and Mintz, 1977).*

Settlement Size and Distribution Given the seasonal fluctuations in the available resources (e.g., water, plant foods, game) in most environments, for-aging societies exhibit seasonal variation in the permanency of encampments and the size of camp groups (Turnbull, 1968; Jochim, 1976; Butzer, 1982). An annual demographic cycle that contains a highly mobile segment (i.e., dispersed mode), where camps are briefly occupied by small numbers of inhabitants, and a less mobile segment (coalesced mode), where camps are occupied for longer periods by a greater number of inhabitants, is typical of foraging societies. In fulfilling elemental social and biological needs (Williams, 1974; Wobst, 1974; Jochim, 1976; Hassan, 1981), aggregation of small, mobile groups into larger, usually less mobile groups appears necessary for the overall viability of a forag-ing population.

This general pattern of seasonal adjustments in the population and mobility of foragers appears to be reflected in the Mushabian settlement strategy. A clear dichotomy in the sizes of the sites is seen when those of the high inland areas (Gebel Maghara, highland Negev, southern Jordan) are compared with coastal sites such as those of Nahal Hadera. Sites of the Gebel Maghara area range in size from +30m² to 200m² (Phillips and Mintz, 1977:149), those of the high-land Negev display primary occupation areas (the estimated site area prior to deflation) of 100m² to 200m² (Marks and Simmons, 1977:234), and the south Jordan sites range from 150m² to 200m². In contrast to these small site areas, Nahal Hadera I and II exhibit areas of 900m² and 1,000m², respectively (Kauf-man, 1976:96–97). In this regard, it is noteworthy that the artifact distributions of the Nahal Hadera sites are apparently not governed by erosion or slope wash, but are in primary context and thus indicative of the original occupational areas of the sites' prehistoric inhabitants (Kaufman, 1976:97).

An estimation of the number of inhabitants for Mushabian sites can be achieved by using equations, developed from Yellen's (1977) ethnographic data, that define the relationship between the occupied area and the number of occupants in contemporary !Kung Bushmen camps. Wiessner (1974, 1979), Casteel (1979), Read (1978), and Hassan (1981) have proposed various equations that describe this relationship mathematically.

Power and exponential curves have been used on the same data set, with both approaches displaying high (r = .93) correlation coefficients (Hassan, 1981:68–70). Although there is little difference between the two curves in the population estimates for camp areas in the 100m²–200m² range, the curves differ significantly at the 900m²–1,000m² level (Table 5.5). Because there is really no way to determine, with the data at hand, which of these procedures offers the best means of defining the mathematical relationship between occupation area and number of occupants, population estimates for the Mushabian sites are presented using both power and exponential curves (Table 5.6).

TABLE 5.5
Population estimates for various site areas based upon power (Casteel, 1979) and exponential (Hassan, 1981) curves. Both curves yield correlation coefficients of .93 for same data set.

| | Population Estimates | |
| | Power curve | Exponential curve |
Site Area (m²)	$(A = .1542\ p^{2.321})$	$(A = 8.9584\ e^{.1414p})$
30	10	9
100	17	16
200	22	22
900	33	41
1000	33	43

TABLE 5.6
The number, minimum, and mean ($\bar{x}$) distances between hearths for three Sinai Mushabian sites. Data taken from site plans published by Phillips and Mintz (1977) and Bar-Yosef (1977).

Site	Number of Hearths	Distance(s) Between Hearths (m)	$\bar{x}$ Distance (m)
Mushabi V	4	2,2,2,3	2.25
Mushabi XIV	2	2	2.00
Mushabi IV	2	8	8.00

In fitting Mushabian site areas to the curves, the small ($+30m^2-200m^2$) sites would have had an estimated 9–22 occupants—with the majority of these having about 15 occupants—and the large ($900m^2-1,000m^2$) sites would have been occupied by some 33–43 persons.

Another method of developing a population estimate for the Mushabian sites entails comparing the mean distances (m) between hearths within the sites. Hassan (1981:72) finds, again using Yellen's ethnographic data, that the mean distance between hearths increases directly with the number of camp occupants. In comparing the mean distances between hearths from three small Mushabian sites (Mushabi IV, V, and XIV) to the regression line computed from Yellen's data by Hassan, estimates of site occupants range from 5 to 28 persons with an average of about 10 persons (Table 5.6). These population estimates, therefore, are remarkably similar to those based upon occupation areas.

If, as suggested, these differences in the areas of Mushabian sites are expressions of the seasonal coalescence and dispersion of Mushabian groups, then the coalesced camps would have been formed by the merging of two to five dispersed groups. If the population estimates are correct, such a coalescence would have been demanded in order to achieve group population levels that were socially and economically viable (Wobst, 1974:170, 173).

When combined with an understanding of the differences in the availability of resources for the region, the seasonal and demographic reconstructions of Mushabian occupations can be used to design a comprehensive model of Mushabian settlement and subsistence strategies. On the basis of these considerations, the settlement-subsistence pattern of Mushabian groups is most likely to have followed an annual cycle that entailed a late winter (February–March) through midsummer (June–July) occupation of the interior uplands (e.g., Gebel Maghara, Negev Highlands, Jordanian Plateau) followed by a late summer (August–September) through mid-winter (December–January) occupation of the coastal lowlands. These seasonal shifts in environmental setting are also likely to have been accompanied by demographic adjustments that involved reduced mobility and coalescence of Mushabian groups as they moved from upland interior areas to the coast.

Although evidence related to establishing the seasonality of occupations indicates that the interior uplands were inhabited during winter and summer months, it was probably only in the late winter, when temperatures began to moderate, that the uplands would have been settled. The much colder temperatures, some 6°–8°C lower than today's, of Late Glacial times would have made mid-winter occupation of the higher elevations unlikely. After several months of a long dry season, the winter rains would have prompted the growth of new vegetation, and by the late winter/early spring the inland areas would have become attractive for plant and animal exploitation by Mushabian foragers. From another perspective, it was only during or immediately following the rainy season that a widespread occupation of the interior would have been possible away from the more permanent water sources (e.g., springs, seasonal lakes). Those sites (Mushabi I, IV, V) located in the southwestern part of the Mushabi Basin away from the seasonal lake are probable expressions of this segment of the settlement cycle. In this context, one might recall that seasonal evidence from these sites suggested a winter occupation. Those sites recorded in the Har Harif and Ramat Matred as being found far from permanent water are probably related to the same settlement segment, but because of their higher elevations they were perhaps occupied somewhat later in the spring. Similarly, the high elevation Madamaghan rockshelters of southern Jordan were also likely occupied in the late winter and spring.

With the continued occupation of the interior during the spring and into the summer, Mushabian groups would have become increasingly dependent upon permanent water sources. The lakeside sites of Mushabi XIV and XIX, interpreted as summer occupations, would be representative of this segment as would the site of D101b, which is located near perennial springs in the Nahal Zin. As the dry season progressed, those areas in the vicinity of springs and seasonal lakes would not only have provided the only available water but would also have been attractive because of their higher density of game.

By mid-to-late summer, surface water would have virtually disappeared from the interior with the drying up of isolated pools and seasonal lakes. Only a few perennial springs would have continued to supply water. Even with these meagre water sources still available, however, the dying-off of vegetation after several months without rain would have caused game to begin moving toward the better watered and more heavily vegetated coastal lowlands. It seems a reasonable conjecture, therefore, that Mushabian groups would have been drawn in a similar fashion to the Mediterranean and Red Sea coasts as water and food resources declined in the interior. The two large sites of Nahal Hadera I and II, located about .5km north of a major perennial tributary on the coastal plain, are probably expressions of this segment of the Mushabian annual cycle.

Origin and External Relationships

Within the Levant, there exists no real evidence for a source of the Mushabian. The principal characteristics of the Mushabian material culture (arched backed bladelets, scalene bladelets, La Mouillah points, geometric microliths, and microburins) are virtually absent from those Epipaleolithic and late Upper Paleolithic assemblages that precede the Mushabian Complex. This observed lack of typological and technological continuity with the Paleolithic succession of the Levant has prompted scholars to look outside the region for a Mushabian origin. Similarities noted between the Mushabian and industries from North Africa and the Nile have precipitated suggestions of a western origin for the complex (Henry, 1974; Phillips and Mintz, 1977; Bar-Yosef, 1981a).

The microburin technique, used in fashioning *piquant triedres* and La Mouillah points, is common to the Iberomaurusian II or Classic Industry (Gobert, 1962; Tixier, 1963; Brahimi, 1970; Phillips, 1973, 1975) of the Maghreb and to the Silsilian Industry of Upper Egypt (Phillips and Butzer, 1973; Henry, 1974). Geometric microliths are also found in both industries (Phillips, 1975). Whereas the Iberomaurusian II apparently dates to after ca. 14,130 years ago, as evidenced by a series of dates from Taforalt in Morroco (Camps, 1975), the Silsilian dates from as early as 16,000 B.P. to as late as 14,430 B.P. (Wendorf and Schild, 1976:267; Smith, 1968:396; Butzer and Hansen, 1968:114; Phillips and Butzer, 1973). In comparing the Iberomaurusian II and Silsilian chronologies to that of the Mushabian Complex (14,170−12,700 B.P.), it seems improbable that the Iberomaurusian would have contributed to the development of the Mushabian. On the other hand, Silsilian peoples could well have accounted for the origin of the Mushabian either through direct contact via expansion of a population from Upper Egypt northeastward into Sinai and the Negev or merely through diffusion of ideas. Unfortunately, we know little of the prehistoric occupation of the Egyptian eastern desert along such a proposed route of expansion.

Regardless of the origin of the Mushabian, the evidence at hand can be used to trace its cultural development in three regions of the southern Levant beginning ca. 14,000 years ago. One region, representing the Sinai Mushabian Industry, would have included northeastern Sinai, the lowland Negev, and the coastal plain as far north as the Nahal Hadera. Another region, representing the Negev Mushabian, would have been comprised of the Negev Highlands and the southern Hebron Hills. The third region, linked to Madamaghan, would have included southern Jordan and perhaps extended northeast as far as the Azraq Basin. Cultural evolution and development appears to have continued with little change until after ca. 12,500 B.P., at which time Mushabian groups came into contact with Early Natufian communities. The conservatism in material culture over this 1,500-year pre-Natufian period is particularly surprising given that Mushabian groups shared some of their overall territorial range with contemporary Geometric Kebaran peoples. It was only after coming into contact with Early Natufian communities, however, that the Mushabian material culture began taking on some of the characteristics attributable to neighboring peoples.

In a situation where different populations share geographic territories and yet remain culturally distinct, material culture is likely to be promoted as a symbolic advertisement of ethnicity and thereby to enhance group solidarity (Hodder, 1979). In many ways, those groups lacking a territorial boundary that corresponds to an ethnic boundary are obligated to identify themselves more fully through behavior and material items. As with many simple foraging societies, Mushabian and Geometric Kebaran groups were likely to have had loosely defined territories with flexible boundaries. The distribution of the sites for these two complexes, in fact, points to considerable geographic overlap in northeastern Sinai, the Negev, and southern Jordan for approximately 1,500 years. Clearly, such proximity over such a length of time should have resulted in a social mixing of the two populations had not a deliberate and persistent effort at social distinctiveness been practiced. From this perspective, it may be easier to understand why populations inhabiting the same geographic area and practicing a similar economy maintained quite different material cultures, at least with regard to chipped stone tools, for such a long time.

With the emergence of the Natufian, the relationship between the Mushabians and their neighbors changed. First, the territorial and ethnic boundaries between the two populations were concordant, thereby reducing the emphasis upon behavioral advertisements of ethnicity. Secondly, the social complexity and stratification of the two populations were no longer symmetric in that the Natufians represented a complex foraging society with large, sedentary, ranked communities in contrast to the simple foraging system of the Mushabians. Thirdly, the different territorial distributions of the two populations and the concomitant lack of redundancy in available resources appear to have prompted a trading relationship between them.

Mushabian groups apparently provided Natufian hamlets with marine shells found along the Mediterranean and Red Sea coasts. Such shells, found in abundance in Natufian sites, were used extensively as jewelry and symbols of status. Whereas the catchments of Natufian hamlets would have included the Mediterranean shoreline in the Carmel (El Wad, Kebara, Nahal Oren) and western Galilee (Hayonim) sites, other major hamlets located in the eastern Galilee (Ein Mallaha), Samaria (Shukbah), Judea (El Khiam, Ain Sakhri, Erq el Ahmar), the Highland Negev (Rosh Zin, Rosh Horesha), and the Jordanian Plateau (Wadi Hama 27, Wadi Judayid, and Beidha) would have lacked access to the Mediterranean coast. And none of the Natufian sites would have had direct access to the Red Sea. The site of Wadi Judayid, closest to the Red Sea coast, is some 80km distant.

Mushabian groups may well have supplied such hamlets with shells from both the Red Sea and the Mediterranean. In support of this idea, the sources of dentalium in the Sinai Mushabian show a clear shift through time from almost exclusively local Mediterranean species to a balance between Mediterranean and Red Sea forms. Such a shift might be expected if the shells had been used locally during the early Mushabian but had taken on significance as a trade item during the late Mushabian.

In addition to the effects of trade between Early Natufian and late Mushabian groups, the differences in social and economic complexity between the two populations are likely to have led to the adoption of Natufian traits by Mushabian groups. In examining a similar relationship, although at higher levels of social stratification, between the inhabitants of the Valley of Oaxaca and the Olmec, Flannery (1968:105) discovered a remarkable cross-cultural regularity in this pattern. He points to a number of commonalities in noting that data from several parts of the world suggest that a special relationship exists between consumers of exotic raw materials and their suppliers, especially when the suppliers belong to a society which is only slightly less stratified than that of the consumers. First, it seems that the upper echelon of each society often provides the entrepreneurs who facilitate the exchange. Second, the exchange is not "trade" in the sense that we use the term, but rather is set up through mechanisms of ritual visits, exchange of wives, "adoption" of members of one group by the other, and so on. Third, there may be an attempt on the part of the elite of the less sophisticated society to adopt the behavior, status trappings, religion, symbolism, or even language of the more sophisticated group—in short, to absorb some of their charisma. Fourth, although the exchange system does not alter the basic subsistence pattern of either group, it may not be totally unrelated to subsistence. It may, for example, be a way of establishing reciprocal obligations between a group with an insecure food supply and one with a perennial surplus (Flannery, 1968:105).

It is not difficult to imagine how Mushabian groups, as relatively impoverished simple foragers, would have been impressed with the apparent wealth and status associated with Natufian hamlets. Shells from the Mediterranean and the Red Sea would have made easily portaged trade items that could have been exchanged for surplus foods such as nuts and grains during the upland-interior segment of the Mushabian settlement cycle. Such an exchange at this time of the year would have made for ideal scheduling for both parties. For the Natufians this would have been a time when the previous year's surplus could be measured against the current year's harvest and any shortfalls could be avoided. And for the Mushabians, the summer dry season would likely have represented the least productive part of their annual cycle, making Natufian surpluses an attractive supplement to their diets.

The interaction between Natufian and Mushabian groups may also explain the presence of Helwan retouch, a Natufian stylistic trait, in Mushabian assemblages. From a diachronic perspective, the cultural interaction between the two societies may also furnish an explanation for the ultimate disappearance of the Mushabian as an archaeological entity and a distinct social system. With the deterioration of the environment in Sinai, accompanying the northward migration of storm-tracks about 13,000 years ago, Mushabian groups would have become increasingly dependent upon the uplands to the north (e.g., Highland Negev, Judean Hills, southern Jordan) during the interior segment of their annual cycle. Mushabian groups would have been forced northward out of Sinai to these better watered uplands and were likely to have become increasingly attracted to Natufian surpluses of foodstuffs.

In that the uplands would have been controlled by the larger and more politically complex Natufian hamlets, Mushabian groups would ultimately have been incorporated into the Natufian social system if they were to have access to the uplands and to survive. A possible archaeological expression of the absorption of the Mushabian into the Natufian social system may be seen in the temporal and spatial distribution of the microburin technique in the Natufian. This

technique, most strongly identified with the Mushabian, shows a clinal increment in utilization in Natufian assemblages from south to north and from early
to late times. If the diachronic relationships between Mushabian and Natufian
populations as presented here are accurately reconstructed, then by Late Natufian times (after ca. 11,000 B.P.) the Mushabian would have ceased to exist as a
distinct social system, thus explaining its disappearance from the archaeological
record.

6
The Geometric Kebaran Complex

The Geometric Kebaran is the most widespread and diverse of the Levant's late Epipaleolithic complexes. The considerable artifactual variability of the complex in part reflects the adaptive responses of Geometric Kebaran groups to different environments. Unlike the Mushabians, who were confined to the steppe and desert zones, Geometric Kebaran groups inhabited the Mediterranean woodlands as well as parts of the arid zones. These wide differences in environmental settings probably induced local adjustments in activities that, in turn, influenced the composition of the material culture. Geometric Kebaran groups also appear to have experienced some regional cultural divergence quite apart from that induced by environmental pressures alone. Regional pockets of cultural development may have stemmed from an adaptive strategy based on transhumance. By exploiting several closely packed, but vertically differentiated resource zones, Geometric Kebaran groups were able to subsist within relatively small territories. This acted to reduce the extent of cultural dispersion and prompted the emergence of relatively small cultural enclaves.

Two factors, however, acted to counter those forces contributing to the cultural heterogeneity of the Geometric Kebaran peoples. An origin within the Kebaran and two major periods of population movement provided a common cultural background and episodes of social remixing. These factors enabled Geometric Kebaran peoples to retain a general level of social cohesiveness and thus remain an archaeologically recognizable entity some 12–13,000 years later.

As with most prehistoric cultures, it is inaccurate to say that the Geometric Kebaran disappeared some 12,500 years ago. The Geometric Kebaran people continued to exist, their genetic material was passed on, and some of their behavioral patterns undoubtedly persisted, but overall they underwent a fundamental evolution in their strategy of adaptation sometime between 12,000 and 13,000 years ago. Near the end of the Ice Age, the expansion of the Mediterranean woodlands into the Levantine uplands made available new resources that when exploited induced sedentary lifeways. This adaptive shift prompted such marked changes in the economy, demography, and social organization of the Geometric Kebarans that their culture and its material residue were transformed to the extent that a new high order social and archaeological taxon emerged, as seen in the Natufian.

The evolutionary path of the Geometric Kebaran, however, was not a direct one. When the patterned variation in artifacts is examined against the dimensions of time and space, at least four industry level variants (i.e., cultures) can be identified as sub-sets of the complex. Whereas one of these shows a direct, smooth cultural evolution to the Natufian, the others show a more abrupt transition. This would suggest that the specific cultural patterns of the Geometric Kebaran population that first bridged the transformation were then rapidly adopted by other Geometric Kebaran groups as they evolved from mobile to sedentary foragers. The specific mechanics of this process are unclear, as are the precise linkages between adaptation and ethnicity in this case. What is clear, however, is that with the Geometric Kebaran to Natufian transition there occurred the amalgamation of a culturally heterogeneous population into an ethnic entity of marked cultural homogeneity.

BACKGROUND

The term "Geometric Kebaran" was introduced by Bar-Yosef in his study of the Epipaleolithic of Palestine in 1970. In this work he provided the first systematic overview of the Levantine Epipaleolithic. Of particular importance was his proposed cultural-historical classification, which was based upon the quantitative comparison of certain technological and typological attributes of chipped stone assemblages. Prior work had focused upon the presence or absence of guide fossils and had implicitly explained variability in lithic assemblages as a consequence of their evolution through time.

Bar-Yosef's (1970) initial classification of the Geometric Kebaran distinguished between two industries: A and B. Whereas the Geometric Kebaran A was well defined and exhibited relatively tight techno-typological parameters, the Geometric Kebaran B included a group of assemblages that were not only archaeologically heterogeneous but also poorly defined conceptually. At a very general level, these assemblages shared certain affinities with the Natufian that prompted Bar-Yosef (1970:173) to suggest that the Geometric Kebaran B represented either an industrial facies of the Geometric Kebaran or the residue of Natufian seasonal camps.

Subsequent research has assisted in resolving this conceptually awkward classification in which a single material culture taxon (the Geometric Kebaran

B) served as a behavioral correlate for two exclusive sociocultural systems. The discovery of the Mushabian did much to clarify the issue insofar as the Geometric Kebaran B assemblages that were most strongly identified with the Natufian (Ramat Matred 190 and 141) are now placed within this newly defined complex. Other Geometric Kebaran B assemblages from surface scatters (e.g., Poleg 18M) have been shown to be mixed assemblages (Henry, 1973a), and the remaining assemblages (e.g., Ein Gev IV) fall within newly defined industries of the complex. In short, the Geometric Kebaran B has ceased to be recognized as a taxon, as is indicated by its exclusion from recent syntheses (Bar-Yosef, 1981; Henry, 1983).

Bar-Yosef's (1981a:396−97) most recent classification divides the complex into two "groups" (I and II) on the basis of the patterned variation in geometric microliths and the dimensions of bladelets and non-geometric microliths. It is important to note that this division does not correspond to the older Geometric Kebaran A and B scheme. The geometric component of Group I assemblages mainly consists of trapeze-rectangles, but triangles are occasionally present in low frequencies. Group II assemblages, on the other hand, are made up only of trapeze-rectangles. Additionally, Group I assemblages display much narrower bladelets and backed bladelets than do Group II assemblages.

In building upon Bar-Yosef's classification, two additional industries can be recognized within the complex, again on the basis of differences in the geometric component. Group III assemblages are defined by a predominance of triangles, whereas Group IV assemblages have a dominant proportion of lunates. As discussed in Chapter 4, these four industries display different, although partially overlapping, geographic distributions and temporal ranges.

Chronologic and Geographic Distributions

Geographically the four Geometric Kebaran industries display both regional and environmental related patterns (Figure 6.1). The assemblages of the Group I Industry are found mainly in the core Mediterranean zone but extend into steppe-desert settings. They are confined to an area west of the Rift Valley stretching from as far north as the western Galilee Mountains southward to northeastern Sinai. Unlike the Group I Industry, Group II assemblages are restricted to the steppe-desert zone. The industry has a broad geographic distribution in following an arc from the Sinai and Negev deserts in the west to the Jordanian and Syrian deserts in the northeast. This distribution of sites closely parallels the modern 300mm isohyet (the boundary separating the Mediterranean and steppe zones) resting just inside the arid zone.

The assemblages of Group III and IV are much more restricted than the others. Group III, represented at only three sites (Nahal Oren, Ein Gev IV, and Kefar Darom 28), appears to be confined to the northern sector of the Rift Valley

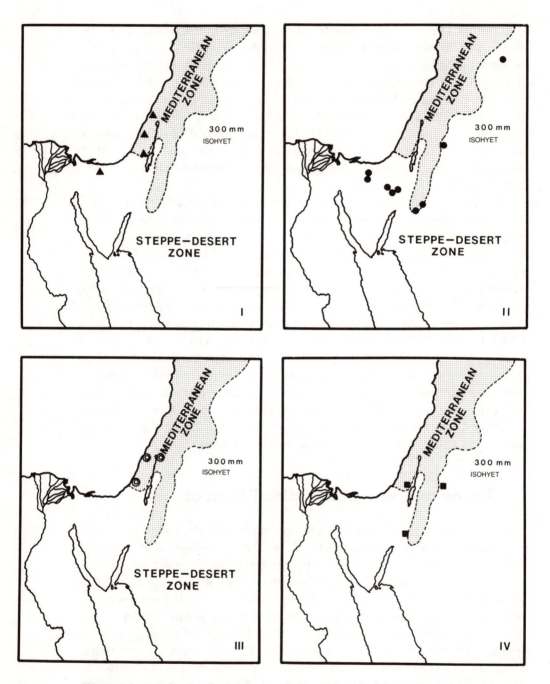

Figure 6.1. *Map showing the distribution of sites within each of the Geometric Kebaran Complex industries (I, II, III, and IV). Note how these distributions compare to the modern boundary between the arid and wooded zones.*

and to the Mediterranean coast of northern Israel. Group IV has a larger distribution in extending along the Rift Valley from the Dead Sea and south to the mountains of southern Jordan. In looking at the overall distribution of Geometric Kebaran sites, it is noteworthy that the Rift Valley, although a clear and in · most sections formidable geographic boundary, had little effect upon the territorial ranges of the industries of the complex. As shall be discussed later, however, the Rift Valley did act as a territorial divide *within* the Group II Industry.

CHRONOLOGY

Although sixteen radiocarbon dates have been obtained for the complex, delimiting a chronology from 12,610 to 14,330 B.P., all but three of these dates come from Group II Industry sites located in the Sinai and the Negev. Except for the single problematic date for the Group III assemblage from layer 7 at Nahal Oren and the two dates from Neve David, the industries of the complex remain undated.

Stratigraphic successions allow for further tightening of the chronology, however. In Jordan east of the Rift Valley, two sites (El Quweira-J203 and Kharaneh 4) contain deposits in which Group IV assemblages stratigraphically overlie Group II assemblages (Henry, 1982, 1987a, 1987b; Muheisan, 1983; Jones, 1983). And at El Khiam, located just west of the Dead Sea, Group IV assemblages (i.e., layers 7,8) stratigraphically overlie a Group I (i.e., layer 9) assemblage (Echegaray, 1966). Unfortunately, Group III assemblages are without either good radiometric dates or firm stratigraphic associations.

The available evidence then suggests that Group I and Group II Industries are partially synchronous, with both industries succeeded by Group IV in that area from the Dead Sea south. On purely technological grounds (i.e., the narrow bladelets), the Group I Industry shows much stronger affinities with the preceding Kebaran than does Group II. Upon growing out of the Kebaran within the core Mediterranean woodlands, the Group I Industry appears to have given rise to the Group II Industry as Geometric Kebaran peoples expanded into the steppe and desert zones. Group IV, apparently the latest industry of the complex, not only falls stratigraphically between Group II and Early Natufian horizons, but it also displays techno-typological characteristics that bridge the two complexes. The Group IV Industry then most likely fills the gap between 13,000 and 12,500 B.P. in representing the transitional interval between the Geometric Kebaran and the Natufian.

POPULATION MOVEMENTS

During the period from roughly 14,500 to 13,000 B.P., the southern reaches of the southern Levant appear to have experienced climatic conditions that were somewhat moister than those of today. The greater available moisture in the southern extremes of the region at this time is indicated by the presence of large numbers of Mushabian and Geometric Kebaran sites.

Beginning around 13,000 B.P., near modern desert conditions appear to have developed in the lower elevations of the southern reaches of the region as winter storm paths assumed a northward migration. Whereas desert conditions emerged in Sinai, the northward retreat of storm paths increased the moisture budgets of the central and northern sections of the region, especially in the uplands fronting the Mediterranean littoral. A rise in worldwide temperature at this time would also have caused an expansion of the Mediterranean woodlands into the uplands such as those found along the hilly spine of Palestine and on the Jordanian Plateau.

These climatic and environmental changes can be meshed with the diachronic shifts in the geographic distributions of the Geometric Kebaran industries, which, in turn, are viewed as expressions of population movement. During the period between 14,500 and 13,000 B.P., the moister conditions of the arid zone would have allowed for an expansion of Geometric Kebaran groups into the Negev, Sinai, and southern Jordan from the Mediterranean woodlands. With this expansion requisite adaptive adjustments and interaction with Mushabian peoples are likely to have induced some cultural divergence from the founding population. The Group II Industry, restricted to the steppe-desert zone, is thought to represent the archaeological expression of this line of cultural development.

With the deterioration of the climate after about 13,000 B.P., the southern desert appears to have become relatively abandoned as reflected in the absence of Group I and Mushabian sites. Geometric Kebaran occupation of the region continued in the Mediterranean woodlands of the north and in enclaves at high elevations (i.e., 800–1,300m) in the south. Group IV assemblages, in showing a techno-typological continuity between Group II and the Early Natufian, probably represent some part of this population that retreated from the southern deserts to the edge of the Mediterranean woodlands after about 13,000 years ago.

Material Culture

Like that of the Mushabian, the material culture of the Geometric Kebaran Complex is dominated by chipped stone artifacts, although rare items of groundstone, worked bone, and ornamental shell have also been recorded. The patterned variation in the lithic artifact assemblages, however, not only provides a means of tracing the temporal and spatial relationships within the complex, but it also furnishes a way to reconstruct aspects of the economy, demography, and social organization of Geometric Kebaran peoples.

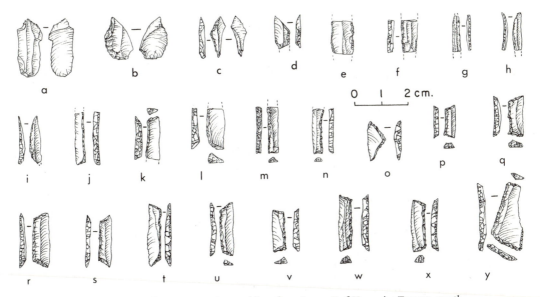

Figure 6.2. *A Geometric Kebaran Group I assemblage from Layer E of Hayonim Terrace, northern Israel (after Henry and Leroi-Gourhan, 1976). Microburins (a–c), La Mouillah point (d); medial segments of backed bladelets (e,f,g); straight backed and pointed bladelet (g); arched backed bladelets (h,i), straight backed and truncated opposite snap (j–n), triangle (o), trapeze-rectangles (p–x); varia (y).*

GROUP I INDUSTRY

Group I assemblages that have been analyzed and published in detail come from only five sites: Mushabi XIV,2 and Lagama Ic (Bar-Yosef and Goring-Morris, 1977), Hayonim Terrace E (Henry and Leroi-Gourhan, 1976; Henry, et al., 1981), El Khiam 9 (Echegaray, 1966), and Hefsibah (Ronen, et al., 1975). Other assemblages included within the industry by Bar-Yosef (1981a:397) consist of Haon III, Malikh V, Fazael III, Hamifgash, Azariq II, and Azariq VII. Bar-Yosef also places El Khiam 8 within the industry, but the dominance of lunates in the assemblage would tie it to the Group IV Industry instead. Finally, the important recently discovered site of Neve David (Kaufman, 1986), located on the slope of Mount Carmel, should probably be included in the industry.

Lithic Artifacts The industry is generally characterized by tool-kits that are composed of geometric microliths and backed bladelets, with the latter predominating (refer to Table 4.9 and Appendix B). The geometric microliths are typically madeup of trapeze-rectangles, but lunates and triangles are occasionally present (Figure 6.2). The backed bladelets mainly occur in the form of straight-backed types with many of these apparently snapped intentionally.

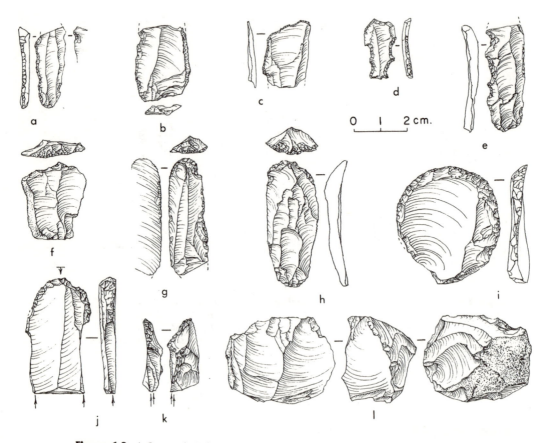

Figure 6.3. *A Geometric Kabaran Group I assemblage from Layer E of Hayonim Terrace, northern Israel (after Marks, 1976). Straight backed bladelet (a); backed flake (b); retouched flake (c); denticulates (d,e); endscrapers (f–i); burin-endscraper (j); burin (k); bladelet core (l).*

Other tools, such as scrapers, burins, notches, and denticulates, are present in low or moderate frequencies (Figure 6.3).

Technologically, the industry's most distinguishing trait is the production of narrow bladelets from predominantly single platform cores. Metric data for bladelet dimensions are unavailable, but data published for microliths indicate mean widths of 10–11mm (refer to Table 4.10) in comparison to mean widths of over 13mm for Group II assemblages. Microburins occur in low numbers in most assemblages, but the indices are not sufficiently high to indicate that the technique was habitually used. Instead of being made with the microburin technique, the narrow bladelets of Group I assemblages were apparently broken transversely and then fashioned into microlithic tools.

Other Items of Material Culture The sites of Hefsibah and Neve David, both located along the Mediterranean coast of northern Israel, yielded the most elaborate artifact inventories beyond flint tools. At Hefsibah, a wide variety of groundstone items made of basalt and limestone were found. These included pestles, deep mortars, and handstone mullers. Although none of the mortars were complete, the largest would have weighed about 18 kg! The nearest source of basalt is some 15–20km to the north in the Carmel Mountains. Deep mortars, bowls, and flat grinding slabs were also recovered from Neve David and, as at Hefsibah, these were made from both basalt and limestone. Three of the specimens were found associated with the burial of a 25–30-year-old-male, the only human remains known for the Geometric Kebaran Complex.

Shells are reported from most Group I occupations (Bar-Yosef and Goring-Morris, 1977; Marks, 1976; Simmons, 1977; De La Campa, 1966; Reese, 1982; Kaufman, 1986). Most are marine shells, and many of them have been perforated for stringing or sectioned into beads. In contrast to the Mushabian occupations, Group I sites display fewer shells and a more limited range of species. Also, where their origins have been established, the shells come exclusively from the Mediterranean (Reese, 1982).

Architecture Any form of architecture is rare for the Geometric Kebaran, with the best evidence coming from the site of Neve David (Kaufman, 1985). Two small structures were uncovered during the initial work at the site. These consist of a slightly arched wall and an oval structure (ca. 1m in diameter), both constructed of large undressed limestone slabs. The oval structure appears to have had an internal hearth.

GROUP II INDUSTRY

A long list of assemblages is attributed to this widespread industry. Those studied in the greatest detail have been recovered from sites in the Highland Negev (Marks, 1976; Simmons, 1977; Goring-Morris, 1978), the low western Negev (Phillips and Bar-Yosef, 1974), northeastern Sinai (Bar-Yosef and Goring-Morris, 1977), southern Jordan (Henry, 1982; Jones, 1983), eastern Jordan (Muheisan, 1983; Garrard, et al., 1986), and central Syria (Fujimoto, 1979). Many of these assemblages have undergone detailed typological, technological, and even microscopic use-wear analyses, but subtle differences in analytic procedures hinder synthesizing the available data. It seems likely that a broad comparative study based upon a common set of detailed attributes would reveal regional clusters beyond those identified within this study for Sinai, the Negev, and southern Jordan.

As in Group I, the distinguishing characteristics of the Group II Industry are found in the patterned variation of geometric microliths and in the dimensions of bladelets. Geometric microliths consist almost entirely of trapeze-rectangles; other geometrics (e.g., lunates and triangles) are absent or account for less than 1% of the class. The bladelets of Group II assemblages are relatively wide, averaging slightly over 13mm, and somewhat shorter than those of other Geometric Kebaran industries.

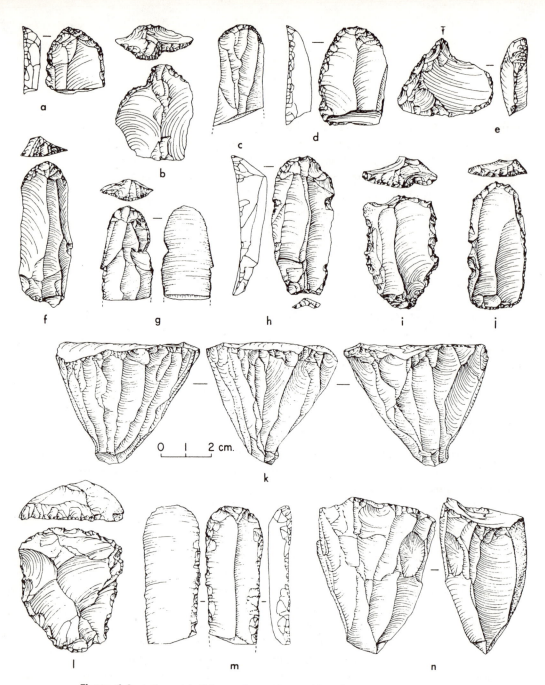

Figure 6.4. *A Geometric Kebaran Group II assemblage from Site D5, central Negev, Israel (after Marks, 1976). Scrapers (a–d, f–j, m)—both g and m show bilateral sheen; perforator (e); cores (k,n); denticulate (l).*

Lithic Artifacts Backed bladelets and geometric microliths compose the majority of the tool-kits, with scrapers, burins, notches, and denticulates appearing in much lower frequencies. The most common types of backed bladelets consist of backed and truncated specimens opposite snaps, medial segments, and backed and double truncated specimens (Figures 6.4 and 6.5). Of these, the medial

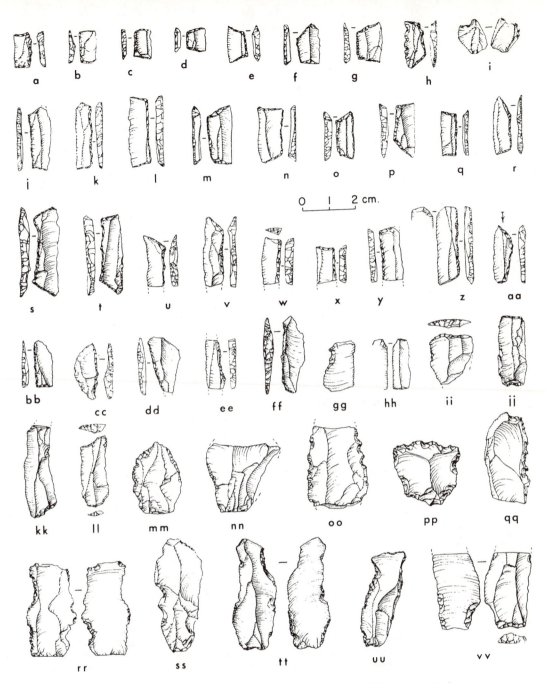

Figure 6.5. *A Geometric Kebaran Group II assemblage from Site D5, central Negev, Israel (after Marks, 1976). Geometrics (a–h, j–bb); microburin (i); backed pieces (cc–ee); La Mouillah point (ff); perforator (gg); truncated pieces (hh, jj, ll); endscraper (ii); retouched pieces (mm, nn, uu); denticulates (oo–qq); notched pieces (rr–tt); bec burin (vv).*

segments were apparently remnants of broken tools, whereas the other two types represented complete specimens that are likely to have served as tips for projectiles.

Geometrics, formed exclusively of trapeze-rectangles, not only assist in the definition of the Group II Industry but also form the basis of stylistic attribute and wear-pattern studies. Low magnification use-wear analysis of trapeze-rectangles indicates that the type was probably used to tip arrows. Given this interpretation, it is not surprising that attribute studies reveal regional clusters of assemblages. The subtle design differences in the trapeze-rectangles probably functioned as ethnic symbols advertising social boundaries.

Both discrete and dimensional attributes point to differences among Group II assemblages from the Sinai, the Negev, and southern Jordan (Table 6.1). In the Negev, trapeze-rectangles were fabricated mainly through normal abrupt retouch, with much less use of fine, semi-steep, or bipolar retouch. Although the assemblages from southern Jordan show a similar retouch pattern, the specimens from these assemblages are much narrower than those from the Negev. The assemblages from Sinai contrast sharply with those of the Negev and Jordan with respect to retouch varieties, especially in the greater use of bipolar backing.

Such geographically linked variation in attributes of trapeze-rectangle manufacture is thought to reflect stylistic preferences among the Group II peoples who inhabited these three contiguous areas. These attributes are more likely to have been stylistic than functional, given the environmental redundancy of the three settings.

The presence of mastic on several specimens from Sinai (Bar-Yosef and Goring-Morris, 1977:124), in conjunction with certain patterns of edge damage on specimens from Douara Cave in Syria (Fujimoto, 1979:61–62), provide clues as to how the tools were mounted and used. The mastic, described as a pinkish substance, is noted to cover as much as two-thirds the width of specimens and their full length. This distribution indicates that the trapeze-rectangles were either mounted transverse to a shaft, a common orientation for arrow tips in ethnographic and historic contexts, or mounted in a groove parallel to a shaft

TABLE 6.1
Comparison of the patterned variation in retouch varieties and widths of trapeze-rectangles recovered from sites in Sinai, the Negev, and southern Jordan.

Attributes	Sinai[a]	Regional Site Clusters Negev[b]	Southern Jordan[c]
Variety of retouch			
Normal abrupt	53–66	86–91	61–100
Fine & semi-steep	0–5	5–12	13–15
Bipolar	13–33	1–3	5
Widths in mm			
Range	5.5–10.0	5.5–10.0	5.5–10.0
Mean	7.0	—	5.0

[a]Bar-Yosef and Goring-Morris, 1977.
[b]Marks, 1976; Simmons, 1977; Goring-Morris, 1978.
[c]Jones, 1983.

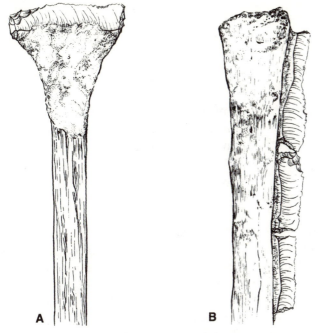

Figure 6.6. *A schematic illustration of two ways in which trapeze-rectangles are likely to have been mounted as arrow tips (A) and reaping implements (B).*

for use as a scythe or reaping implement (Figure 6.6). The results of a microscopic examination of specimens for edge-wear and striations are consistent with the interpretation that trapeze-rectangles were used as transverse mounted arrow tips.

Trapeze-rectangles were strongly associated with large, bifacial edge damage and striations oriented perpendicular to the unretouched edge. The presence of edge damage on both surfaces of the geometric imply a cutting action, and the striations running perpendicular to the edge indicate that the direction of cutting was transverse to the edge. Therefore, the nature and direction of the action revealed by the analysis is precisely what one would expect to find on a geometric microlith that was used to tip an arrow.

Technological studies of assemblages from the Negev (Marks, 1976) and southern Jordan (Jones, 1983) show that a billet or punch technique was used to detach bladelets from the predominantly single platform cores. Microburins are either absent or present in such low numbers as to suggest that the technique was never consistently employed for sectioning bladelets.

Other Items of Material Culture When compared to the Group I assemblages, those of Group II are relatively impoverished in material culture items beyond stone tools. Only two groundstone artifacts, ornamental marine shells, and some ochre make up this category. The marine shells, however, show an interesting distribution. Those recovered from sites in the Negev and Sinai are of Mediterranean origin; those from southern Jordan come from the Red Sea. The shells then follow a similar pattern of regional distribution as defined by the attribute study of geometric microliths.

GROUP III INDUSTRY

Assemblages of this industry are defined mainly on the basis of their typological characteristics, particularly by the dominance of triangles in the geometric microliths. The industry is known from only three sites: Ein Gev IV (Bar-Yosef, 1970), Kefar Darom 27 (Bar-Yosef, 1970), and Nahal Oren VII (Noy, et al., 1973). They define a territory in northern Israel stretching from the eastern shore of Lake Tiberias (i.e., Ein Gev IV) to the Mediterranean coast.

Lithic Artifacts Of the four Geometric Kebaran industries, the Group III assemblages show the greatest balance in tool classes. Backed bladelets and geometric microliths form the dominant classes, as in the other industries, but they are about equally represented. The presence of high frequencies of broken and obliquely truncated backed bladelets denotes typological parallels with the other industries, but pointed types (e.g., micro-gravettes and narrow micro-points) occur in markedly higher frequencies than in the rest of the complex. It is the geometrics, however, that furnish the best means of defining the industry. Triangles, constituting 54–99% of the class, occur in sharply higher frequencies than in any other industry of the complex. Scrapers and burins, although much less numerous, are nevertheless well represented when compared to other assemblages of the Geometric Kebaran.

Technological data for the industry are available only for the assemblage from Ein Gev IV (Bar-Yosef, 1970; Henry, 1973a, 1975). This assemblage is characterized by the production of relatively narrow bladelets from single and opposed platform cores in addition to an intensive use of the microburin technique. The technique was used mainly for the production of small triangles and was applied in a manner distinctive to Ein Gev IV (Henry, 1975).

Other Material Culture and Architecture Numerous marine and freshwater shells were recovered from the site of Ein Gev IV, with the marine shells all coming from the Mediterranean. Their origin thus confirms the ties to the coastal sites as indicated by artifact similarities. Ein Gev IV also yielded evidence of rudimentary architecture in the form of a low wall that outlined a shallow hut dug into the slope of the site.

GROUP IV INDUSTRY

This industry is known from only four sites: Qa Salab (J202) and El Quweira (J203) in southern Jordan (Henry, 1982; Jones, 1983), Kharaneh IV in eastern Jordan (Muheisan, 1983), and El Khiam in the hills of Judea just west of the Dead Sea (Echegaray, 1966). These sites suggest a distribution for the industry that follows the Rift Valley from the Dead Sea south and stretches eastward to the edge of the Syrian desert.

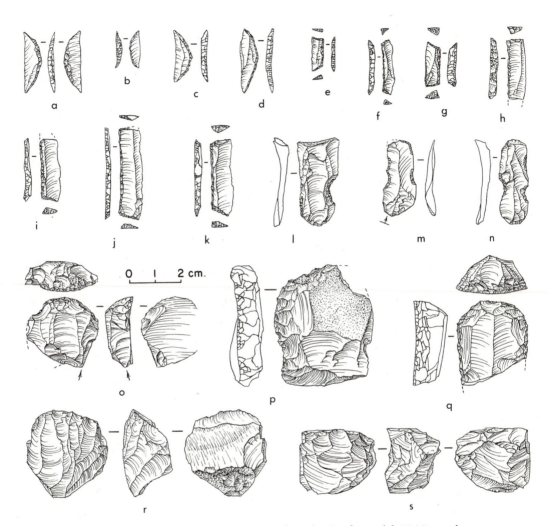

Figure 6.7. *A Geometric Kebaran Group IV assemblage from the site of Qa Salab (J202), southern Jordan (after Henry, 1983). Lunates (a–d); trapeze-rectangles (e–g,j,k); backed and truncated bladelets (h,i); notches (l,n); burin-scraper (o); thick endscrapers (p,q); bladelet cores (r,s).*

Lithic Artifacts The high frequency of lunates in their geometric class causes these assemblages to stand apart from the other industries of the Geometric Kebaran Complex (Figure 6.7). Lunates would also appear to form a progressively greater proportion of the geometrics through time, as indicated by the stratigraphic trends recorded in the Qa Salab rockshelter deposit.

Technologically, Group IV assemblages differ from those of the other industries with respect to bladelet dimensions, core varieties, and microburin indices. Bladelets are narrower and shorter in Group IV assemblages than in the other industries. They were struck mainly from multi-platform cores as opposed to the single platform varieties that dominate the other industries. The microburin indices, while generally high, parallel those reported for the Group III Industry, but the specific applications of the technique differ markedly between the two industries. For Group IV assemblages, the technique employed resembles that which was used in the Natufian (a lateral notch and snap) for the production of lunates.

The techno-typological characteristics of Group IV assemblages are especially important in defining a smooth transition between the Geometric Kebaran and Natufian complexes. This is most clearly expressed in the stratigraphic trends at Qa Salab (Henry, 1982; Jones, 1983), where lunates progressively replace trapeze-rectangles coincident with rising microburin indices.

Other Items of Material Culture Aside from flint artifacts, the material culture is limited to ornamental marine shells and ochre. At El Khiam the shell, represented principally by dentalium, comes exclusively from the Mediterranean, but at Qa Salab both Mediterranean and nearby Red Sea species are present. In this regard, the Group IV Industry differs from the rest of the complex in showing a widespread exchange system in which Mediterranean shells found their way to sites close to the Red Sea. This may provide the first hint of the widespread social interaction that would come to take place throughout the Levantine uplands and culminate in the Natufian.

Economy, Demography, and Social Organization

Although the Geometric Kebaran Complex is represented at more than fifty sites scattered over a large geographic area and encompassing some 1,500–2,000 years, certain economic and demographic patterns characterize the complex as a whole. Regardless of the local setting, Geometric Kebaran groups apparently followed a mobile foraging strategy with episodes of seasonal aggregation and dispersion that normally corresponded to differences in elevation. This vertical nomadism or transhumance would have enabled groups to bring resources that were seasonally out-of-phase and located within different elevational belts into a schedule of annual availability.

The vertically zoned and closely packed resources also appear to have prompted the development of relatively small territories of social interaction. Certain stylistic attributes and trade items associated with Geometric Kebaran assemblages point to the presence of networks of social interaction at three geographic scales. Interestingly, the relative and absolute sizes of these prehistoric territories closely parallel those described for the San Bushmen of the Kalahari. These similarities suggest that Geometric Kebaran groups may have maintained a hierarchy of social networks resembling those of the contemporary Bushmen.

TRANSHUMANCE: PATTERNS WITHIN AND BETWEEN SITES

Within each of the Geometric Kebaran industries there is a clear dichotomy between sites that corresponds to differences in elevation (Table 6.2). The two kinds of sites differ in size, depth of cultural deposit, and artifact density. Large sites with thick cultural deposits and high artifact densities occur at relatively low elevations, whereas small sites with thin cultural deposits and low artifact densities are found at high elevations. Absolute elevations are not as important to this pattern as are the relative elevations dictated by the local topography. For example, in Group I and III Industries lowland sites are found near sea level along the Mediterranean coast (e.g., Hefsibah, Neve David, and Nahal Oren) and even below sea level in the Rift Valley (e.g., Ein Gev IV and Haon), whereas their "upland" counterparts are situated only 300–400m higher (e.g., Hayonim Terrace). In contrast, the "lowland" sites of Group II and IV industries in southern Jordan are found at 800–900m above sea level, with their upland counterparts resting at 1,000–1,200m.

This asymmetry among sites is viewed as an expression of the differences in occupational intensity between lowland and upland camps in a transhumant settlement system. The relative occupational intensities of the sites are likely to have been determined by a combination of factors. These would have included the number of occupants, the length of residence, and the frequency of habitation. It is difficult or even impossible to determine the relative weights of these factors as they pertain to a particular site, but this is not an especially important obstacle to identifying prehistoric transhumance.

Perhaps the clearest picture of Geometric Kebaran transhumance is revealed in the site and artifact patterns displayed between the different elevational belts on the southern edge of the Jordanian Plateau (Henry, 1982, 1987b). Here sites belonging to Group II and IV industries are found at elevations ranging from 800 to 1,200m. Upland sites are confined to the piedmont that skirts the edge of the Jordanian Plateau at elevations between 1,000 and 1,200m. Lowland sites are situated on the floor of a wide valley beneath the piedmont at 800–900m elevation. The sites found in the piedmont, without exception, display small occupational areas, thin cultural deposits, and low artifact densities (Table 6.2). Lowland sites, on the other hand, exhibit large occupational areas, thick cultural deposits, and high artifact densities.

The pattern seen in southern Jordan is repeated along the Mediterranean coast among Group I sites. Here the shoreline site of Hefsibah has an occupational area of 1,300–2,000m^2 with a cultural deposit over 2m thick (Ronen, et al., 1975). In contrast, the site of Hayonim Terrace, located in the Galilee Mountains, furnishes evidence of an upland occupation that extends over less than 300m^2 in a deposit less than 40cm thick (Henry, et al., 1981). Similarly, one can point to the small occupational areas and shallow deposits (never exceeding 130m^2 or 30cm, respectively) recorded for the upland sites of Sinai (Bar-Yosef and Goring-Morris, 1977) and the Negev (Marks, 1976; Simmons, 1977).

TABLE 6.2
A comparison of Geometric Kebaran sites located in the piedmont and the lowland zones of southern Jordan with regard to size, thickness of cultural deposit, direction of exposure, and artifact density.

Site No.	Site Size (m²)	Cultural Deposit (cm)	Exposure (o = open)	Artifact Density (n/m³)	Total No. of Artifacts
Piedmont					
21	100	5	o	36	1,019
22	120	5	o	13	343
26	100	20	E	17	1,018
31	180	30	E	19	1,319
$\bar{x}$	125	15	—	21	924
Lowland					
504	600	+30	SW	341	4,696
503	260	30	S	227	1,354
201	320	80	S	228	5,051
202	400	60	S	641	5,908
203	550	80	SW	37	1,296
$\bar{x}$	426	56	—	295	3,663

Beyond identifying patterned variation in the intensity of occupation between different elevational belts, a question emerges as to when the belts were occupied over an annual cycle. Patterns of exposure and local setting perhaps provide the best clues for establishing seasonality. These data consistently indicate that the uplands were occupied during the warm season and the lowlands were inhabited during the colder part of the year.

In southern Jordan, for example, the sites of the piedmont are located in the open on the floor of the large Judayid Basin and along the base of an east-facing escarpment that forms the basin's western margin. Lowland sites are found exclusively on the south and southwest faces of inselbergs that dot the floor of the Wadi Hisma. These sites generally occupy shallow rockshelters overlooking dry lake beds that are never more than .5km away. The piedmont sites would have made unlikely winter camps. At elevations of 1,000–1,200m, they would have been exposed to cold north-northwest winter winds. Also, in falling within the shadow of the escarpment, those sites along the western margin of the basin would have been further denied the warmth of afternoon sunshine. The lowland sites, however, would have furnished ideal settings for winter camps. In addition to their lower and hence warmer elevational setting, their south-southwest exposures would have afforded protection from the wind, and brought the warmth of solar radiation as well. The dark red sandstone forming the cliff faces creates a natural solar furnace in that it collects heat during the afternoon and then radiates heat overnight as temperatures reach their daily lows.

Evidence for seasonality is also provided by intra-site patterns in artifacts and features in the upland occupation of Mushabi XIV (level 2), located in the Gebel Maghara of northeastern Sinai (Bar-Yosef and Goring-Morris, 1977). Excavation revealed a zone of ash distributed to the south and southwest of a large firepit. This denotes a wind blowing from the north-northeast, the prevailing direction of wind during the summer in the area. The artifact scatter provides an additional hint of a warm season encampment at the site. Artifact plots suggest that activities were conducted within the smoke of the fire, a practice that may well have served to ward off swarms of insects that would have infested such a lakeshore camp in the midst of the warm season.

In addition to being small and rarely reoccupied, upland sites were apparently inhabited only briefly. Sites in both the Negev and Sinai display intra-site patterns that denote a clear succession of unbroken activities in small areas of the sites. Bladelets were struck from cores, fashioned into tools, and then used, with all of these activities occurring within a few square meters. This continuity in production and use of flint tools within a confined area implies a brief episode of occupation. The clarity of these artifact distributions, not having been distorted by other activities, has prompted the sites to be interpreted as "ephemeral hunting camps" (Bar-Yosef and Goring-Morris, 1977) and "ephemeral occupations" (Marks, 1976; Simmons, 1977; Goring-Morris, 1978).

Estimates of the numbers of residents indicate that the lowland camps contained some 2–4 times the population of upland camps. As estimated from the occupational areas of the sites using both power (Casteel, 1979) and exponential (Hassan, 1981) curves, as discussed in Chapter 5, upland camps would have contained some 14–17 persons and lowland camps some 25–50 persons. If the 14–17 occupants of upland camps are viewed as representing a single band (a reasonable assumption given that the average size of a foraging band in ethnographic contexts is about 25 persons), then the larger lowland sites must reflect an aggregation of some 2–4 bands.

ANNUAL CYCLE OF TRANSHUMANCE

The locations and composition of Geometric Kebaran sites thus indicate an annual cycle of transhumance into the uplands during the spring and summer months followed by a migration to lowland settings in the autumn and winter. This pattern was governed by seasonal differences in resources and creature comfort. The higher elevations would have made comfortable habitats and furnished surface water only during the spring and early summer. Temperatures in the uplands would have risen to comfortable levels at this time, and water from winter rains would have still been available in streams and pools. This would also have coincided with the period of new plant growth, resulting in the most extensive and diverse season for plant resources in the uplands. These resources would have been important foodstuffs in their own right in conjunction with attracting game animals to the higher elevations. By middle to late summer, after several months without rain, both water and edible plants would have become hard to find in the uplands. At this time, the better watered areas of the lowlands would have become more attractive to game as well as to prehistoric foragers. Groups then were likely to have remained in the warmer lowland settings over the winter months until they could return to the uplands following the rainy season.

The spring-summer segment of the annual cycle appears to have been a time when the Geometric Kebaran population was dispersed into small, highly mobile groups. During the autumn and winter, these groups apparently came together into larger social units that resided in long-term encampments. The proposed larger populations and longer residence in these lowland sites is consistent with their settings on the seacoast and lakes where resources would have been more diverse and abundant. The presence of artifacts associated with plant processing at Hefsibah, Neve David, and Ein Gev IV perhaps point to a greater emphasis on storable foods in this more sedentary segment of the cycle.

From an evolutionary perspective, this lowland segment of the transhumant pattern of Geometric Kebaran populations was a precursor to what was to become the year-round pattern for settled Natufians. In this regard, it is particularly interesting to recall that wild cereals would have been confined to these warmer lowland settings during most of the Geometric Kebaran interval. Although not as abundant as in later times, wild cereals would nevertheless have provided an important, easily procured, storable resource. Therefore, in many ways, the transition from long-term Geometric Kebaran camps to settled Natufian hamlets can be explained by the terminal Pleistocene temperature elevation that triggered the expansion of wild cereals into the uplands. What is important here is that the reconstruction of Geometric Kebaran transhumance provides a specific understanding of how the changes in climate and resources at the end of the Ice Age are likely to have influenced the evolution of adaptive strategies.

SCALES OF ETHNICITY AND SOCIAL ORGANIZATION

When the Geometric Kebaran and its constituent industries are evaluated with respect to temporal-spatial distribution and associated economic-demographic data, two significant conclusions can be reached. First, it is clear that the material culture classification used in the definition of the complex and its industries is truly detecting patterned variation in prehistoric ethnicity and not merely functional variability. That is to say, the classificatory units (complex, industry, phase/facies) differ from other units of the same scale because of the differences in the identity of prehistoric interest groups as opposed to functional differences *within* such interest groups. In this context, "ethnicity" is viewed as the "mechanism by which interest groups use culture to symbolize their within-group organization in opposition to and in competition with other interest groups" (Hodder, 1979:452).

Secondly, several scales of ethnicity were apparently present among Geo-metric Kebaran peoples as in other societies where interest groups are defined at various temporal and spatial scales. At the highest and most general scale, the Geometric Kebaran Complex reflects those material culture symbols that differ-entiated Geometric Kebaran from the contemporary (and in part geographically overlapping) Mushabian peoples. At this scale it is important to note that even though the assemblages included within the complex are drawn from diverse environmental settings over a broad area, they nevertheless share attributes that distinguish them from Mushabian assemblages that were contemporary and of-ten located in nearby similar environments. Ethnic differences, therefore, were apparently maintained even in settings of pronounced environmental pressures for functional similarity.

At an intermediate scale, at least four industries nested within the Geometric Kebaran Complex are defined. In having partially overlapping spatial and tem-poral distributions, they nevertheless show specific artifact patterns. Further-more, these industry specific patterns are maintained across various site types indicative of different segments of an annual cycle. At an even more refined scale, nested within the Group II Industry, three facies can be identified in as-semblage groups from Sinai, the Negev, and southern Jordan. Again, it is note-worthy that the artifact patterns are uniform across the assemblages of each facies even though a functional dichotomy was maintained by the activities as-sociated with lowland and upland segments of an annual transhumant cycle.

If, as proposed here, the material culture units mirror different scales of pre-historic ethnicity, a question emerges as to how these units correlate with differ-ent levels of social organization. One approach to addressing the question rests in comparing common measures of different levels of social organization drawn from ethnographic and archaeological contexts. This comparison focuses on the number of persons and the sizes of territories that are associated with social organizational hierarchies.

The ethnographic evidence is drawn from various studies of Kalahari Bush-men groups (Wiessner, 1983; Lee, 1979; Heinz, 1979; Silberbauer, 1972; Bar-nard, 1979) that, like the Geometric Kebaran groups, live as simple foragers in a semi-desert environment. Although the subsistence strategies employed and the environmental settings encountered by Geometric Kebaran groups are likely to have been similar to those of the contemporary Bushmen groups, such general similarities do not necessarily imply that similar levels of social organization would have been shared by the two societies. It is recognized not only that ele-ments common to prehistoric social systems may not be present in contempo-rary foraging societies (Wobst, 1978), but also that even among contemporary foragers, such as the Kalahari Bushmen, there is considerable variability with respect to social organization (Barnard, 1979). What is common to Bushmen groups, however, is the hierarchical arrangement of social units into five levels—nuclear family, band, band cluster, dialect group, and language group (Wiessner, 1983). These different levels of social organization are associated with differences in the degrees of social interaction and in the sizes of social networks. As the intensity of social interaction declines and the sizes of networks increase in the social organizational hierarchy, the temporal and spatial scales of the social organizational levels are similarly enlarged. For example, a band involves fewer members distributed over a smaller area than a language group, and the temporal life of a specific band is much shorter than that of a language group. Ethnicity, serving to reinforce the cohesion of social networks and to define their boundaries, exists at each of the levels. Thus ethnic symbols expressed in material culture would be expected to parallel the trend of increasing time and space scales seen in the hierarchy of social organization.

Among the Bushmen groups, the lowest level of social organization is the nuclear family, the primary economic unit charged with satisfying basic daily subsistence needs. The band or camp is the next highest level; composed of a number of nuclear families, it forms the primary residential unit. Although the sizes of bands and the areas they inhabit vary according to the distribution of resources (Wiessner, 1983; Barnard, 1979), the ranges in band membership and sizes of exploited areas among various Bushmen groups are remarkably similar. Bands average about 25 persons, with a range of 8–40 members among the !Kung (Lee, 1979; Marshall, 1976), 22–60 members among the G/wi (Silberbauer, 1972), and 35–40 members among the !Xo (Heinz, 1979). In regard to areas inhabited, the average !Kung band occupies some $300–600km^2$ (Lee, 1979), an average G/wi band exploits some $450–1,000km^2$ (Silberbauer, 1972), and an average !Xo band commands about $300–600km^2$ (Wiessner, 1983 estimated after Heinz, 1979).

The next highest level of social organization among the Bushmen is the band cluster, which is made up of a number of bands. This level shows the greatest variability among Bushmen groups with respect to how strongly it is recognized as a formal interest group and how precisely its territorial boundaries are defined. Band clusters are apparently weakly developed among the !Kung, but Wiessner (1983) notes that 4–10 bands do identify certain areas for which they have worked out a regular pattern of cooperative land-use and also tend to aggregate regularly at the same permanent water holes during the dry season. Among the !Xo, band clusters consist of 3–7 bands and form an almost exclusive territorial unit (Heinz, 1979). The G/wi band cluster appears to be better defined than that of the !Kung, but social interaction between clusters is common (Silberbauer, 1972, 1981). Social interaction between bands relates principally to exchange partnerships that allow for extended visiting and for obtaining marriage partners. Wiessner (1983) notes, for example, that among the !Xai/Xai, 42% of all exchange partnerships involved persons within a common band cluster. With respect to marriages, among the !Xo some 70–80% of marriages took place within the same band cluster, an interest group that is considered to be the ideal pool for wives, while among the !Kung only 50% of the marriages take place within the band cluster (Wiessner, 1983). In that some 3–10 bands form a band cluster, a band cluster would be expected to contain some 100–250 members and to occupy some 2,600–6,500km².

The dialect and language groups, the highest levels of social organization among Bushmen, encompass vast areas and relatively great numbers of members. The land areas of the San linguistic groups as estimated from Wiessner's (1983) map range from 96,000km² to 625,000km². Whereas the Nharo, G/wi and !Xo occupy roughly equivalent areas (ca. 96,000–125,000km²), the !Kung command a much larger area (ca. 625,000km²). Even though the dialect groups cover vast areas, Wiessner (1983) notes that !Kung, !Xo and G/wi informants do recognize their membership in a specific linguistic group and have terms for these groups. She goes on to list several factors that hold the groups together—exchange networks, intermarriage, male initiation rites and other ceremonies, a common language, and a shared kinship system. All but two of the four San linguistic groups have common borders. Frequent contact occurs along the borders, with relations varying from friendly to reserved and conflict being limited to only a few points (Wiessner, 1983).

In moving to the archaeological context, an examination of the geographic areas associated with the various levels of the material culture hierarchy (assemblage, facies, industry, and complex) show a significant correspondence to those areas related to the various levels of San Bushmen social organization (Table 6.3).

The correlation of the two hierarchies is seen in both the absolute and the relative sizes of the territories represented at the various levels. The increments in magnitude of the areas between the successive levels of both hierarchies are dramatic and non-ambiguous. These correspondences in the two hierarchies suggest that similarities existed in the areal scope and the degree of social interaction at various scales in Geometric Kebaran and San Bushmen societies.

It is proposed that the small upland sites of the Geometric Kebaran were occupied by bands numbering 15–17 persons based upon population estimates from the occupation areas of the sites. The larger lowland sites, estimated to have contained 25–50 persons, would have represented aggregations of 2–3 bands that formed part of a larger territorial unit, a band cluster. Two methods can be

TABLE 6.3
A comparison of the territorial areas associated with material culture and social organization hierarchies for the Geometric Kebaran Complex and San Bushmen.

Material culture level	Geometric Kebaran Group II Industry Territorial area (km²)	Social organization	San Bushmen Territorial area (km²)
Industry	153,000	Dialect group	96–625,000
Facies	7,850	Band cluster	2,600– 6,500
Assemblage/site	266–777	Band/camp	450– 1,000

used to estimate the sizes of the site catchments. One method follows the procedure used by Vita-Finzi and Higgs (1970) in which site catchments were determined by a two-hour walking distance from a site. This method consistently results in such catchments having about a 10km radius and an area of about 314km² (Vita-Finzi and Higgs, 1970). Another method merely employs a population density measure, thereby enabling a catchment area to be calculated from the population of a given site. Hassan (1981) calculated a population density of .045 persons/km² for a semi-desert biome whereas Lee (1969) reports a population density of .06 persons/km² for the !Kung. These population densities would indicate that the upland sites, with residents averaging about 16 persons, would have maintained catchments of 266–355km², whereas the larger lowland sites, averaging about 35 persons, would have commanded catchments of 583–777km². As seen in Table 6.3, the range in the sizes of catchment associated with Geometric Kebaran sites considerably overlaps the range of site catchment areas reported for San Bushmen camps.

At the next material culture level, three geographic facies are recognized in the Group II Industry of the Geometric Kebaran. The facies are centered in the Gebel Maghara area of Sinai, the Highland Negev, and along the southern edge of the Jordanian Plateau. The Sinai and Negev facies are situated about 100km apart as are the Negev and southern Jordan facies. Although the positions of the boundaries separating the facies are uncertain, an arbitrary midpoint (50km) was selected for calculation of the sizes of the territories. Such boundaries would define territories that each have a 50km radius and an area of 7,850km². This figure, slightly exceeding the upper limits of those areas contained within San Bushmen band cluster territories, does not take into account unused lands resting between territories and thus may be over-estimated.

A certain degree of social interaction would have taken place across the band cluster territorial boundaries, but the most intensive interaction would have occurred among those bands that formed an interest group concerned with providing marriage partners and economic security within a defined territory. The patterned variation in artifacts points to differences in *degree* rather than *kind* of interaction. All three facies share the same range of stylistic attributes, but they each display clear proportionate differences. Although interaction across band cluster boundaries is indicated by the general similarities in stylistic attributes of lithic artifacts, the distribution of ornamental shell implies that it was exchanged only *within* band clusters. Whereas the Sinai and Negev facies contain only shells derived from the Mediterranean, the southern Jordan facies contains shell only from the Red Sea.

At the next highest material culture level, that of industry, the Group II Industry is seen to encompass about 153,000km², thus falling within the range of 96,000–625,000km² displayed by the four San Bushmen linguistic groups. The other three Geometric Kebaran industries command territories that range from 20,000km–88,000km². The smaller territories (those of Group III and Group IV

Industries), however, may not be accurately delimited owing to the few sites attributed to these industries.

The proposition that the successive levels of material culture hierarchy of the Geometric Kebaran are reflective of social organizational levels representing band, band cluster, and linguistic group finds additional support from Wiessner's (1983) study of Kalahari San projectile points. In examining distributional patterns of stylistic attributes, she found that stylistic differences could first be detected at the band cluster level and were consistently present at the level of dialect group (Wiessner, 1983:267).

Wiessner's study raises other important points that are pertinent to the interpretation of stylistic patterns in the Geometric Kebaran. First, she found that among the Kalahari San the stylistic attributes that are emphasized vary between band clusters and linguistic groups. In this regard, it is worthwhile recalling that the three facies of the Group II Industry are distinguished on the basis of stylistic profiles drawn from a combination of three kinds of retouch and the widths of geometric microliths. Secondly, Wiessner (1983) compares the distributional patterns and the social association of two categories of style: emblemic and assertive. In building upon other studies (Wobst, 1977; Conkey, 1978, 1980), she argues that emblemic styles are expressive of social identity with specific referents, have clearly defined spatial boundaries, are not reflective of interpersonal interaction, and are associated with present/absent as opposed to clinal distributions. Assertive styles, on the other hand, are those that convey personal identity and as such are reflective of interpersonal interaction, thus displaying clinal distributions that cross-cut social boundaries at various scales.

As Wiessner (1983:259) notes, "emblemic style . . . gives information about ethnic boundaries, and assertive style in other features gives a measure of degree of contact across boundaries." With regard to the Geometric Kebaran, it would seem that the stylistic patterns manifested by the lithic artifacts are of the assertive variety as they reveal clinal distributions that crosscut various spatial and presumably social organizational boundaries. The ornamental shell, confined to the territories of facies, is more likely to have been associated with an emblemic style that defined a specific interest group—in this case a band cluster.

Origin and Evolution of the Geometric Kebaran

Unlike the Mushabian Complex, the Geometric Kebaran is relatively well understood, with regard to its origin and evolution at least at a general level. The Geometric Kebaran clearly grew out of the Kebaran and ulimately evolved into the Natufian within an interval of some 2,000 to 2,500 years. Although the Geometric Kebaran continued the basic economic, demographic, and social patterns of the Kebaran, it differed from the preceding complex in its geographic distribution and material culture. The Geometric Kebaran, in developing from the

Kebaran, was initially limited to the core Mediterrarean zone, but with the improved climatic condition of ca. 14,000 years ago it expanded into the modern steppe-desert zone. The principal changes in material culture were related to the introduction and increasing utilization of geometric microliths that progressively replaced the microlithic point varieties (e.g., microgravettes, broad and narrow micro-points) common to the Kebaran.

At a general level, the complex fills an intermediate position in the unilinear evolutionary sequence leading from the Kebaran to the Natufian. But, at a more detailed level, the complex consists of at least four industries that display different temporal-spatial distributions and generic relationships that are indicative of a multilinear evolutionary succession. The complexity of the Geometric Kebaran succession at the industrial level seems to have been derived from the interplay of two opposing forces with regard to cultural homogeneity. On one hand, the transhumant adaptive strategy employed by Geometric Kebaran groups contributed to the formation of relatively small territories of social interaction that in turn resulted in the development of regional pockets of autonomous and partially isolated cultural evolution. This regional cultural heterogeneity can be seen in the multiple facies of the Group II Industry and in the numerous industries (at least four) within the complex. In opposition to the cultural heterogeneity, regional differences were periodically overlaid by common behavioral patterns associated with massive population movements. The first such movement was associated with the expansion of Geometric Kebaran groups into the arid zone, whereas the second major movement occurred when Geometric Kebaran groups abandoned the arid zone between 13,000 and 12,500 years ago.

Evidence for regional evolutionary tracks is seen in the development of at least three Geometric Kebaran industries from a Kebaran Complex base (Figure 6.6). The sequence identified at the series of sites (I–IV) near the spring, Ein Gev, located on the eastern shore of Lake Tiberias defines one such track that leads to the formation of the Group III Industry. A more widespread development, related to the formation of the Group I Industry, is denoted by the typological and technological continuities seen between Group I and earlier Kebaran Complex assemblages. Another possible regional development from a Kebaran Complex base is seen within the stratigraphic sequences of several sites represented by the Hamran Industry in southern Jordan. Alternatively, this succession could be explained by an expansion of Group II populations into the mountains of southern Jordan.

With the emergence of the Group II Industry, the Geometric Kebaran apparently had three parallel and partially synchronous industries. The Group I and Group III industries were principally confined to the core Mediterranean zone whereas the Group II Industry reflects an arid zone adaptation. The uncertain chronology of the Group I and III industries prohibits a precise definition of the duration of the parallel succession. It can be established, however, that the arid zone was abandoned by Geometric Kebaran populations after about 13,000 B.P., leaving the area to be occupied by Late Mushabian groups. Concurrent with this episode of abandonment, the Group II Industry gave rise to the Group IV Industry along the margin and within the core Mediterranean zone. In all likelihood, Group I and Group III peoples continued to inhabit the core Mediterranean woodlands at this time. By 12,500–12,000 years ago, the Natufian Complex had come to replace the Geometric Kebaran in all regions of the Levant. The Group IV Industry shows the greatest typologic (e.g., lunate production) and technological (e.g., bladelet dimensions and microburin technique) similarities with the Natufian, thus suggesting a source for this new, highly uniform, and widespread taxon. After emerging, the Natufian appears to have rapidly amalgamated a number of distinct regional cultures, as represented by Group I and III Industries, into a single markedly homogeneous sociocultural system. Such an amalgamation process can be seen in several stratigraphic sequences where Group I (Hayonim Terrace), Group III (Nahal Oren), and Group IV (El Khiam) horizons are overlaid by Natufian occupations.

7
The Natufian Complex

The Natufian, the richest and best known of the Epipaleolithic complexes of the Levant, was discovered in 1928 during the excavation of the cave of Shukbah (Garrod, 1942). By the mid-1930s, additional occupations had been found in the caves of El Wad (Garrod and Bate, 1937; Waechter, 1949) and Kebara (Turville-Petre, 1932), located on the Mediterranean coast in the vicinity of Mount Carmel, and at several sites (Neuville, 1934, 1951) in the Judean Hills south of Jerusalem. These excavations produced a remarkable array of artifacts including groundstone items, sickle blades, ornamental elements, bone tools, and *art mobilier*, in conjunction with architectural features and burials. These extraordinary finds prompted Garrod (1957:212) to view the Natufian as an intrusive culture "full-grown with no traceable roots in the past." In placing a greater emphasis on chipped stone assemblages, Neuville (1934:251) disagreed and argued that though the Natufian was in many ways unique it nevertheless continued the tradition of the Levantine Upper Paleolithic.

Subsequent work has shown that Neuville was correct, for the Natufian did evolve in place within the Levant from the preceding Geometric Kebaran Complex. What had misled Garrod was the rapidity with which so many new material culture items appeared, apparently without roots in the past. On the surface such marked changes in material culture in the context of a Paleolithic foraging society would seem to be best explained by an intrusion of peoples or at least of their ideas. However, had Garrod fully understood the importance of the economic and social changes that accompanied the emergence of the Natufian, she probably would have been less surprised by the evolution in material culture. For some time scholars have freely accepted the changes in material culture between the Natufian and Neolithic horizons as the consequences of food-production. But, they have been less willing to view the even more dramatic changes in material culture that followed the appearance of the Natufian as being indicative of a fundamental shift in the adaptive evolution of Paleolithic foragers.

The Natufian adaptive shift, rather than being seen in the context of a "Pre-agricultural Revolution" (Henry, et al., 1981), has generally been interpreted as the end of a series of gradual cumulative changes that set the stage for incipient food-production. The problem with this interpretation, as noted in Chapter 1, is that the evidence points to sudden, not gradual, shifts in economy, demography, and social organization. The economic and behavioral characteristics of the Natufian then were as poorly rooted in the past as were many of the material culture elements that so puzzled Garrod.

The failure to recognize the evolutionary break between the complex foraging Natufians and their simple foraging ancestors has another, perhaps even greater, consequence. This relates to misreading the stability and security of the Natufian adaptive system. In comparing the rich material culture and elaborate settings of Natufian sites with those of the Geometric Kebaran and earlier times, one is easily drawn to the conclusion that the Natufians enjoyed unusual success as foragers. What is hidden in this interpretation, however, is that their success was based upon a fundamentally different approach to adaptation. And this approach had a much higher level of risk relative to the system's long-term survival.

In disregarding the systemic differences between simple and complex foraging, the Natufian was seen as resulting from either an unusually rich environment (especially aquatic resources) or a broadening of the diet. As noted in Chapter 1, neither of these notions is borne out by the evidence. Although a climatic change did induce a shift in resources, the overall biomass (including aquatics) remained relatively constant; and the Natufian diet was actually more specialized than that of preceding populations.

From an evolutionary perspective, the Natufian represented a fundamental change from the preceding system, i.e., simple foraging. In most respects the Natufian adaptive strategy had a stronger resemblance to that of early food-producers than to that of foragers. Though not yet capable of culturally controlling the distribution and density of resources, Natufians nevertheless had come to depend upon intensified exploitation and storage of resources for their survival. Mobility and its linkage to natural fertility controls had been sacrificed for permanent settlements. Furthermore, a social organization and ideology supportive of the intensified collection and rigid control of resources had come to replace those associated with conservation and reciprocal access to resources.

Archaeologically, these changes are manifested in various items of material culture, site contexts, and settlement patterns. Around 12,500 years ago, the Natufian emerged within the core Mediterranean zone to rapidly amalgamate several regionally distinctive Geometric Kebaran groups into a tightly bound culture. During the next 1,500 years population increases resulted in the colonization of areas on the very margin of the Mediterranean zone. This acted to bring an expanding Natufian population into contact with simple foraging Mushabian groups in the southern Levant and most likely similar groups elsewhere along the fringes of the Mediterranean woodlands. And these contacts prompted the development of a symbiotic relationship between two radically different social systems.

At the peak of their expansion, Natufians began to experience a general deterioration of their habitat, especially along the southern and eastern margins. In conjunction with continued population growth, the dramatic reduction of the Mediterranean zone, with its cereal and nut resources, destabilized the Natufian adaptive system. Natufian settlements in the marginal areas were abandoned, with their inhabitants returning to a mobile simple foraging strategy. Within the Mediterranean zone, an alternative strategy was adopted; one that enabled Natufian communities to continue their sedentary patterns and in which a system dedicated to intensification could thrive. Here we see the first physical evidence of agriculture in those Natufian sites near permanent water sources some 300–500 years after the communities in the marginal areas had collapsed. But even within the core, Mediterranean area sites adjacent to less secure water sources were abandoned.

Therefore, over a period of 2,500 years, a new adaptive system emerged, flourished, and disappeared. Although the contexts and artifactual contents of Natufian sites differ markedly from those of preceding complexes, these differences veneer a continuity seen in the lithic artifacts. Ironically, these changes in material culture that seemingly point to an extraordinarily stable system were for the most part indirectly linked to sedentism—the single most important factor in rendering the Natufian adaptive system unstable. Quite apart from the impact of the drastic decline in resources associated with the deteriorating climate, the Natufian would have inevitably collapsed as a result of the combined tensions between intensified collection, population growth, and a fixed ceiling on natural resources. However, a complex foraging strategy was especially vulnerable to the kinds of environmental perturbations that are so common to the region and to which simple foragers were virtually immune.

In this light, the relative stability of the two strategies is most clearly reflected in the dramatic break in settlement continuity that occurred at the end of the Natufian. An examination of sheltered sites, which are generally resistant to depositional biases, shows that most contain a near-continuous sequence of occupation from Middle Paleolithic times through the Natufian. But at the end of the Natufian this sequence was broken with the abandonment of virtually all of these sites. This demarks a change in settlement unparalleled for most of the Paleolithic, even though it spanned many significant climatic changes. Therefore, it would seem that the simple foragers of the Paleolithic were able to adjust to environmental changes and maintain a continuity in settlement. In contrast, during the relatively brief interval constituting the emergence and collapse of complex foraging, we see a disruption of this pattern for the first time.

Chronologic and Geographic Distributions

Geographically, Natufian sites are found in the hill zone of Israel, Lebanon, Syria, and Jordan (Figure 7.1). Although assemblages from Egypt (de Morgan, 1926) and Turkey (Bostanci, 1962) have been attributed to the Natufian, these connections were based solely on the presence of Helwan retouch and not on comprehensive total assemblage analyses. Geographically, the sites of Tel Murey-bet (Cauvin, 1977, 1979) and Abu Hureyra (Moore, 1975), both located along the Euphrates in northern Syria, also fall outside the main cluster of Natufian sites. And there is disagreement as to whether they should be considered as Natufian. Cauvin (1977) views Mureybet as a sedentary Natufian community based upon foraging. But Moore (1979) and, most recently, Olszewski (1986) argue that Abu Hureyra and similar north Syrian sites were incipient agricultural settlements distinct from the Natufian. The rich botanical inventories recovered from these sites, however, point more to foraging than agicultural economies (Van Zeist, 1970; Hillman, 1975). Futhermore, the artifactual differences be-tween these sites and those of the southern Levant that prompted Olszewski (1986) to propose a distinct taxonomic label, the "Hureyran," are likely to have been caused more by differences in local resources than ethnicity. While other studies (Goring-Morris, 1987; Byrd, 1987) have also identified ties between pat-terned variation in artifacts and geographic/environment settings, these again appear to have a functional basis. Given the geographic scope of the Natufian, some variability in tool-kits and reduction strategies should be expected. The important question is whether similar geographic patterns exist within those artifactual characteristcs that were likely to have been governed more by ethnic than functional forces. As yet such patterns have not been identified.

From an environmental perspective, Natufian sites fall within the Mediter-ranean zone as it existed some 12,500–10,500 years ago. This pattern of settle-ment is clearly expressed in the trend of sites resting at progressively higher elevations to the south and southeast. In moving to these drier settings away from the better watered areas close to the Mediterranean coast, Natufian groups would have had to establish their hamlets at increasingly higher elevations in order to enjoy a Mediterranean environment.

At a local scale, Natufian base camps or hamlets also shared several environ-mental and topographic features (Figure 7.2). They were typically located near the boundary separating level grassland settings (e.g., coastal plain, broad inte-rior valley) from the wooded slopes of the Mediterranean hill zone. Major water sources in the form of springs or wadis were always nearby. The strategic place-ment of hamlets in such locations provided for resource catchments that included an open habitat favored by gazelle and a forest habitat containing deer, cereals, and nuts. Such settings also furnished a predictable water supply along with sources of flint in the wadi gravels and limestone deposits.

Chronologically, Natufian assemblages are remarkably well dated because of

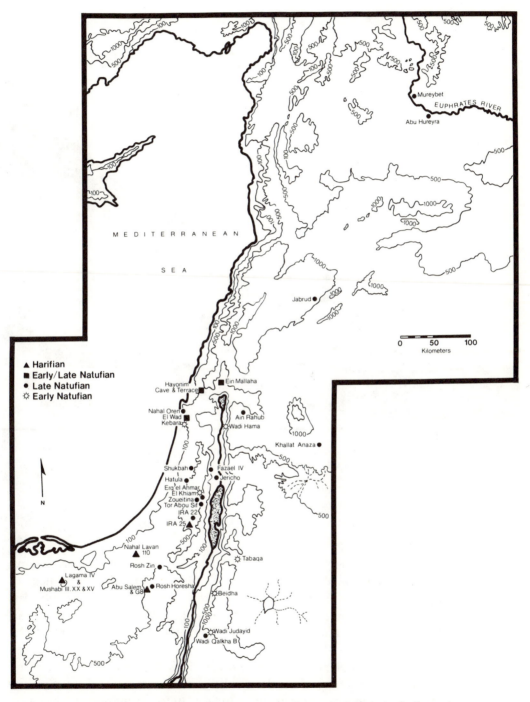

Figure 7.1. *Map showing the distribution of the major Natufian and Harifian sites in the southern Levant. Note the absence of Early Natufian sites in the arid zone (i.e. the Negev and the Eastern Desert of Jordan) and the concentration of Harifian sites within the arid zone west of the Rift.*

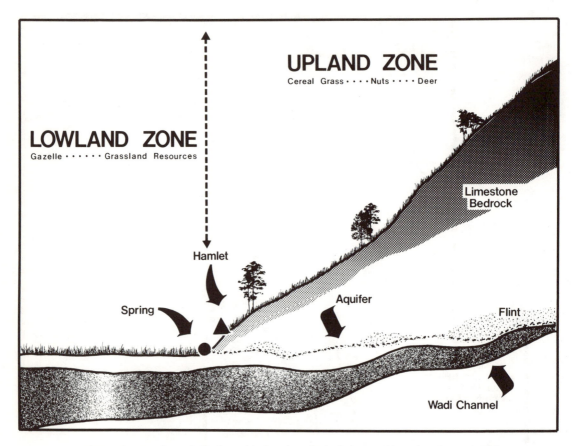

Figure 7.2. *A schematic diagram showing the principal topographic and environmental features common to Natufian hamlets. Note the proximity of important resources to such a setting.*

multiple lines of evidence tied to radiocarbon dates, stratigraphic successions, and artifact seriation. Sixty-two radiocarbon dates from eighteen occupations define a duration (using point dates only) from as early as about 12,900 years ago to as late as about 9,800 years ago (Table 4.15). In addition to the radiocarbon chronology, seriation schemes based upon retouch varieties (Henry, 1973a, 1981) and geometric dimensions (Bar-Yosef and Valla, 1979) have also been proposed for chronologically ordering occupations. Of these, the variety of retouch used in fashioning microliths has the greatest temporal sensitivity (Figure 4.23). The progressive replacement of Helwan (bifacial) by normal abrupt retouch is confirmed by both stratigraphic and radiometric dating. Although there is a general tendency for the lengths of geometrics to decline through time, there are several exceptions to this trend (Figure 4.23). A recent study of the Wadi Judayid succession, for example, shows that Helwan retouch was gradually replaced by normal abrupt retouch throughout 45cm of deposit, but geometric lengths reveal a stochastic time-trend (Sellars, personal communication, 1987). Byrd (1987:336) also questions the use of lunate dimensions in seriating Natufian assemblages.

If the point at which Helwan and abrupt retouch became roughly balanced is used as a divide between Early and Late Natufian, we find that this falls at about 11,000 B.P. on the radiocarbon calendar (Table 4.15, Figure 4.24). Specifically, if the mean of the point-dates and the mean of their associated single sigmas are considered, the Early Natufian would have persisted from 12,360 to 11,510 B.P. and the Late Natufian would have lasted from 10,845 to 10,389 B.P. (Table 4.16).

Nested within the Natufian Complex, the Harifian Industry is radiocarbon dated from 10,430 to 10,212 B.P. Whereas the Harifian appears to have grown out of the Late Natufian communities that failed within the marginal habitat of the Negev, Harifian groups were coeval with those Late Natufian settlements that continued to exist within the better watered areas of northern Israel.

Material Culture

Although the Natufian is most noted for its elaborate artifacts of worked bone, groundstone, and *art mobilier*, the chipped stone industry has actually provided the greatest information about the culture.

CHIPPED STONE INDUSTRY

Assemblages are characterized by a microlithic technology based upon the production of rather broad bladelets from multi-platform cores. Typologically, the industry displays significant inter- and intra-site variability, but technological patterns are remarkably homogeneous. The typological diversity was induced by both functional and stylistic forces. For example, the frequency profiles of tool-kits show strong correlations with environmental settings (Henry, 1973a, 1977), site types, and specific activity areas within sites (Henry, 1973a, 1973b; Bar-Yosef and Tchernov, 1966). And, as discussed earlier in regard to seriation schemes, certain styles of retouch clearly reveal time-trends.

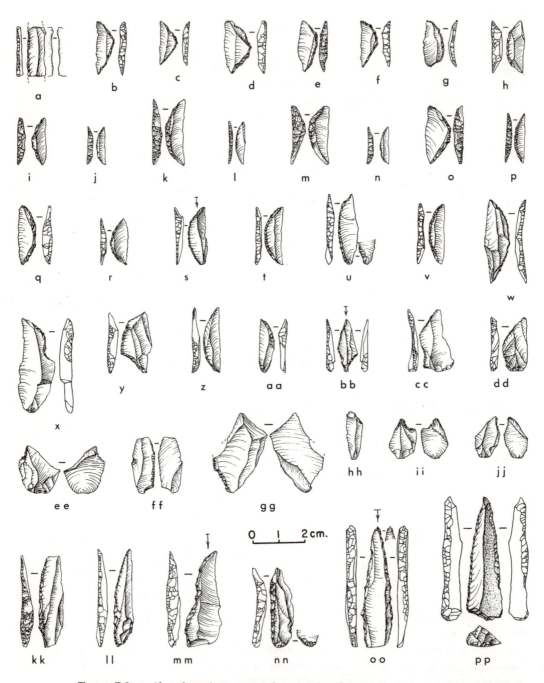

Figure 7.3. *Artifacts from the Late Natufian site of Rosh Zin (after Henry, 1976). Sickle blade (a); triangles (b–f); lunates (g–w); atypical and incomplete geometrics (x–z); truncations (aa, cc, dd); various backed pieces (bb); microburins (ee–gg,ii,jj); piquant triedre (hh); backed pieces (kk–nn); perforators (oo,pp).*

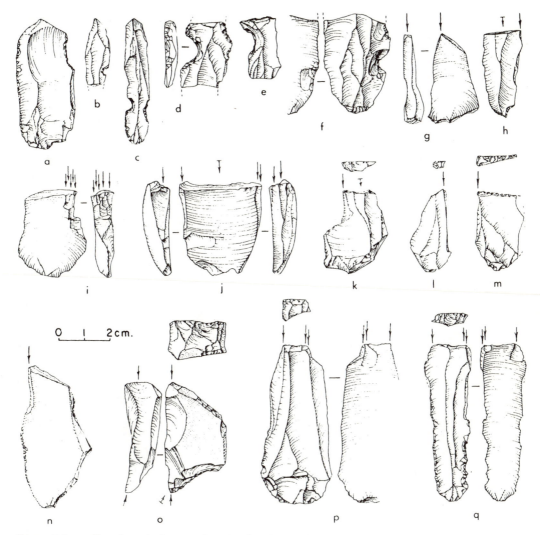

Figure 7.4. *Artifacts from the late Natufian site of Rosh Zin (after Henry, 1976). Notches (d–f); retouched piece (a); burins on snaps and old surfaces (g–j,n); burins on truncations (k–m,p,q); multiple mixed burin (o).*

Tool-kits Natufian tool-kits are typically dominated by geometric microliths, with lunates accounting for 60–98% of the class (Table 4.14; Figure 7.3). The balance of an average tool-kit is about evenly represented by backed bladelets, burins, scrapers, and notches-denticulates (Figures 7.4 and 7.5). Assemblages also normally contain a few "massive tools" that stand sharply apart from the microliths (Figures 7.6 and 7.7). Sickle blades, although generally accounting for less than 5% of a tool-kit, are nevertheless consistently present in Natufian assemblages.

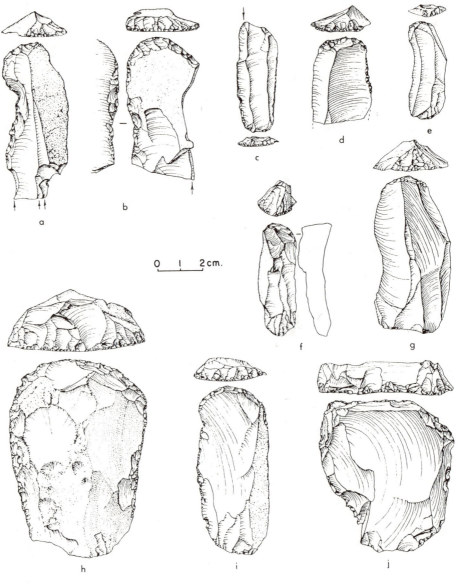

ABOVE:
Figure 7.5. *Artifacts from the Late Natufian site of Rosh Zin (after Henry, 1976). Burin scrapers (a–c); endscrapers (d,e,g,i); carinated scraper (f); massive scraper (h,j).*

TOP RIGHT:
Figure 7.6. *Artifacts from the Late Natufian site of Rosh Zin (after Henry, 1976). Denticulated endscraper (a); denticulates (b,c,e,f); strangled denticulate with transverse burin.*

BOTTOM RIGHT:
Figure 7.7. *Massive scraper from the Late Natufian site of Rosh Zin (after Henry, 1976).*

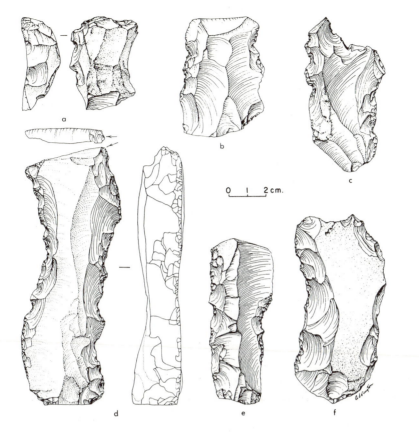

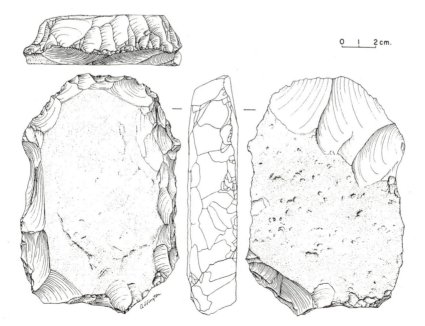

TABLE 7.1
The relationship between the percentage of geometrics in the tool kit and rainfall. Note that those sites in the 400–800 mm zones generally have low percentages whereas those in drier 100–300 mm settings have high percentages.

Site[a]	HC	HT	EM	NO	AU	EW	SK	HA	FZ	EA	IR	RZ	RH	WJ
Geometrics	10	14	11	14	20	67	46	11	21	48	27	37	41	62
Isohyet	800	-------------------------------------					400		300	------------------------------				100

[a](HC) Hayonim Cave, (HT) Hayonim Terrace, (EM) Ein Mallaha, (NO) Nahal Oren, (AU) Abu Usba, (EW) El Wad, (SK) Shukbah, (HA) Hatula, (FZ) Fazael IV, (EA) Ergel Ahmar, (IR) Ira 10, (RZ) Rosh Zin, (RH) Rosh Horesha, (WJ) Wadi Judayid.

A 1973 study employing a cluster analysis of ten Natufian tool-kits revealed four major groups, with three of these showing correlations with differences in environmental settings (Henry, 1973a, 1977). Since this initial study, detailed quantitative analyses have been completed on assemblages from six additional sites (Ein Mallaha, Hayonim Terrace, Nahal Oren, Wadi Fazael, Hatula, and Wadi Judayid). When data from these assemblages are considered, tool-kit clusters are still seen to be strongly tied to environmental settings, but the new data also indicate that one of the clusters is more likely a product of recovery bias than of functional responses to environmental conditions.

Although all of the major tool classes were considered in the original cluster analysis, the geometric class was the most discriminating variable. With the new data, a pattern emerges in which the frequency of geometrics in tool-kits is inversely correlated to modern isohyetic belts (Table 7.1). The only tool-kits that do not fit this pattern are from the sites of El Wad and Shukbah, both excavated by Garrod in the 1920s and 1930s. The high proportion of geometrics for assemblages from these sites is likely to result from the preferential recovery of lunates at the expense of less formal tools (retouched pieces, notches, etc.). The huge backdirt pile fronting the cave of El Wad, for example, is filled with cores, blades, and flakes, ample evidence of the nonsystematic recovery procedures employed by Garrod.

Therefore, it would appear that geometrics formed a proportionately greater part of the tool-kits found in drier settings. As previously argued for Mushabian and Geometric Kebaran tool-kits, geometrics are also likely to have served as arrow tips in the Natufian. Recent microwear studies, in fact, confirm such an interpretation (Valla, 1984; Anderson-Gerfaud, 1983:81). Lunates from Ein Mallaha, El Wad, Mureybet, and Abu Hureyra show patterns of wear and residue of mastic indicating that they were employed as composite arrowheads; i.e., mounted transversely or as barbs. The geographic distribution therefore shows that hunting-related implements formed a larger part of the tool inventory in drier settings. Given that Natufian hunters concentrated on gazelle and that these small antelopes favor an open setting, such an interpretation of the variability in tool-kits is consistent with the site distribution. The Natufian groups that colonized the drier, less wooded areas on the margin of the Mediterranean zone most likely adjusted their economy by placing a greater emphasis on hunting.

The correlation between geometric frequencies and environment also can be seen diachronically. If the stratigraphic successions of Hayonim Cave, Hayonim Terrace, and Ein Mallaha (all located within the core Mediterranean zone) are examined, geometrics form an increasingly larger part of the tool-kits through time (Table 7.2). This trend corresponds to a climatic deterioration in which a drier, more open setting progressively replaced the Mediterranean woodlands. As discussed earlier, this was most strongly expressed about 11,000 years ago, coincident with the transition from Early to Late Natufian. The irony here is that with the evidence for more intensive hunting and the growth of the gazelle habitat, nutritional data actually argue for a decline in meat consumption. As noted in Chapter 2, population growth and intensification through time would have led to the over-exploitation of resources within the catchments of Natufian hamlets. Even though environmental changes apparently induced an enlargement of gazelle habitats within the catchments, gazelle herds nevertheless would have soon been diminished by hunting pressure. The progressive scarcity of gazelle then would have driven the intensification of hunting to increasingly higher levels. Therefore, an explanation is provided for the seemingly contradictory evidence of more hunting and less meat.

TABLE 7.2
The percentage of the tool-kits represented by geometrics for several stratified assemblages from three Mediterranean zone sites. Note that geometric percentages tend to increase through time.

Site	Percent Geometrics
Hayonim Cave	
Phase III, locus 4	21
Phase II, locus 5 (upper)	17
Phase II, locus 5 (lower)	12
Phase I, locus 3	4
Hayonim Terrace	
Layer B	15
Layer C, upper	14
Layer C, middle	18
Layer C, lower	13
Layer D	11
Ein Mallaha	
Ib	11
III	7
III–IV	8

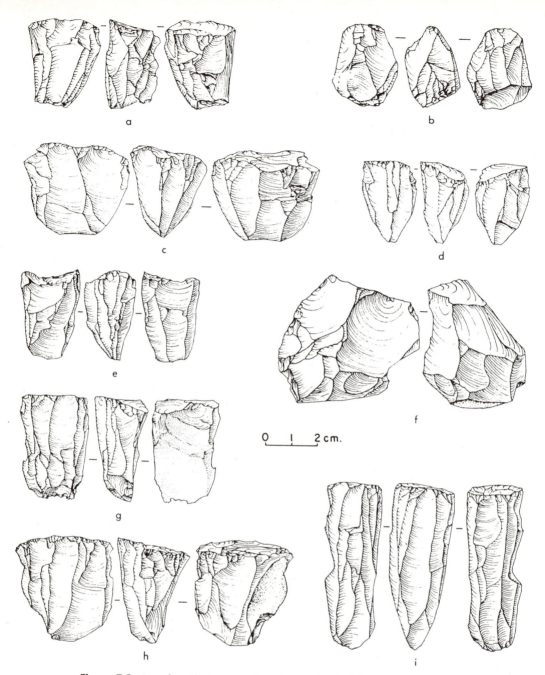

Figure 7.8. *Cores from the Late Natufian site of Rosh Zin (after Henry, 1976). Opposed platform cores (a,b); single platform pyramidal cores (c–e,h,i); ninety-degree core (g); irregular flake core (f).*

Lithic Technology The most striking aspect of the Natufian lithic technology is its standardization. From assemblage to assemblage, regardless of temporal and spatial contexts, the procedures employed in the production of bladelet blanks were remarkably uniform (Henry, 1973a, 1977, 1981). Production of relatively short, broad bladelets from predominantly multiple platform cores characterizes the industry (Figure 7.8). The dimensions of Natufian bladelets vary little between assemblages, averaging between 25 and 31mm in length and

TABLE 7.3
The relationship between restricted microburin indices (rIMbt) and rainfall. Note that those sites in the 400–800 mm zones generally have low indices, whereas those in drier 100–300 mm settings have high indices.

Site[a]	HC	HT	EM	NO	AU	EW	SK	HA	FZ	EA	TS	RZ	RH	WJ
rIMbt	0	70	1	15	31	10	0	1	50	0	30	80	70	44
Isohyet	800	------	------	------	------	------	400		300	------	------	------	------	100

[a] (HC) Hayonim Cave, (HT) Hayonim Terrace, (EM) Ein Mallaha, (NO) Nahal Oren, (AU) Abu Usba, (EW) El Wad, (SK) Shukbah, (HA) Hatula, (FZ) Fazael IV, (EA) Ergel Ahmar, (TS) Tor Abu Sif, (RZ) Rosh Zin, (RH) Rosh Horesha, (WJ) Wadi Judayid.

9.6 and 11.6mm in width. Bladelet platforms are predominantly unfacetted or crushed; bulb shapes are typically unlipped.

As initially noted by Garrod (Garrod and Bate, 1937), Natufian assemblages reflect the preferential use of certain raw materials for the fabrication of specific tools. Fine-grained, translucent chalcedony was employed for the production of microliths, whereas coarse-grained cherts were used in the manufacture of larger implements such as scrapers and massive tools.

One aspect of Natufian lithic technology does show patterned variation. Microburin indices tend to be much higher in sites on the margins of the Mediterranean zone and in Late Natufian occupations (Table 7.3). This pattern was initially viewed as evidence for the diffusion of the technique from Mushabian to Natufian groups as they came into contact in the Negev (Henry, 1974). Although the cultural chronologies of the two complexes are still consistent with this interpretation, the recent work in Jordan suggests that the diffusion front covered a much larger area. Also, once the technique had been adopted by Natufians, purely functional forces may have governed its patterned variation in time and space. In that the microburin technique was mainly used by the Natufians to fashion geometric microliths, the environmental factors that influenced geometric frequencies would also have guided microburin indices. Therefore, like geometrics, microburins are found in proportionately higher frequencies in drier settings.

Stylistic Attributes The various ways in which Natufians retouched their tools, especially the geometric microliths, would appear to reflect stylistic preference as opposed to any kind of functional requirement. In that these variations in retouch are incredibly subtle it seems unlikely that their differences could have had any functional importance. Furthermore, certain kinds of retouch are maintained in the same proportions across different tool classes (e.g., geometric microliths, backed bladelets, and sickle blades) even when the classes vary greatly in their proportionate representation.

It is not surprising, then, to find that these varieties of retouch provide the basis for the artifactual seriation of the Natufian, as discussed earlier. While most of the forms of retouch that occur in the Natufian have broad temporal and spatial distributions, one form is much more limited. A kind of marginal bifacial retouch, traditionally termed "Helwan" because of its presence at the Egyptian site of the same name, is geographically restricted to the Levant and temporally bracketed to a period between about 13,000 and 10,000 years ago. It is most commonly associated with Natufian assemblages, especially of the Early Natufian (ca. 12,500–11,000 B.P.), in which it constitutes 50% or more of the retouch on geometrics (Figure 7.9). It declined in use until its virtual disappearance by the end of the Late Natufian.

Figure 7.9. *Artifacts from the early Natufian layers of Hayonim Terrace (after Henry and Leroi-Gourhan, 1976). Microburin (a); lunate with bipolar backing (b); lunate with inverse retouch (c); Helwan backed lunates (d–g); backed and truncated bladelets opposite snaps (h–k); arched backed and pointed bladelet (l), La Mouillah point (m); notched and truncated pieces (n–p); Helwan retouched bladelet with sickle sheen (q); bilaterally backed bladelet with sheen (r); perforator (s); cores (t,u).*

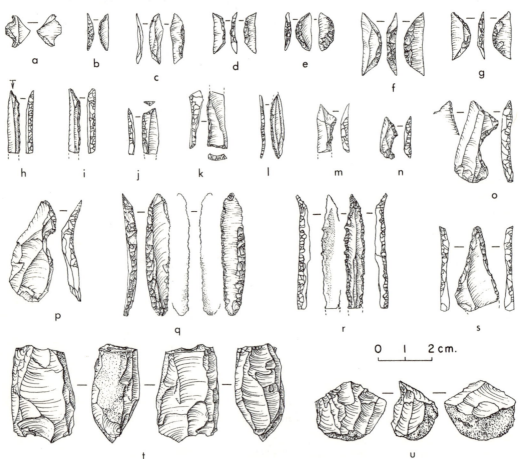

Although Helwan retouch is most closely linked to the Natufian, like so many stylistic elements it was also adopted by other contemporary groups such as the Mushabians. But what of its origin? Here again we find a line of evidence pointing to a tie between the Natufian and the preceding Geometric Kebaran. Though not common to the Geometric Kebaran, Helwan lunates have been recovered from horizons at Hayonim Terrace (Henry, et al., 1981) and at Qa Salab (Henry, 1982) in contexts that are thought to immediately predate the Early Natufian.

GROUNDSTONE ARTIFACTS

Of all Levantine Epipaleolithic complexes, the Natufian furnishes the most diverse and elaborate groundstone inventory. This may be explained in part by an increased dependence on wild cereals and nuts, but the greater permanence of Natufian communities would have also relaxed the need for portable utensils and thus indirectly given rise to heavy stone bowls and pestles, bedrock mortars, and various other groundstone implements.

Natufian groundstone artifacts include several forms that were used as containers or surfaces for either pounding or grinding. These consist of mortars, bowls, cup marks, querns, slabs, and grooved stones. Of these, the deep-hole conical mortars are the most common and their shape appears unique to the Natufian. They occur in bedrock and as free-standing forms that have been either finely finished or left unaltered. The bedrock mortars, 10 to 30cm in diameter and some 40 to 90cm deep, are often found to have penetrated the limestone boulder or slab into which they were drilled. At this point most were abandoned, but some were rejuvenated by sealing the openings with flint cores. Boulder mortars were sometimes used as grave furniture (Bar-Yosef and Goren, 1973) and tombstones (Stekelis and Yizraeli, 1963), but were more commonly incorporated into walls after they had been exhausted. Kenyon (1959:41) speculated that such deep-hole mortars may have served as bases for posts or even totem poles, but they were more likely to have been used simply for pounding or grinding activities. In that conical mortars are so common to Natufian sites and found throughout their distribution, the mortars were likely to have served a function very basic to the Natufian economy. A study of wear on their interior walls revealed horizontal striations, a pattern indicating a rotary grinding motion (Henry, 1976). In her ethnographic survey of the uses of groundstone artifacts, Kraybill (1977) found that mortars were utilized for both the pounding and grinding of grains and nuts.

Other groundstone artifacts common to Natufian occupations include grinding slabs, querns, bowls, pestles, mullers, and grooved stones. Grinding slabs and querns are less numerous than mortars and also lack the standardization in form. Stone bowls, perhaps also used as mortars, were often finely finished and even decorated with a "wavy-line" pattern.

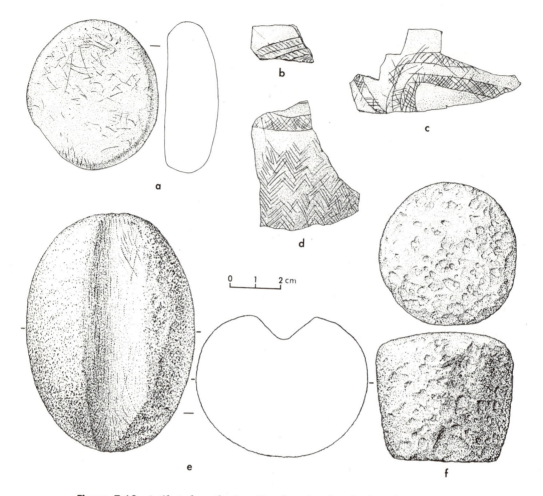

Figure 7.10. *Artifacts from the Late Natufian site of Rosh Zin (after Henry, 1976). Polished quartzite disc (a); decorated-incised ostrich eggshell (b–d); grooved stone (e); pestle (f).*

Pestles, like their mortar counterparts, are the most numerous and standardized of the "active" grinding-pounding implements; mullers and hand stones are less common. They are generally round or oval in cross-section, ranging from 10 to 30cm in length. Some exhibit ochre stains (Bar-Yosef and Goren, 1973).

Grooved stones typically occur as oval or bun-shaped specimens with a 1–2cm wide trough (Figure 7.10e). They were probably used to smooth and straighten arrow shafts or sharpen bone points.

In comparison to the Mushabian and Geometric Kebaran, the Natufian has a much richer and more elaborate groundstone industry. Whereas a groundstone technology was obviously present in these earlier complexes, it was not extensively employed and may have been most often used in the context of grinding pigment. With the expansion of Mediterranean woodlands, the technology was transferred to become the backbone of a new economy based upon the intensive collection, processing, and storage of cereals and nuts.

WORKED BONE ARTIFACTS

Like groundstone items, artifacts made of bone increase markedly in number and variety in the Natufian (Table 7.4). Classifications of worked bone assemblages have mainly followed a functional theme (Bar-Yosef and Tchernov, 1970; Bar-Yosef and Goren, 1973), although Stordeur (1981) recently attempted to identify Natufian cultural facies on the basis of the patterned variation between assemblages.

In Bar-Yosef's classification, implements linked to hunting, sewing, and weaving are the most common. Sickle hafts and ornamental specimens (to be discussed under Decorative and Ornamental Objects) are the next most common categories. Finally, implements associated with skin working, fishing, and hairdressing round out the inventory.

Implements tied to hunting consist of various bone points, including barbed points or "harpoons" (Figure 7.11a–c). Although barbed points have traditionally been associated with fishing, their presence in dry inland settings implies that they were more likely used for hunting. Specimens thought to have been used for sewing or weaving include slender, pierced points, awls, and borers (Figures 7.11 and 7.12). Sickle hafts, typically made from split limb bones, are often decorated with a parallel-line or net pattern common to other bone artifacts (Bar-Yosef and Tchernov, 1970) and even ostrich eggshell (Figure 7.10b–d). Hafts recovered from the caves of El Wad and Kebara were finely sculpted into the forms of deer and goat heads (Figure 7.13). Also at El Wad and at the Judean Desert site of Oumm ez Zoueitina, sickle hafts were found that still contained flint sickleblades bearing lustre. Fishing implements are not widely distributed, but gorgets, at least when found, occur in substantial numbers.

The emergence of an elaborate worked bone industry with the Natufian has been explained as resulting from a "secure economic position" that "enabled the Natufians to direct some of their activities towards an enrichment of their material culture . . . " (Bar-Yosef and Tchernov, 1970:149). Bar-Yosef and Tchernov (1970: 150) go on to state that "with this socio-economic gain the Natufian culture emerged in sharp contrast to the previous Kebaran hunter-and-gatherer groups." In short, this explanation suggests that Natufians would have had a greater amount of time to devote to such labor intensive tasks as bone working. Ethnographic data, however, would argue to the contrary, as mobile foragers are well known for their leisure (Sahlins, 1972; Lee, 1979). Rather than being associated with an inclination to enrich their material culture, the Natufians' interest in working bone was more likely driven by a desire to create material advertisements of status.

The appearance of an elaborate worked bone industry in the Natufian was probably indirectly tied to ranking and prestige, which, in turn, fueled intensified foraging and the development of surpluses. In comparison to most other materials used by foragers (flint, for example), bone has a much greater capacity for communicating the time and effort spent in the manufacturing process. With

TABLE 7.4
Distribution of worked bone artifacts in Natufian sites following the "functional groups" used by Bar-Yosef and Tchernov (1970).

Tool Group	Hayonim Cave	Ein Mallaha	El Wad	Kebara	Shukbah	Erq el Ahmar	Qumm ez Zoueitina	Jericho	Hayonim Terrace	Rosh Horesha	Hatula
I. Skin working											
a. Burnisher	×		×								
b. Spatulae											
1. Plain	×	×							×		
2. Pierced											
3. Decorated	×										
II. Sewing/weaving											
a. Awl	×	×	×	×		×			×	×	×
b. Point (awl)	×	×	×	×					×	×	×
c. Pierced point		×	×	×	×				×		
d. Elongated point						×					
III. Hunting											
a. Fully shaped point	×	×	×	×	×	×			×	×	
b. Bi-point	×	×		×							
c. Barbed point											
1. One barb						×					
2. Row of barbs			×	×				×	×		
IV. Fishing											
a. Gorget	×		×	×		×					
b. Hook				×							
V. Sickle hafts											
a. Plain	×	×	×	×							
b. Decorated	×		×				×				×
VI. Hair dressing											
a. Comb				×							
b. Barrette				×							
VII. Pendants											
a. Phalange		×	×	×		×					
b. Tooth	×		×	×					×		
c. Shaft	×		×						×		
VIII. Varia											
Decorated	×		×		×		×				

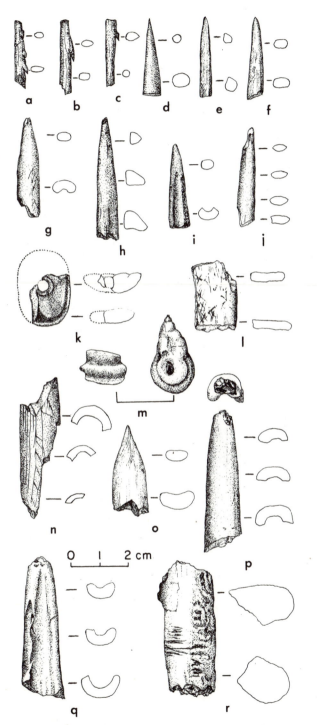

Figure 7.11. *Worked bone tools and ornaments from the Natufian layers of Hayonim Terrace (after Henry and Leroi-Gourhan, 1976). Barbed points (a–c); point tips (e–j); pendant (k); decorated fragments (l,n,r); borers (m,o); punches (p,q).*

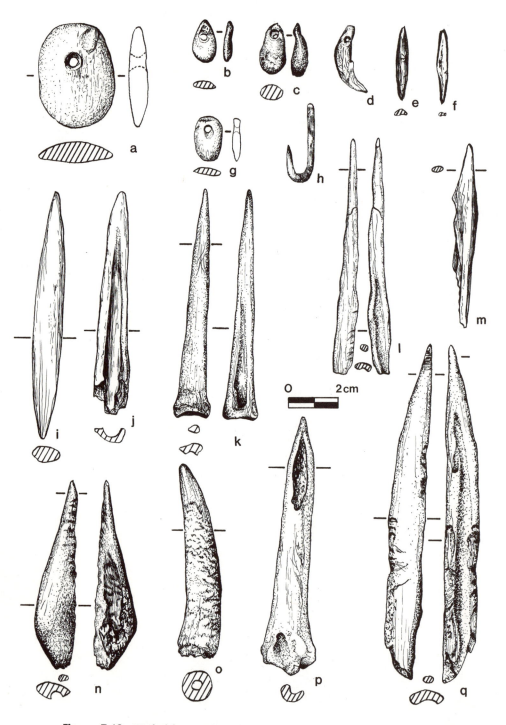

Figure 7.12. *Worked bone tools and ornaments from the Natufian layers of Hayonim Cave (Bar-Yosef and Tchernov, 1970) and Kebara (Turville-Petre, 1932). Pendants of bone and tooth (a-d,g); gorgets (e,f); fish hook (h); bi-point (i); awls (j,m,n,q); points (k,l,p); polished horn (o).*

a

0 1 2 3cm

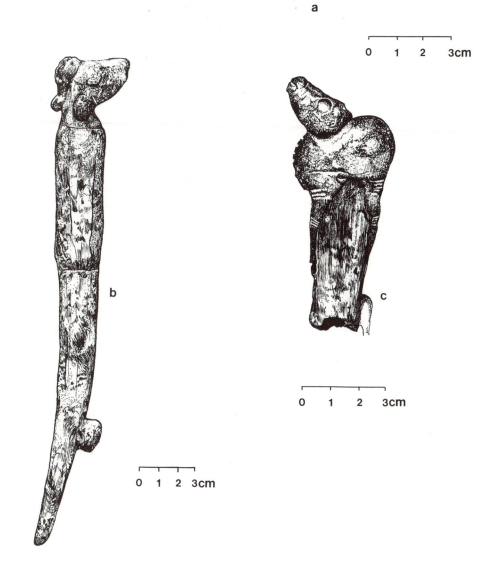

b

c

0 1 2 3cm

0 1 2 3cm

Figure 7.13. *Natufian sculpted objects. Limestone statuette of ruminant from Oumm ez Zoueitina (a); sickle haft from Kebara (b); sickle haft from El Wad (c).*

the rise of ranking, then, Natufians were attracted to bone as a new material culture medium. This was not for any direct functional reason, but because bone provided a material that could clearly advertise the labor invested in its fabrication. Worked bone items thus furnished ideal status objects. Three points support this interpretation. First, most of the Natufian worked bone artifacts are in the form of ornaments rather than utilitarian pieces. Secondly, a great number of the utilitarian pieces are elaborately decorated. Thirdly, the richest worked bone sites or areas are those associated with burials.

DECORATIVE, ORNAMENTAL, AND ART OBJECTS

With the Natufian, we see the first extensive evidence of decorative and artistic expressions in the material culture of the Levant. Decorative elements include those designs and motifs that appear on potentially utilitarian objects, e.g., stone bowls and ostrich eggshell containers. Ornamental objects consist of specimens that were used for adornment, such as pendants and beads. Art objects are mainly figurines and statuettes.

From an anthropological perspective, art is often seen as a means of social communication, and this is the dimension that concerns us here. Like the analysis of other forms of communication, an examination of Natufian decorative styles and art objects is directed toward understanding the structure of the system, identifying any diachronic changes that may have occurred, and determining the system's boundaries.

A survey of decorative elements isolates eight relatively complex designs (Figure 7.14). Only two of these (D and G) appear to have been time-transgressive, present in both Early and Late Natufian occupations, and to have had a wide geographic distribution (Table 7.5). The other six designs, in fact, are found restricted to single sites: A and C to Ein Mallaha, B and H to Rosh Zin, and E and F to Hayonim Cave. This raises the question of why there was such heterogeneity within decorative designs when so many other lines of evidence within Natufian material culture (chipped stone, groundstone, and worked bone) were so standardized. The explanation may rest in determining what was being communicated by the decoration and how this was transmitted. The site-specific designs appear on stone bowls, ostrich egg bottles, and hide-working tools, objects most likely to have been made and used by females. Though the designs may have served as symbols of local groups, it is difficult to determine at what scale. They could have denoted hamlets, clans, or even joint families. If women were responsible for the decorations, the distribution of the designs indicate that Natufian women must have typically resided in their hamlet of birth throughout life. This pattern then is consistent with the proposal, based upon other lines of evidence, that Natufians were matrilocal.

Ornamental objects are common to most Natufian artifact assemblages. They were typically fashioned from bone, shell, and tooth into beads and pen-

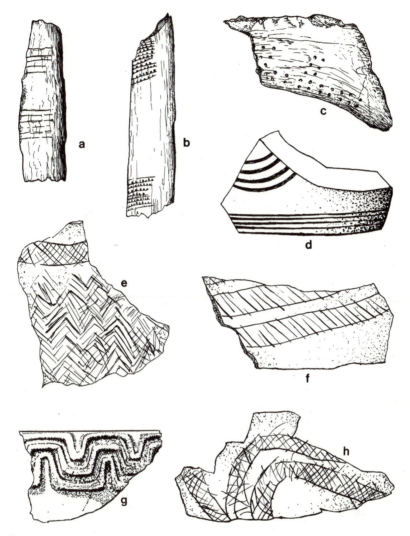

Figure 7.14. *Illustration showing eight designs found within the Natufian.*

TABLE 7.5
The distribution of the major Natufian design styles by time and material.

Design Style	Natufian Phase Early	Late	Stone	Material Bone	Ostrich eggshell
A	X		X		
B		X			X
C	X		X	X	
D	X	X	X	X	
E	X			X	
F	X			X	
G	X	X		X	X
H	?	X		X	X

dants. These were mainly incorporated into objects of adornment such as head-dresses, necklaces, garters, and bracelets as identified in burials.

The most commonly used shells were the tusk-shaped dentalium that are present in great numbers in all Natufian deposits. They occur unmodified, pierced with holes, and sectioned into beads. At El Wad various styles of head-dress fashioned from dentalium were found still adhering to four skulls (Figure 7.15). Several dentalium necklaces, bracelets, and garters were also recovered from the El Wad burials. Other finds of dentalium shell ornaments include a headdress attached to a skull at Ein Mallaha (Perrot, 1966), a bracelet on a burial at Nahal Oren (Noy, et al., 1973; Reese, 1982), and a necklace on a female burial at Erq el Ahmar (Neuville, 1951). Three species of dentalium were used: *D. dentalis*, *D. vulgare*, and *D. elephantinum*. All were recovered from the Mediterranean except for the large *D. elephantinum*, which comes from the Red Sea. Various other marine shells including, among others, *Columbella, Mitrella, Conus,*

Figure 7.15. *Photograph of burial at El Wad showing dentalia shell headdress adhering to skull (from Garrod and Bate, 1937).*

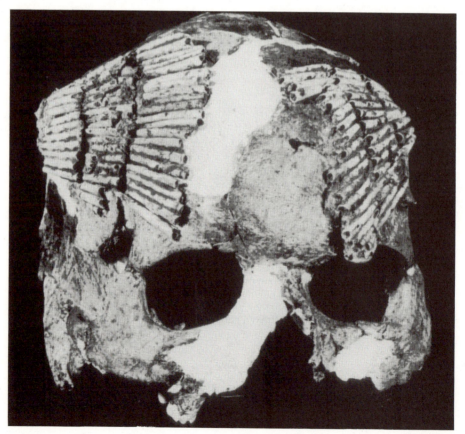

Arcularia, and *Acanthocardia* occur in substantial numbers in Natufian occupations (Reese, 1982; Bar-Yosef and Tchernov, 1966; Tchernov, 1976; Mienis, 1977). These have typically been holed apparently for stringing as beads or pendants. The only freshwater shell to be consistently present is *Theodoxus jordani*, a species common to the Sea of Galilee.

An examination of the shell collections from Natufian sites reveals a pattern of increasing utilization of shells from distant sources through time. Early Natufian occupations rarely include species from both the Mediterranean and the Red Sea, and they are dominated by shells indigenous to the nearest water body. El Wad, Kebara, the early horizons of Hayonim Cave and Terrace, and Ein Mallaha contain shells only from the Mediterranean (and the Sea of Galilee), while Wadi Judayid is dominated by Red Sea species. In contrast, Late Natufian occupations contain shells from both local and distant sources. For example, Red Sea species first make their appearance in the upper deposit of Hayonim Cave (Bar-Yosef and Tchernov, 1966), and a mixture of species from the Red Sea, the Mediterranean, and the Sea of Galilee were found in the Negev sites of Rosh Zin and Rosh Horesha (Tchernov, 1976; Mienis, 1977). If shells were used as ornaments symbolizing status, which is certainly indicated by the burials, then their greater circulation through time might have been an expression of the increasing concern of the Natufians with matters of rank and prestige. As noted earlier, such interests would have been fueled by the need for intensified exploitation in the context of progressive population growth and resource scarcity.

Pendants of bone and tooth compose another major category of ornaments. The bone pendants mainly occur in three forms: oval, phalange, and club-like. Oval forms, fashioned from segments of long bones, and truncated phalanges have the widest distribution, being present at El Wad, Kebara, Hayonim Cave, Ein Mallaha, Erq el Ahmar, and Ain Sakhri (Stordeur, 1981). The club-like pendants are confined to El Wad; those made of canine teeth have been found only at El Wad and Hayonim Cave.

Objects of art unrelated to utilitarian implements are limited to statuettes, phallic objects, and figurines recovered from the sites of El Wad, Ein Mallaha, Oumm ez Zoueitina, and Ain Sakhri. The three representations of human heads from El Wad and Ein Mallaha are remarkably similar in overall form although the Ein Mallaha specimens are much more finely executed. All are sculpted from stone. They depict prominent broad, flat noses and exaggerated continuous eyebrows. The eyes, disproportionately large, are outlined by two or three lines with no attempt to define pupils. Garrod characterized the El Wad head as unique and cautioned against viewing the sculpture as a portrait of a Natufian (Garrod and Bate, 1937:39). Given the similarities between this head and the subsequent discoveries at Ein Mallaha, however, it may be that these are fairly realistic representations of Natufians or at least of how they perceived themselves. The prominent broad, flat noses and pronounced brows are consistent with Ferembach's (1977) description of Natufian faces based upon skeletal remains. And one might also note that the Natufians' artistic portrayal of animals was also very representational.

At Oumm ez Zoueitina, a remarkably finely sculpted limestone statuette of a deer or gazelle was found by Neuville (Figure 7.13). Unfortunately, the head was missing. Similarly finely executed sculptures in bone were found on sickle hafts at Kebara and El Wad. These depicted the heads of deer, goats, and unidentified bovids. Natufian art also had an erotic element as seen in a calcite statuette, recovered from Ain Sakhri, and phallic objects from El Wad and Rosh Zin.

Interpretation of art from a social perspective is always difficult even among living groups. In depicting anthropomorphic figures, animals, and human sexual organs, Natufian art was most likely linked in some manner to ritual and ceremony. The emergence and florescence of art probably paralleled the heightened ritual and ceremonial acitivities that developed in Natufian communities. Such activities would have served to oil social interaction and reduce tensions in these large, permanent communities where cooperation was basic to their functioning.

MORTUARY PATTERNS, HUMAN OSTEOLOGY, AND SOCIAL ORGANIZATION

More than 200 skeletons have been recovered from burials at El Wad, Kebara, Nahal Oren, Hayonim Cave, Ein Mallaha, Shukbah, and Erq el Ahmar (Henry, 1973a, 1983; Wright, 1978). The mortuary patterns indicate that Natufian society was stratified and that initially rank was principally determined within subgroups (e.g., joint-families or clans) of the community. Through time this practice appears to have given way to ranking based upon status on a community-wide scale.

Subgroups and Rank In his study of Natufian mortuary patterns, G. Wright (1981) notes several attributes that are typically tied to ranked societies. In following Binford's (1971) ethnographic survey of mortuary practices, Wright (1981) points to: the different types of group burials, the presence of grave furniture that cross-cuts sex lines, the recurrence of a specific symbolic artifact (dentalium shells) in a few burials, and the association of elaborate grave goods with children as evidence for inherited status and subgroup differentiation within the Natufian. He goes on to suggest that with the emergence of large permanent communities and the necessary redistribution of storable surpluses, status positions are likely to have developed. Such positions and their attendant authority to coordinate activities and to reduce intra-community conflict would have become a necessary component of Natufian society. Subsequent population growth and dwindling resources may well have further elevated ranking as a mechanism for intensifying the economy, controlling resources and reducing conflict.

The evolution from an egalitarian to a ranked society is likely to have been based initially upon kinship. That is, the earliest Natufian hamlets were probably composed of two or more joint-families or perhaps clans within which most economic, social, and political decisions were made. As the communities grew, competition over resources would have increased and managerial activities would have become more complex. At this point, status positions that crossed subgroup boundaries would have become more effective.

This proposed development from kin-bound to community-wide ranking is perhaps reflected in the evolution of interment practices between Early and Late Natufian times. During the Early Natufian, the dead were buried together in small groups; in the Late Natufian the dead were buried individually in cemeteries. Within these burials the definition of subgroup affiliation may be detected in the different mortuary patterns. The Early Natufian burials at El Wad, for example, reveal two quite distinct patterns of interment. In the cave area, a group burial (which was reopened twice) contained skeletons of adults, children, and infants in an extended position accompanied by grave furniture, limestone, and hearths; but no dentalium. On the terrace of the cave, five separate group burials (none of which were reopened) contained skeletons of adults and children in a flexed position with one member of each group always wearing dentalium; but hearths and limestone were absent from these burials. It is noteworthy that the individuals wearing dentalium shells included men, women, and children. Similar mortuary patterns were observed in Early Natufian burials at Erq el Ahmar (Neuville, 1951; Vallois, 1936), Ein Mallaha (Perrot, 1966), and Hayonim Cave (Bar-Yosef and Goren, 1973). Wright (1981) suggests that these patterns denote the transferral of high status through inheritance within one subgroup of a Natufian community.

By Late Natufian times mortuary practices had changed to predominantly single interments. This shift, initially observed by Garrod at El Wad, is paralleled by 45 individual burials at Shukbah and about 50 single interments at Nahal Oren. At Hayonim Cave, two of the three burials in Phases 4 and 5 (both Late Natufian) are individual interments, whereas all of the Early Natufian graves are group burials (Bar-Yosef and Goren, 1973).

Ethnographic data collected from cross-cultural surveys show that mortuary patterns closely mirror the social and geographic domains of those interred (Binford, 1971; Goldstein, 1981). Specifically, a linkage between corporate groups, resources, and the formal disposal of the dead has been noted on a consistent basis (Saxe, 1971; Saxe and Gall, 1977; Goldstein, 1981). In her survey of 30 societies, Goldstein (1976:61) found that a permanent, spatially defined burial area is always representative of a corporate group that has "rights over the use and/or control of crucial but restricted resources." She further discovered that this control is maintained by means of "lineal descent from the dead, either in terms of actual lineage or in the form of a strong, established tradition of the critical resource passing from parent to offspring" (Goldstein, 1976:61). The findings of Goldstein and others, then, would suggest that Natufian burials most likely contain members of corporate groups that controlled crucial resources and that this control was inherited. The crucial resources probably consisted of land-rights to cereal stands and nut plots. The transition from group burial to individual burial in cemeteries may well have reflected an evolution from kin-based (e.g., clan, joint-family) to community-wide ownership of resources.

Endogamy and Matriliny Interestingly, analysis of the skeletal remains themselves provides another clue to Natufian social organization. A study of 17 skeletons from the burials at Hayonim Cave revealed that third molar agenesis was present in 47% of the sample (Smith, 1973). Because the congenital absence of the third molar is a genetically determined trait, inherited as a Mendelian recessive characteristic that occurs at relatively low frequencies (0–20%) for other populations, significant inbreeding or endogamy is indicated for the Hayonim Cave population. The persistence of abnormally high frequencies of third molar agenesis throughout the five phases of occupation (bridging Early and Late Natufian times) implies a long duration of intra-community endogamy, perhaps on the order of 1,000 years. This pattern, extending over as many as thirty generations, implies that the practice was a habitual part of the community's social fabric. The geographic scale of the practice appears to have been restricted to the community level because the high frequency of third molar agenesis that characterizes the Hayonim Cave population is found at normal frequencies in the skeletal samples from six other Natufian sites (Ein Mallaha, Nahal Oren, El Wad, Kebara, Shukbah, and Erq el Ahmar).

Universally, kin group endogamy is quite rare, with only 67 of 862 societies being listed in Murdock's (1967) *Ethnographic Atlas* as prescribing a form of endogamous marriage. When present, however, endogamy is almost always associated with sedentary, matrilocal communities (Murdock, 1949, 1967; Levinson and Malone, 1980). Matrilocal residence patterns are similarly highly correlated with matrilineal descent. These strong correlations between marriage, postmarital residence, and descent patterns in the ethnographic record therefore suggest that, given the evidence for endogamy, Natufian communities were most likely composed of one or more matrilocal groups that traced their descent matrilineally. This proposal also finds support in the previously discussed distribution of decorative styles in which the designs on female-related objects were shown to be specific to certain Natufian communities. This contrasts sharply with the distributional patterns in the styles of male-related objects (e.g., flint tools), which show little variation between communities.

It is tempting to argue that the matrilocal-matrilineal pattern was related to the important role that women must have played in procuring and processing the plant resources on which the Natufian adaptive system depended. Local knowledge and ownership of such resources by women may well have given rise to their staying in the community of their birth after marriage. However, the economic role of women as the contributing factor to matriliny has been challenged on the basis of cross-cultural data (Ember and Ember, 1971:573). This has prompted Harris (1980:281) to argue that it is actually the variation in male activities (warfare, hunting, and trade) that accounts for differences in post-marital residence patterns. He proposes that when warfare, hunting, and trade practices shift from short-distance forays to long-distance expeditions, matri-locality emerges as a "permanent core of mothers, daughters, and sisters" who oversee the economic and social needs of the family and community (Harris, 1980:281). There is evidence to support such a shift with the emergence of the Natufian. The prevalence of gazelle remains in Natufian sites situated well out-side the antelope's natural habitat, along with basalt and seashells from distant sources, indicates long-distance hunting and trading expeditions.

Besides being linked to sedentary, matrilocal communities, endogamy has been "functionally" related to concentrating control over resources by keeping heritable authority within the group (Hammel, 1964; Goody, 1970, 1976; Kloos, 1963; Goody, et al., 1970; Levinson and Malone, 1980). This may well have become an increasingly important factor to Natufian communities as they experienced declining resources. In comparing the Natufian data to ethnographic evidence, Mussi (1976) argues for a social organization that promoted formal claims over goods and resources.

A synchronic parallel to the diachronic changes proposed for Natufian social organization may well be seen in the clinal patterns observed among the com-plex foragers of the Northwest coast of North America. Riches (1979:150) notes that among these groups the south-to-north decline in resources was accompa-nied by shifts from intra-group to inter-group rank, from cognatic to matrilineal descent, and from intra-community to inter-community exchange through trade and ceremony. In short, the social responses to scarcity were to concentrate and formally fix authority over resources while simultaneously enlarging the sphere in which resources might be exchanged. While a practice of matriliny appears to have been in place early in the Natufian, the previously discussed change from group to individual burials likely reflects the transition from intra-group to inter-group rank. Correlations between stress on resources and increased formality in the disposal of the dead are noted in several ethnographic sources (Chapman, 1981). For example, Saxe and Gall (1977) have recorded a change in burial custom among the Temuan of Malaysia in which a decline in resources was accompanied by the emergence of supra-household proto-lineages and the for-mal disposal of the dead in cemeteries. The progressive enlargement of the ex-change spheres of Natufian communities is also indicated in the archaeological record by the increasing use of shells from distant over local sources.

Summary of Social Organization The general economic, social, and politi-cal organization of Natufian communities is likely to have closely resembled that described as a "chiefdom" by Service (1962) and Sahlins (1968). In examining chiefdoms archaeologically, Renfrew (1973:543) lists twenty features com-

TABLE 7.6
The occurrence of chiefdom characteristics in the Natufian. The characteristics are drawn from a list developed by Renfrew (1973).

Common Characteristics of Chiefdoms	Present in the Natufian
1. A ranked society	x
2. Increase in the total number in the society	x
3. Increase in the size of individual residence groups	x
4. Greater productivity	x
5. More clearly defined territorial borders	
6. Redistribution of produce organized by the chief	
7. Greater population density	x
8. A more integrated society with a greater number of sociocentric statuses	x
9. Centers that coordinate social and religious as well as economic activity	
10. Frequent ceremonies and rituals	
11. Rise of priesthood	
12. Relation to a total environmental situation	x
13. Specialization, not only regional or ecological	x
14. Organization and deployment of public labor	
15. Improvement in craft specialization	
16. Potential for territorial expansion	x
17. Reduction of internal strife	
18. Pervasive inequality of persons or groups	
19. Distinctive dress or ornament for those of high status	x
20. No true government to back up decisions by legalized force.	x

monly found in ethnographic contexts (Table 7.6). Evidence for eleven of these features is found in the Natufian. For the remainder, data are unavailable or ambiguous, but of the data available all are consistent with the Natufian having been organized as a chiefdom.

At a more detailed level, Natufian communities would appear to have been composed of matrilocal subgroups (e.g., joint-families or clans) that traced their descent matrilineally. Natufian society was apparently ranked, with high-status individuals coming from a certain subgroup (at least in Early Natufian times). In many ways this may have resembled the social divisions of Northwest Coast complex foragers in which communities were divided into the hereditary categories of "privileged ones" (chiefs or nobles) and commoners (Drucker, 1965:47). In this system each individual occupied a unique position in a graded scale from highest to lowest. Perhaps also as in the Natufian, differences in rank were denoted by articles of clothing and ornaments, such as "chief's hats, necklaces, and ear pendants" (Drucker, 1965:48). It is a remarkable historic coincidence that, as with the Natufian, dentalium shells were seen as high-status ornaments and valuable trade goods by these Northwest Coast chiefdoms (Drucker, 1965; Kroeber, 1976).

Natufian social organization apparently underwent a change from identifying status and authority within subgroups of a community to defining such roles at the community level. This transition is paralleled by an enlargement of the sphere for trade and exchange. Both of these changes are viewed as social responses to problems resulting from population growth and dwindling resources.

ARCHITECTURE

Architecture, the most striking feature of these earliest permanent village communities, is best known from Ein Mallaha (Perrot, 1966; Valla, 1981; Figure 7.16), Hayonim Cave (Bar-Yosef and Goren, 1973) and Rosh Zin (Henry, 1976). Other, more limited, examples of structures and features come from El Wad (Garrod and Bate, 1937), Hayonim Terrace (Henry and Leroi-Gourhan, 1976),

Figure 7.16. *Photograph of House 131 and adjoining structures at the Natufian site of Ein Mallaha (provided by Centre de Recherche Français de Jerusalem and F. R. Valla). Note the storage pits, internal hearths, and footings for roof-supports.*

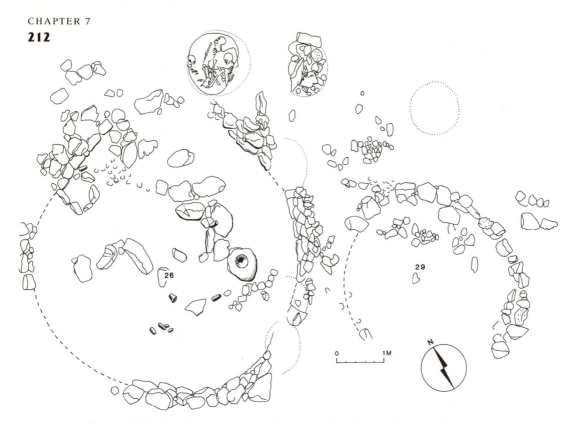

Figure 7.17. *Plan of structures 26 and 29 at the Natufian site of Ein Mallaha (redrawn after J. Perrot, 1966). Note the mortars, pestles, and storage areas in structure 26; and also note the external group burial.*

Wadi Hama 27 (McNicoll, 1985), Abu Hureyra (Moore, et al., 1975), and Mureybet (Cauvin, 1972; Gilot and Cauvin, 1973). Unfortunately, the overall size and organization of any Natufian hamlet is poorly understood because of the differences in the preservation of architecture and the limited areas that have been excavated. Where architectural features have been identified in the southern Levant, semi-subterranean circular and curvilinear structures, built of unmodified stones, have been found in two patterns: linear and clustered. At Ein Mallaha, structures arranged in a linear pattern in the earliest phase are subsequently replaced by clustered structures (Valla, 1981), and the Late Natufian site of Rosh Zin shows this same clustered pattern (Henry, 1973a, 1976). Sites along the Euphrates (Abu Hureyra and Mureybet) also contain circular and curvilinear structures, but rather than being built of stone they are either fashioned of clay and timber (Mureybet) or cut into the subsoil (Abu Hureyra).

The significant variability in the sizes of the structures (ranging from 2–9m in diameter) point to their having served different functions. Beyond being used as dwellings (Figure 7.17), they probably served as places for storage of goods and even for conducting ceremonies. The small walled structures within Hayonim Cave have been interpreted as storehouses, whereas the largest of the structures at Rosh Zin was associated with unique ceremonial features. Unlike the other structures at the site, its floor was paved and a monolithic limestone

Figure 7.18: *Photograph of Locus 4 at the Natufian site of Rosh Zin showing part of pavement, walls, and base of pillar at right center (after Henry, 1976). Note bedrock mortar in lower right corner and displaced top of pillar at top center.*

column (1m long and .4m in diameter) had been erected just inside the wall (Figure 7.18). At the base of the phallic-shaped column, a cache was found containing a matched pair of grooved stones (carefully placed with their grooves together), a polished limestone disc, and five unusually large chalcedony cores.

Apart from the walled structures, Natufian sites display various other architectural features or facilities including storage pits (some of which are lined with plaster), terrace walls and curbs, and stone pavements. When these facilities are considered along with the structures, a picture of rather intensive construction activity emerges. Not only were a great number of limestone blocks and slabs brought into the sites for building walls and pavements, but a considerable amount of earth was removed in the construction of subterranean houses and storage pits. The intensity of construction activities is also expressed in the multiple phases of building as seen at Ein Mallaha, Hayonim Cave, El Wad, and Rosh Zin.

In examining the architectural patterns of the Natufian, Flannery (1972) suggested a number of parallels with ethnographic communities arranged as "circular hut compounds." He argued that if Natufian communities were organized as compounds then: (1) the houses would have housed only one adult, not a family; (2) the community would have lacked stratification; (3) the community would have been incapable of intensifying the economy and maintaining large numbers of residents (Flannery, 1972:31,48–49). Whereas the architectural patterns of Natufian sites do resemble those of the compounds, other varieties of archaeological evidence indicate that Natufian communities shared little else with those of the compound type. Artifact patterns within Natufian dwellings, for example, point to diverse activities associated with both sexes. And burials beneath the floors of the dwellings contain the remains of males, females, and children, thus suggesting a family as a residential unit. Regarding social stratification, the previously discussed interment patterns in Natufian sites argue for ranking, apparently inherited matrilineally. And in the context of foraging, the storage pits and permanency of the Natufian hamlets clearly denote the community's ability to intensify the exploitation of wild resources. Although community size is difficult to pinpoint, based upon allometric growth models the areas of Natufian sites suggest populations ranging from 45 to greater than 200 persons. Communities with such numbers of year-round residents would certainly have had the social mechanisms for maintaining group cohesion.

Economic Evidence

Natufian subsistence activities can be determined directly from the dietary residue recovered from the sites and from analyses of the teeth and bones of the Natufians themselves. The implements and facilities that were used for collecting, processing, and storing foodstuffs provide another line of evidence for reconstructing Natufian economic patterns.

HUNTING

In those excavations where flotation or fine wet-sieving techniques were used for the recovery of minute bones, a wide range of fauna has been recovered (Bar-Yosef and Tchernov, 1966; Moore, 1975; Henry, et al., 1981, 1983; Valla, et al., 1986). The remains of numerous species of lizards, snakes, tortoises, amphibians, birds, small mammals, and even fishes have been identified in association with larger game. Traditionally, this evidence has been interpreted as denoting a generalized or broad-spectrum dietary pattern. But when the actual meat yield of the various species is calculated, it is clear that the Natufians obtained most of their meat from one animal: the gazelle (Henry, 1975; Bar-Yosef, 1981a). The remains of other large game, including fallow deer, sheep/goat, cattle, wild boar, red deer, roe deer, hartebeest, and equids, have been recovered, but gazelle always constitute the largest part (40–80%) of the large animal assemblages. In those faunal assemblages where meat yield can be estimated, over 98% of the meat can be accounted for by gazelle and one (caprovines or cattle) or two (wild boar and fallow deer) other large animals. Rather than representing a generalized hunting strategy, these data point to a highly specialized strategy focused on gazelle.

Emphasis on Gazelle This emphasis on the exploitation of gazelle has prompted speculation that Natufians were actually managing or keeping herds of the small antelope (Legge, 1972). The high proportion of immature gazelles (50–60%) in the faunal assemblages has been cited as evidence for culling of the herds, a common practice in animal husbandry. However, the seemingly high proportion of immature animals only reflect the age profiles of "natural" gazelle herds (Henry, 1975). And, as noted by Davis (1983:60) in his study of Hayonim Terrace gazelles, the dominance of males associated with culling practices fails to appear; instead, males and females are equally represented. Thus, rather than being over-represented and pointing to the practice of culling, the high proportion of immature gazelle remains in Natufian deposits may imply that the herds experienced catastrophic mortality. That is, the herds were apparently taken *en masse*, resulting in age profiles representative of those for entire herds. Such representative samples in the faunal remains suggest that hunting practices were nonselective in regard to the ages of gazelles. Gazelle then, were most likely hunted by surround or ambush, practices that would have resulted in the taking of a whole herd. Ethnographic accounts note that gazelle are particularly vulnerable to large-scale surrounds (Henry, 1975). Although such strategies would have required a substantial party of hunters, there would have been little difficulty in mustering the necessary number of adult males in a Natufian village.

Domestication of the Dog Canid remains from the Natufian occupation at El Wad were identified as belonging to dog (Garrod and Bate, 1937), but this claim was never fully accepted. A study of recent evidence recovered from Hayonim Terrace and Ein Mallaha, however, confirms the domestication of the dog in Early Natufian times (Davis and Valla, 1978). Davis found that the maximum lengths of the lower carnassial teeth of wolves (both recent and Late Pleistocene) were significantly longer than those of dogs; and that specimens from the Natufian sites fit comfortably within the range displayed by dogs.

Beyond this taxonomic evidence, a burial under the floor of one of the dwellings at Ein Mallaha contains a human skeleton in association with a puppy identified as a dog or wolf (Davis and Valla, 1978). The human skeleton's left wrist rested under its forehead with its hand lying on the chest of the puppy (Figure 7.19). Within the same dwelling a mandible from an adult canid was excavated in association with another human burial. Though neither of these specimens can be definitely attributed to dog, their contexts are more consistent with their being dogs than wolves.

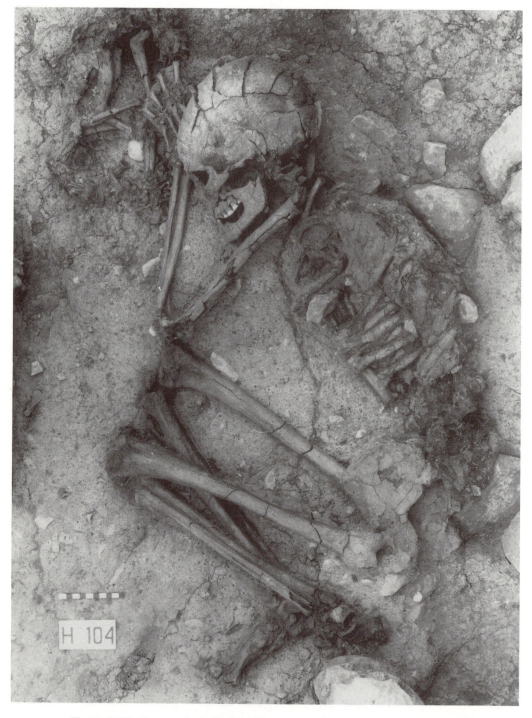

Figure 7.19. *Photograph of a burial with a puppy (of dog or wolf) at Ein Mallaha (provided by Centre de Recherche Français de Jerusalem and F. R. Valla).*

These specimens represent the earliest conclusive evidence for the domestication of *Canis lupus*, dated to about 12,000 years ago, some 3,000 to 5,000 years before the domestication of other animals. It would appear then, that as with other early claims for the presence of dog (Degerbøl, 1961; Turnbull and Reed, 1974), the driving forces behind its domestication were its use in hunting and perhaps a general affection for the animal.

GATHERING

As with most foraging groups, plants formed the greatest part of the Natufian diet. But in the Natufian the abundance, predictability, and seasonally staggered maturation of wild cereals and nuts led to their intensive exploitation and storage. The physical evidence of these plant remains is thus far relatively meager. The carbonized remains of wild barley (*Hordeum spontaneum*), acorns (*Quercus* sp.), lentils (*Lens* sp.), chick peas (*Cicer* sp.), and field peas (*Pisum* sp.) have been recovered from the Jordanian site of Wadi Hama 27 (McNicoll, et al., 1985). And, from the Syrian sites of Mureybet and Abu Hureyra, wild einkorn wheat, barley, and vetch have been recovered along with a long list of other possible food and non-food plants (Van Zeist, 1970; Hillman, 1975). Pollen grains attributed to cereals have been identified from the deposits of Hayonim Terrace (Henry, et al., 1981) and Wadi Judayid (Henry, et al., 1985).

Osteological analyses of the skeletal remains of the Natufians indicate not only that their diet contained significant amounts of stone ground carbohydrates, but also that stone ground foods filled a progressively larger part of the diet through time. In examining the dental disease and attrition patterns of skeletal samples from Ein Mallaha, El Wad, and Kebara, Smith (1972:236–237) concluded that the Ein Mallaha and El Wad populations consumed a high proportion of stone ground foods to the extent that they resembled Early Neolithic populations. Although the Kebara population had relatively low dental attrition scores, strontium/calcium studies of the Kebara and El Wad samples point to equivalent high levels of plant food consumption at both sites (Schoeninger, 1981:85–85). Other studies of the strontium/calcium ratios of Natufian skeletal populations also indicate a high level of plant food consumption (Schoeninger, 1982; Sillen, 1981; Smith, et al., 1985). As might be expected, these studies show that plant food consumption increased during the Natufian over that of earlier Late Glacial populations, but also surprisingly, that plants formed an even greater proportion of the diet in the Natufian than in later food-producing populations.

Indirect evidence for an emphasis upon wild cereals and nuts (and probably peas and lentils) rests in (1) the overall distribution of Natufian hamlets, which corresponded with that of these resources; (2) the presence of facilities for the storage of such resources; and (3) a rich inventory of artifacts functionally tied to collecting and processing such resources. Natufian hamlets are restricted to the Mediterranean hill zone of today, or its extent at the time of occupation. This zone represents an environmental mosaic containing stands of wild cereals and nut producing woodlands. Natufian hamlets have not been found outside of this zone. Storage pits (some plaster lined) and stone-walled storage structures have been recorded at many sites along with mortars, grinding slabs, and querns worked into bedrock. Flint blades bearing silica polish and a diverse inventory of groundstone items further underline the ties between the Natufian and plant resources.

Demographic Data

An examination of the evidence for Natufian demography indicates that the population had grown significantly over that of pre-Natufian times and that it continued to grow during the 2,000-2,500 years of the Natufian. However, an understanding of the absolute number of residents in a Natufian hamlet at any one point in time is difficult to achieve. Hamlets range in area from about 350m² to over 7,000m², with those best defined through excavation covering some 1,000–2,000m² (Henry, 1975). Population estimates based upon these site areas (using the equations discussed in Chapter 5) would range from 33 to about 50 persons. Hassan (1981:90–93), estimating about 3 persons per hut, calculates that Nahal Oren would have had about 40 residents whereas Ein Mallaha would have had about 150. Both of these techniques are hindered by our not knowing the sizes of the hamlets at any one time. What is clear, however, is that the Natufian hamlets were some 5–10 times larger than the mobile foraging camps of the preceding Geometric Kebaran groups. In many ways, it would appear that the smallest Natufian hamlets would have been inhabited by groups similar in size to those that would have briefly come together as band-clusters in Geometric Kebaran times.

Population growth in the Natufian was expressed at both community and regional scales. At the community scale, evidence for growth is clearly defined at the site of Ein Mallaha, where a line of dwellings at the base of a slope subsequently expanded into a cluster of structures surrounding the initial hamlet (Valla, 1981). Also, the areas of Late Natufian hamlets (e.g., Nahal Oren, Ein Mallaha, Shukbah, Rosh Zin, and Rosh Horesha) imply a growth in population as they are generally larger than those of the Early Natufian. At the regional scale, population expansion is documented by comparing the distributions of Early and Late Natufian settlements. Early Natufian hamlets are confined to the core Mediterranean zone, whereas Late Natufian occupations are found in the core and along the margins of the Mediterranean zone. The Late Natufian settlements in the Negev and Black Desert of northeastern Jordan point to the colonization of those settings on the very edge of the Mediterranean woodlands.

SETTLEMENT PATTERN

Unlike the mobile, transhumant settlement strategies of the Geometric Kebaran and Mushabian groups, Natufians were obligated to obtain their resources year-round from a single locus. This resulted in Natufian hamlets being established in strategic locations such that resources from different locations could be tapped at minimum distances. Sites then are typically found along boundaries separating wooded uplands (containing cereals and nuts) from grasslands (gazelle habitat) and are situated near springs or major drainages. The hamlets appear to have been linked to smaller, special-purpose, non-residential sites that served to funnel distant resources back to the hamlets (Henry, 1975, 1985). Sites such as Jabrud III/2 (Rust, 1950), Abu Usba (Stekelis and Haas, 1952), Tor Abu Sif (Neuville, 1951), Wadi Safat (Waechter, 1949), and Taibe (Cauvin, 1974b) are likely to represent such special purpose camps. The settlement structure of the Natufian thus resembled a "radiating pattern," as initially described by Mortensen (1972) for early Neolithic communities, in contrast to the "circulating" pattern of the Geometric Kebaran and Mushabian.

Post-Natufian Societies

Within 2,500 years after the emergence of the Natufian society all but five of the 23 major hamlets were abandoned. The collapse of these communities and the dissolution of Natufian society in general can be attributed to population growth in the face of declining resources. The population responded to this dilemma in two ways. The Natufian colonies in the marginal Mediterranean settings were abandoned, with their inhabitants returning to a mobile, simple foraging strategy. Archaeologically, this transition is reflected by the Harifian Industry. In the core Mediterranean woodlands, those communities adjacent to dependable water supplies were able to remain intact, sustaining their sedentary lifeways by supplementing the declining wild cereal stands with cultivated ones. This transition in the Mediterranean woodlands finds archaeological expression in the Pre-Pottery Neolithic and is denoted by the earliest evidence for domesticated cereals.

HARIFIAN INDUSTRY

This is a little known and often ignored industry found in the arid zone of the southern Levant. As discussed in Chapter 4, it shares strong techno-typological similarities with the Natufian to the extent that it is included in the same complex. Beyond the flint artifacts, Natufian and Harifian groundstone items, bone tools, ornamental elements, and architecture resemble one another. Although poorly dated, the Harifian apparently succeeded the Late Natufian in the Negev and adjacent regions beginning some 10,300–10,400 years ago (Table 4.15, Figures 4.24 and 4.25). The geographic setting and timing of this transition is important, for it confirms the collapse and replacement of Natufian communities along the southern margin of the Mediterranean woodlands some 200–300 years before those communities in the core Mediterranean zone broke up (e.g., El Wad) or adopted horticulture (e.g., Nahal Oren, Jericho). This time-lag between the southern arid margins and the core of the Mediterranean woodlands is consistent with the paleoenvironmental evidence that points to progressive climatic deterioration beginning about 11,000 years ago.

Patterns of Economy and Settlement Unlike the Natufian, Harifian sites are distributed in both lowland and upland settings of northern Sinai (Bar-Yosef and Phillips, 1977), the Negev (Marks, 1973, 1975; Marks and Scott, 1976; Scott, 1977, Goring-Morris, 1987), and the southern Judean Hills (Bar-Yosef, et al., 1974). Although the type site of Abu Salem, located on the Harif Plateau of the Highland Negev, and the nearby Site E8 represent seasonal hamlets, the remainder of the Harifian occurrences consist of small ephemeral camps. The varieties of sites and their distributions indicate that Harifian groups had returned to a mobile foraging strategy and had adopted a transhumant settlement pattern.

During the occupation of the lower elevations of northern Sinai and the western Negev, the population would have been dispersed into small, mobile groups, whereas the occupation of the uplands appears to have been linked to long-term encampments. Alternative models of transhumance have been advanced (Bar-Yosef, 1981a; Scott, 1977), but it would seem that the seasonal distribution of resources would have favored occupation of the uplands from early summer through autumn and the lowlands during the winter and spring months. Such a pattern would have enabled Harifian groups to exploit what remained of the wild cereals and nuts of the uplands in the summer and fall before returning to the lowlands for the winter and spring. At this time the lowlands would have been good for hunting as a result of the new grasses generated by winter rains. With the onset of the dry season, the grasses and shrubs would have progressively died off from the lowlands to higher elevations, thus acting to concentrate game in the uplands by late summer.

Direct evidence for subsistence activities is limited to the the uplands, coming from excavations at Abu Salem. Here the remains of large game (gazelle, wild goat, wild sheep, and onager) were found accompanied by the bones of hare, lizard, rock partridge, and tortoise. A single large carbonized *Pistacia* shell along with cereal pollen point to the utilization of plant resources.

Material Culture The Harifian chipped stone technology continues the pattern of the Late Natufian in being based upon the production of rather wide bladelets from single platform cores and in relying upon the microburin technique for their subsequent modification. Typologically, assemblages are characterized by small lunates and triangles (Figure 7.20) in conjunction with the diagnostic Harif points (Marks, 1973). The points appear to have gradually replaced the geometric microliths as arrow tips. Artifacts other than chipped stone and architectural evidence are confined to the upland hamlets of Abu Salem and Site E8 (Marks and Scott, 1976; Scott, 1977).

Excavations at Abu Salem exposed eight oval structures, but as many as three to four times that number are estimated for the whole site (Scott, 1977). The structures, fashioned from limestone rocks, are reminiscent of Natufian hamlets in both size and configuration (Figures 7.21 and 7.22). Three of the structures range from 3–4m in diameter; the remainder are 1–2m in diameter. Two trash pits filled with bones, tools, and rocks were also found in excavation.

Figure 7.20. *Tools from the Harifian Site G8 (after Scott, 1977). Harif points (a–c); lunates (d,e); triangles (f,g); notch (h); truncated blades (i,j); backed blades (k,l,p,q); arch-tipped blade (m); endscrapers (n,o,r).*

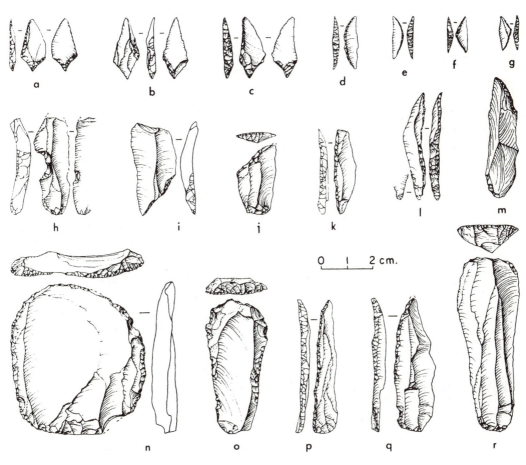

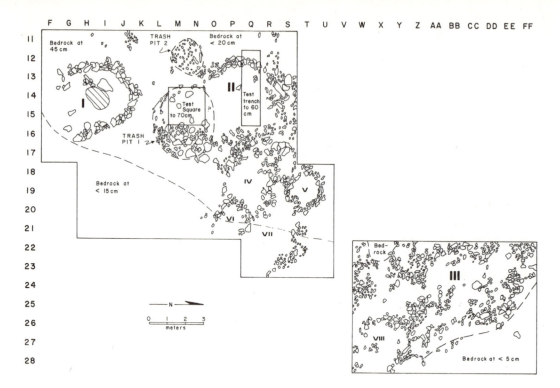

Figure 7.21. *Plan of the architectural features exposed in the excavated areas of the Harifian site of Abu Salem (after Scott, 1977).*

Figure 7.22. *Photograph of Structure I at Abu Salem (after Scott, 1977). The darkened area near the center of the structure is an ill-defined fire area and the large stone slab has twenty cup marks.*

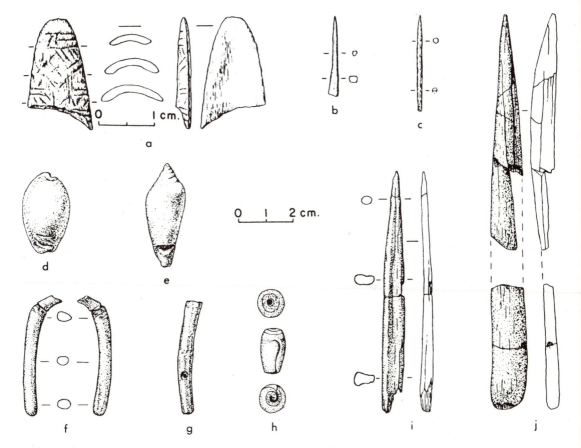

Figure 7.23. *Bone and shell artifacts from the Harifian site of Abu Salem (after Scott, 1977). Bone fragment with incised geometric design (a); bone needles (b,c); perforated shells (d,e); polished shell rod with incised groove (f); Dentalia sp. shell with hole drilled halfway through (g); Conus sp. shell with hole in coiled end (h); bone awl (i); bone punch (j).*

A stone slab found in one of the larger structures contained twenty cup mortars. Several bedrock mortars, identical to those of the Natufian, were discovered at the nearby Site E8. Other groundstone artifacts consist of mortars, grooved stones, mullers, and pestles (including an elaborate bell shaped specimen made of basalt).

Worked bone specimens are limited to needles and awls except for ornamental element with an incised geometric design (Figure 7.23). The design is reminiscent of the "net pattern" engraved on ostrich eggshell at the nearby Late Natufian site of Rosh Zin. Other ornamental items include a wide range of marine shells indigenous to the Mediterranean, the Red Sea, and perhaps even the Indian Ocean (Mienis, 1977). Shells from the Red Sea are the most common. The absence of another shell, *Theodoxus jordani*, is perhaps significant. This shell is indigenous to the Sea of Galilee and common to Natufian sites (including nearby Rosh Horesha). The absence of these shells in Harifian sites may well reflect a break in the social ties and exchange network that had linked Natufian hamlets in the core of the Mediterranean woodlands to those on its margins.

Summary With the progressive deterioration of climate, Natufian communities on the margin of the Mediterranean woodlands were unable to sustain permanent settlements owing to declining resources. Though they continued a foraging pattern and still depended heavily upon the resources of what remained of the woodland habitat at the highest elevations, they were obliged to disperse their population into small mobile groups during part of the year. With a return to mobile foraging, the Harifians appear to have retained many aspects of the Natufian tradition, but at the same time they were unable to maintain ties with the contemporary Natufian communities to the north.

PRE-POTTERY NEOLITHIC

The earliest stage of the aceramic Neolithic in the Levant, traditionally labelled Pre-Pottery Neolithic A (PPNA), is now recognized as containing two distinct industries: the Khiamian and Sultanian (Payne, 1983; Bar-Yosef, 1981b). Although the Khiamian Industry, with its strong techno-typological ties to the Natufian, would appear to be the earlier of the two, the few available radiocarbon dates show considerable overlap for the industries, with the earliest dates falling about 10,300 B.P. (Bar-Yosef, 1981a; Moore, 1985).

Khiamian Industry The industry draws its name from the site of El Khiam (Echegaray, 1966) and is also known from settlements at Nahal Oren (Stekelis and Yizraeli, 1963; Noy, et al., 1973), Salibiya IX (Bar-Yosef, 1980), Hatula (Ronen and Lechevallier, 1985) and Mureybet Ib (M. C. Cauvin, 1974; J. Cauvin, 1976). All of these occupations either overlay or rest near Late Natufian occupations. Bar-Yosef (1981a), however, questions the integrity of Khiamian horizons at El Khiam and Nahal Oren, arguing that the natural mixing in these colluvial deposits may have blended Epipaleolithic and Neolithic layers. Another site, Abu Madi (Bar-Yosef, 1981b), located in southern Sinai, has been attributed to the Khiamian because of the presence of the distinctive point type but may in fact have been more strongly tied to a mobile foraging pattern resembling that of the Harifian Industry.

The lithic artifact assemblages of the Khiamian continue the tradition of the Natufian as reflected by a microlithic technology, lunates, and sickle blades. A distinctive basally-notched point type, the El Khiam point, appears as the guide fossil for the industry. Large, heavy duty implements (e.g., picks, adzes, and planes) also occur, but in low percentages.

Like the flint implements, groundstone artifacts continue the Natufian pattern with mortars, stone bowls, querns, and "cup marks" being found in abundance. Sculpted female figurines from Salibiya IX, Nahal Oren, El Khiam, and Mureybet also share strong similarities with one another and with finds from Natufian and Sultanian occupations (Bar-Yosef, 1981b; Cauvin, 1977).

Khiamian sites vary considerably in size, ranging from about 1,000m² to over 3,000m² in area, but as yet architectural evidence is poorly defined. Subsistence data, confined to faunal remains, point to a continuation of the Natufian pattern with a concentration on gazelle.

Khiamian sites are restricted to relatively low elevations in the core Mediterranean woodlands. All are located near permanent water sources or on major tributaries that are likely to have flowed year-round at the time of occupation. El Khiam is the highest occupation located at 430m above sea level, whereas Salibiya IX is the lowest, situated at 230m below sea level. Of these, El Khiam is the only site not found adjacent to a year-round water supply today, but its location at the confluence of two major tributaries is likely to have provided dependable water during its occupation.

Sultanian Industry The Sultanian is best known from Jericho (PPNA layers), but it is also present at Nahal Oren, stratum II (Stekelis and Yizraeli, 1963; Noy, et al., 1973), Gilgal I (Noy, et al., 1980); Netiv Hagdud (Bar-Yosef, et al., 1980); and perhaps Mureybet II (Cauvin, 1976; Van Loon, 1968).

In contrast to the Khiamian, the Sultanian lithic industry lacks a strong microlithic character, having been based more upon blade production and bifacial flaking (Payne, 1983). The presence of El Khiam points in low percentages at most sites indicates ties with the Khiamian. At Mureybet II, however, these are replaced by a new point type (Helwan Point), which is characterized by a basal tang (Cauvin, 1976; Cauvin, 1974; Bar-Yosef, 1981b). Large heavy-duty implements such as picks, tranchet axes, and adzes also form a substantial part of Sultanian tool-kits along with sickles, other retouched blades, burins, and (at Mureybet) perforators. In general, the lithic assemblages give the impression of increasing specialization. For the first time distant raw material in the form of obsidian coming from Anatolia (Payne, 1983; Bar-Yosef, et al., 1980) was used in making many of the implements, especially those from small blades. Beyond the polished axes of limestone or basalt, which also make their appearance in Sultanian assemblages, other groundstone items (mortars, querns, cup marks) essentially continue the pattern first established in the Natufian.

Although the extraordinary wall, moat, and tower revealed by Kenyon's (1960, 1981) excavation of Jericho tend to overshadow the architectural evidence of other Sultanian occupations, the modest domestic structures are perhaps more informative. They show a regularity in size, form, and layout, but vary widely in construction material. Mud brick, stone slabs, or small stones imbedded in whitish mud were used in the construction of oval (often semisubterranean) structures, with long axes generally 4–6m in length. Internal hearths and plaster floors point to the structures having served for the most part as dwellings. Most occur as single rooms, although examples from Jericho and Mureybet were internally partitioned. Nahal Oren, by far the smallest of the Sultanian sites, provides the best picture of intra-community patterns. Here some 15 semi-subterranean houses were built in rows on four benches of a terraced slope.

In size, Sultanian sites show a marked increment over earlier Khiamian settlements. Except for the small (1,000–2,000m²) hamlet at Nahal Oren, the sites cover 1–3 hectares, with populations estimated as high as 2,000–3,000 persons (Aurenche, 1981). The regional distribution of the sites continues the Khiamian pattern, with settlements established at low elevations, none higher than 300m asl, adjacent to permanent water sources.

Given the size, permanence, and intensity of such settlements outside the natural distribution of cereals, it is not surprising that the first direct evidence for plant cultivation appears at this time. At Jericho, the remains of domesticated emmer wheat (*Triticum dicoccum*) and hulled two-row barley (*Hordeum distichon*) were identified within the Sultanian (PPNA) levels (Hopf, 1969; Renfrew, 1973) dated to about 10,000 years ago, and a single carbonized seed of *T. dicoccum* was reported from the PPNA horizon of Nahal Oren (Noy, et al., 1973). The best sample of charred seeds and grains for this time-frame, however, comes from Mureybet II, where all of the cereal grains (einkorn and barley) and other plant remains are morphologically wild. What is important about the Mureybet II finds is that cereals, although wild, were found outside of their natural habitat located in the uplands some 100–150km northwest of the site (Van Zeist, 1970). As suggested by Hans Helbaek (Mellaart, 1975:46), the paleobotanic evidence from Mureybet II points to the early stages of cultivation when cereals were being maintained in a foreign, man-made habitat but had not yet undergone the morphological changes associated with domesticated cereals. Given the overlapping radiocarbon dates for PPNA Jericho and Mureybet II, the paleobotanic data suggest that incipient cultivation began earlier in the southern Levant than in the northern. This latitudinal "lag-time" in the first steps toward food-production is consistent with the onset of arid conditions earlier in the south than in the north during Late Natufian times. The inhabitants of the southern Levant would have experienced scarcity of resources earlier than those living in the north.

Summary and Conclusions

With the Natufian we see the emergence of a new system of adaptation that differed markedly from the simple foraging system followed by earlier populations. In many ways the germ of this new system can be traced to certain lowland late Geometric Kebaran sites (e.g., Neve David, Hefsibah, and Ein Gev IV).

These appear to have represented a segment of population coalescence and settlement permanence in an annual transhumant cycle. Although the technology for intensive cereal and nut collection was available at this time, it was not until the worldwide temperature elevation of about 13,000 years ago that these resources became economically viable.

With the colonization of the uplands by Mediterranean woodlands, the composition and distribution of cereal and nut resources became economically attractive for concentrated exploitation. Taking advantage of these new resources both allowed and demanded sedentism. With this shift in economy and demography, which apparently took place independently among various Geometric Kebaran groups in the Mediterranean woodlands, a rapid social amalgamation also occurred, as expressed archaeologically in the Natufian. This was accompanied by a higher level of social integration, probably on the order of a chiefdom, and striking changes in social organization.

The most important aspect of this evolution from simple to complex foraging, however, had to do with the loss of natural fertility controls linked to mobility. In sacrificing mobility, the Natufians had crossed the physiological, demographic, social, and even ideological divides that separate foragers and food-producers. Economically they had come to depend upon the development of storable surpluses through the intensified exploitation of resources, but unlike food-producers they were incapable of elevating their resources. They experienced a rapid growth in population, expressed at both community and regional scales, and had expanded to the edges of their habitat when they were confronted with a progressive deterioration of their environment. This imbalance between population and resources is reflected in dietary stress, female infanticide, and declining meat consumption. Endogamy, matriliny, and increased ranking appear to have represented social responses to the scarcity of resources, but these ultimately proved ineffective.

With the continued deterioration of the climate and retreat of the Mediterranean zone, the Late Natufian settlements on the southern and eastern fringes of the woodlands were abandoned. The population that remained along the southern fringes returned to a transhumant, mobile pattern, occupying the highest and best watered areas of the region seasonally as indicated by the upland camps of the Harifian Industry. In the core of the Mediterranean woodland zone, settlement continued after the abandonment of the Natufian hamlets on the margins, but only for 100–200 years. At this point those sites not located on dependable water sources, such as springs or major rivers, also failed. Sites at higher elevations near the headwaters of streams with poor catchments (e.g., Hayonim, Shukbah, Rakefet) were especially vulnerable to the drier conditions, and they were abandoned even though they rest within zones of high annual precipitation today. It was mainly because of these hydrologic factors that those settlements that persisted were at low elevations.

Immediately following the period of abandonment of upland Natufian sites, the population was apparently concentrated into settings in the lowlands that were near dependable water sources. But the sizes of these Khiamian settlements remained essentially unchanged from Natufian times (i.e., from 1,000m² to 3,000m²). Like the Harifian, Khiamian communities were outgrowths of the Natufian, but unlike the Harifian groups the Khiamian apparently maintained a sedentary way of life in certain select, well watered settings.

Although we have little direct economic evidence for the Khiamian, data from the following Sultanian sites point to the first steps of cultivation as having occurred in final Natufian and Khiamian times. The transition from plant collection to cultivation was essentially driven by a separation of cereal and nut resources from dependable water sources. Although occupation of those sites near permanent water continued, the resources of the Mediterranean woodlands would have become increasingly scarce and unpredictable within their catchments. In that these sites were confined to the lowlands, the woodland habitat would have become increasingly remote as it retreated upslope in response to the drier conditions. In short, the settings that had enabled Natufians to exploit a wide range of resources from a single locus year-round were no longer suitable for the exploitation of the two most critical resources—water and cereals.

Cereals, however, are likely to have volunteered themselves to limited areas of rubbish and damp ground in the vicinity of the sites. With some 2,000 years of experience in collecting cereals, the inhabitants of these sites would have undoubtedly recognized the economic advantage of maintaining cereal stands in settings close to the settlements as a means of compensating for the progressive decline of wild stands within their catchments. It should be stressed that this model argues for the gradual replacement of wild plant foods with cultivated forms. And, ironically, like many evolutionary steps, this one was driven by an effort to maintain the *status quo*.

By Sultanian times, probably only 200–300 years after the dissolution of the Natufian, we see the first major shift in demography with the dramatic increase in settlement size. But it is instructive to note that even late in this period, cultivated plants account for only about 6% of the seed and fruit remains (Van Zeist and Bakker-Herres, 1979).

8
Considering a Universal Cause for Agriculture

At this point it may be worth considering what the development of agriculture in the Levant can tell us about the emergence of agriculture in other parts of the world. Most contemporary universal models of agricultural origins hold that prehistoric populations were driven to broadening their diets, reducing their mobility, and ultimately producing their food because of an imbalance between their numbers and their resources. As discussed in Chapter 1, various ideas have been put forward seeking to explain how such imbalances may have come about.

On the population side of the equation, emigration from rich to poor environments (Binford, 1968; Flannery, 1969) and slow growth (P. E. L. Smith, 1972; Smith and Young, 1983; Cohen, 1977) have been suggested as forces that destabilized the balance between the numbers of people and their resources. However, these ideas have not only been challenged theoretically (Bronson, 1977; Hassan, 1981; Rindos, 1984), but they can be shown to be inconsistent with field data. For example, Flannery (1986) has pointed out that the suspected population differences between the rich and poor environments of the Levant, which he once argued for, are not supported by recent data from surveys conducted in the 1970s. Similarly, Binford's (1968) proposal of a Natufian expansion from coastal to inland areas has come to be rejected with a better understanding of the Natufian chronology.

Also, suggestions that populations in various parts of the world ultimately reached levels that demanded a broadening of diet are also inconsistent with recent field evidence. As shown in this study, the population of the Levant was relatively stable prior to the Natufian and diets became increasingly specialized rather than diversified. In synthesizing the demographic and subsistence data collected by MacNeish (1964, 1967) and his associates in the Tehuacan Valley of

Mexico, Reed (1977:891) reaches a similar conclusion in noting that "neither the density nor pressure of population would seem to have been important in the introduction of agriculture. . . . " Likewise, Flannery (1986) has also failed to find any evidence for a rise in population prior to food-production in his study of foraging and early agriculture in Oaxaca. He points out that the populations in highland Mexico were so small when agriculture began that such notions as "overpopulation" and "food crisis" cannot be reasonably entertained (Flannery, 1986).

On the other side of the equation, scholars have suggested that a decline in resources prompted prehistoric populations to broaden their diets and ultimately adopt food-production. One model holds that with the extinction of so many megafauna at the end of the Ice Age, prehistoric populations were obligated to exploit small animals and plants to a much greater extent, and that this finally prompted agriculture (M. Harris, 1977). Taking a slightly different approach, Hayden (1981) argues that periodic responses to resource stress progressively broadened human diets throughout the Pleistocene. And an episode of stress at the end of the Pleistocene is thought to have led to a concentration on r-selected species (e.g., small animals, fish, plants) followed by food-production.

But again in turning to empirical data from the Levant and Mexico, we find that none of the resource stress models can be supported. The massive wave of extinction that affected Pleistocene megafauna worldwide appears to have had little impact on the predation patterns of the prehistoric populations in these regions. As shown in the present study and that of Bar-Yosef (1981a), the faunal remains from Levantine prehistoric deposits indicate that human prey species remained essentially unchanged across the Pleistocene-Holocene boundary. And, from Mexico, Flannery (1986:9) notes that "the late Pleistocene stratigraphic levels from Coxcatlan Cave make it clear that the Indians of that era did not rely solely on large fauna but hunted dozens of small species and even engaged in communal drives of jackrabbits." Finally, when considering climate as a factor governing resource stress, we find that both the Levant and highland Mexico experienced warmer and moister conditions at a time when according to the models resources should have been declining.

Therefore, in the two regions of the world where we have the greatest understanding of the transition from foraging to early agriculture, we find evidence that is inconsistent with the models that have been advanced to account for the rise of food production universally. Furthermore, when the factors that are viewed as contributing to the emergence of agriculture in each of these areas are compared, some clear and fundamental differences are apparent. Sedentism, seen as a critical factor in triggering the development of food-production in the Levant, does not appear in Mexico until some 2,000–3,000 years after the first evidence of agriculture (Reed, 1977). And the broad spectrum economy so well documented for the preagricultural horizons in Mexico was not present in the Levant in a similar context. If universal models can be rejected by regional evidence and this evidence also fails to show parallels in critical areas, is it possible that a universal explanation for the rise of agriculture does not exist? And if not, how do we then explain the rough worldwide synchroneity in agricultural origins?

In many ways, I think we have answers for both of these questions, but we have confused the issue by not distinguishing between those conditions that were *necessary* and those that were *sufficient*, or proximate in following Flannery's (1968:518) discussion of the problem with the "master."

Conditions That Were Necessary

Essentially two conditions were necessary for the development of plant cultivation: the technology for collection, processing, and storage; and the presence of potential domesticates in economically viable settings. Emphasizing the first condition can lead to circular reasoning, unless it can be shown that the technology was in place *before* it was applied to the intensive exploitation of plants, specifically the milling of cereals and pulses.

EMERGENCE OF A MILLING TECHNOLOGY

The most abundant evidence for a milling technology comes in the form of specialized grinding stones from Middle and Upper Paleolithic deposits in southern Africa, Europe, and Russia (Kraybill, 1977: 512–513). These implements, dating to between 33,000 and 49,000 B.P., include both the upper and lower parts of a grinding tool complex. They were used for the processing of pigment (as indicated by the presence of ochre stains on many specimens), and perhaps of seeds, given their distribution in steppe and grassland regions (Kraybill, 1977:513). Earlier evidence, perhaps linked to the pounding of roots and nuts, is dated to the Middle and even Early Pleistocene deposits of the Near East and Africa, but the milling activities associated with hard hulled grass seeds are not indicated.

Therefore, the technology necessary for the processing of the earliest domesticates was in existence some 25,000–30,000 years before we see the first evidence for its intensive use in the milling of wild cereals along the Nile and in the lowlands of the Levant. This timing answers one question but raises another. Technological limitations would have restricted the intensive exploitation of wild cereals and pulses to the temporal sweep of the last 50,000 years, but why was this activity delayed on a broad scale until only some 13,000 years ago? To answer this question we have to move to the second necessary condition.

EXPANSION OF THERMOPHILOUS PLANTS

The second condition is tied to a refinement of Wright's (1977) observation that the wild cereals and other potential domesticates of the Near East are warmth loving, thermophilous plants and that they would have been confined to refuges at low elevations during most of the the Pleistocene. It was only with the warmer conditions at the end of the Ice Age that these plants would have colonized higher elevations and thus achieved their modern distributions. The same argument can be made for both maize and rice, the world's other major cereals.

The expansion out of Pleistocene refugia would have increased the economical importance of these plants far beyond that derived from their merely being distributed over a larger area. Perhaps the single most important factor in the shift in distribution of these warmth-loving grasses came from their colonization of higher elevations. With their enlarged elevational amplitude, the maturation of their seeds would have been stretched over a longer period of time, thus increasing their attractiveness as a dependable, predictable food source. The upslope expansion of such plants would also have acted both to increase the number and reduce the width of food niches. Thus, on a worldwide scale, mountainous areas would have experienced a restructuring of their environments and associated resource belts at the end of the Ice Age. A greater number of closely packed, elevationally zoned environments would have emerged that contained important food sources linked to thermophilous plants.

POSSIBLE GENETIC AND PHYSIOLOGICAL CHANGES

Another argument has been advanced that would further account for a change in the economic importance of cereals (and perhaps legumes) at the end of the Pleistocene. This relates to the genetic and morphological changes that may have occurred in such plants with their expansion from Ice Age refugia. Wright (1977), in noting that cereal grasses are genetically malleable and sensitive to selective pressures, speculates that the robust heads and dense stands that we attribute to wild cereals of today may be a post-Pleistocene phenomenon.

Whyte (1977:209), along similar lines, suggests that "annual grasses and legumes did not appear as significant components of the vegetation of Asia until the Neothermal, some 11,000 B.P." And, of course, it is the large seed heads of the annuals that make these plants attractive as a human food source. Whyte's proposal is based upon the observation that the much warmer and generally drier conditions of the Holocene would have selected for annual over perennial species. He points out that similar differences in modern environments can be linked to "contrastive effects on plant physiology and genetical taxonomy: those that favor the perpetuation of perennial species of gramineae in particular, and those that promote either a change from a perennial to an annual habit, or a situation in which a few existing annuals may become co-dominant or dominant in mixed communities" (Whyte, 1977:214). He goes on to note that annuals are absent or rare on the great steppes and grasslands of the world but become more common in the hot, arid settings of North America, Africa, and Asia. And in such settings studies have traced the ancestry of annual species to perennials living nearby. Whereas Whyte's theory is somewhat off with regard to its specific chronology (given the direct and indirect evidence for intensive plant collection in Early Natufian deposits dating from 12,500 B.P.), it could provide another reason as to why the exploitation of cereals became so important after about 13,000 years ago.

EVIDENCE FROM THE NEAR EAST

Beyond the Levant there is a considerable body of data to support the idea that a global rise in temperature induced the expansion of economically important plants and in turn promoted complex foraging. An important factor in support of this model rests in the timing of adaptive changes for the different populations in the region. These transitions were not synchronous throughout the region; instead, the succession from simple foraging to complex foraging to plant cultivation followed a temporally staggered cline from southwest to northeast. Prior to some 13,000 years ago, both direct and indirect evidence associated with cereal collection, processing, and storage is restricted to low elevations along the coast and within the Rift Valley of the Levant, but it was some 2,000 years later that a similar adaptive pattern appeared in the Zagros mountain region. And a similar lag-time apparently existed between these two regions of the Near East at the onset of plant cultivation (Hole, 1984; Moore, 1986).

The later emergence of complex foraging in the Zagros can be explained by the region's more northerly latitudinal position (35–36°N as opposed to 30–33°N for the Levant) and its more inland setting, both of which would have acted to slow the effects of global warming and to retard the expansion of thermophilous plants into the piedmont zone of the Zagros mountains. One might recall how palynological evidence points to a similar lag-time in forest expansion between the two regions, appearing about 12,500 years ago in the extreme southwest and about 2,000 years later in the northeast (Wright, 1984:508; Chapter 3).

Beginning about 10,800 years ago, we see the first evidence for a shift toward complex foraging in the Zagros region. Although the sites included in the Proto-Neolithic show remarkable general parallels with the Natufian, a detailed comparison of material culture inventories indicates an independent, indigenous development.

At the sites of Zawi Chemi Shanidar (R. L. Solecki, 1964, 1969, 1981) and Shanidar Cave, Layer B1 (R. S. Solecki, 1964), a large and diverse inventory of cereal harvesting and processing tools were found in association with rudimentary architecture. Similar finds have been made at Karim Shahir, Tell M'lefaat, Asiab and Gird Chai in Iraqi Kurdistan (Braidwood and Howe, 1960; Howe,

1983; Hole, 1984). Radiocarbon dates from the occupations at Shanidar Cave and Zawi Chemi Shanidar are radiometrically synchronous at about 10,800 B.P. And another date on charcoal from Asiab would place the early part of that occupation to about 10,000 B.P. (Howe, 1984:116).

At the Shanidar Cave and village sites, groundstone items consisting of mortars, querns, handstones, and grooved stones are accompanied by sickle blades and hafts. Both sites also contained cemeteries, with grave goods reminiscent of the Natufian. Burials yielded a grinding quern and a bone sickle haft that displayed a microlith still fixed in place with bitumen. Beyond these items, similarities with the Natufians include the practice of inbreeding or local endogamy (Ferembach, 1970) and a generally poor level of health (R. S. Solecki, personal communication, 1987).

Whereas storage pits were exposed in both of the Shanidar sites, formal architecture consisted only of a line of stones forming an arc at Shanidar Cave and a single-course, circular stone wall enclosing a small (2m diameter) structure at Zawi Chemi. Also at Tell M'lefaat, an ovoid (3.6 by 2.7m) pithouse with stone floor was discovered. The ephemeral nature of the Proto-Neolithic architecture coupled with the elevational differences of the Zawi Chemi (425m asl) and Shanidar Cave (822m asl) sites have prompted suggestions of transhumance (R. S. Solecki, 1964; R. L. Solecki, 1981; Hole, in press). This may have entailed wintering in caves such as Shanidar and summering in the open, a pattern followed by contemporary Kurdish herders who inhabit the area (R. S. Solecki, 1964). Although sedentism may not have approached the same level as that enjoyed by the Natufians, settlement permanence appears to have increased markedly during the Proto-Neolithic over that of earlier Zarzian groups (Howe, 1984). This is denoted not only by the appearance of rudimentary architecture but also by the dramatic growth in the size of the Proto-Neolithic sites (R. L. Solecki, 1981).

EVIDENCE ON A WORLDWIDE SCALE

Although there is evidence for the limited exploitation of wild cereals in low, warm settings (i.e., the Nile and Rift valleys) during the Late Pleistocene, the earliest evidence for their intensive use comes from intermontane and piedmont settings after about 13,000 years ago. Wild wheat, barley, rice, and maize first come to be intensively exploited in upland settings during a 4,000-year interval on a worldwide scale. This occurred in the Levantine uplands about 12,500 years ago, along the Zagros flanks about 10,800 years ago, in the piedmont zone of southeast Asia between 9,000 and 13,000 years ago (Gorman, 1977:342), and in intermontane settings in Mexico between 7,000 and 9,000 years ago (Reed, 1977; Flannery, 1986:7–8). These global data, then, are consistent with the argument that the second necessary condition for wild cereals to have been intensively exploited was their distribution in upland settings and that such a distribution was most recently triggered by the rise in temperature that ended the Ice Age.

But what of earlier intervals of high worldwide temperature such as occurred during the Last Interglacial some 90,000–130,000 years ago? Why did these not stimulate episodes of intensive exploitation of wild cereal grasses? According to the model presented here, the plant processing technology of large hammerstones and spheroids available at that time was just not adequate for efficiently milling the seeds of wild cereal grasses, even if they had been present. The first necessary condition, a cultural one, then made the second condition, a climatic one, significant.

According to the recent theory of Rindos (1984), the intensive exploitation of wild cereals (his "specialized domestication") developed as a result of the coevolution of these plants and their human predators after millions of years of "incidental domestication." He traces a number of important interrelated factors that may have contributed to certain plants becoming "relatively more fit" and ultimately evolving into "what we today call the domesticated plant." But Rindos does little to answer the riddle of why, after so long a time of casually exploiting plants, humans became intensive collectors and food-producers within a roughly synchronous and relatively brief temporal sweep. It is argued here that the near synchronous development of intensive plant exploitation on a worldwide scale and the temporal correlation of this event with a worldwide rise in temperature are strong reasons to suspect that climatic-environmental factors governed this transition. This argument only offers an explanation of why prehistoric foragers came to intensively exploit plant foods; it does not attempt to address the question of the origin of food-production. For that, we need to examine the conditions that were sufficient to promote agriculture.

Conditions That Were Sufficient

With the conditions necessary for the development of intensive plant exploitation satisfied, what factors are likely to have accounted for the origin of agriculture? The answer to this question is complex, multivariate, and, I think, ecologically specific to different regions around the world. The road to agriculture described in this study of the Levant certainly traces each of these facets of the problem. And when examined against other regional studies, especially those of highland Mexico, it points to the sufficient conditions as having been regionally specific. Therefore, it seems unlikely that universal causes will be found at this level.

The multivariate models that have been advanced by Hassan (1977, 1981), Reed (1977), Redman (1978), D. R. Harris (1977), Flannery (1969, 1986), and others probably contain most of the answers to why populations in various parts of the world adopted agriculture. But although each of these models may be close to providing the answer for a specific region of the world, none of them furnishes an explanation for all regions. This is simply because there was no single factor or set of factors that prompted the emergence of food-production worldwide (Shnirelman, 1982, 1985). The regionally specific nature of the shift from foraging to food-production may well account for the differences in lag-time between the stage of intensive plant collection and incipient agriculture in various parts of the world.

An examination of several pivotal notions and associated evidence related to incipient agriculture in various regions of the world reveals few parallels. In the Levant, agriculture grew out of an intensive specialized exploitation of plants and animals, whereas broad spectrum economies are recorded at this stage in southeast Asia and Mexico. While we find evidence for sedentism followed by rapid population growth and plant domestication in the Levant, settlement mobility and general population stability are indicated for highland Mexico. And where there are indications of resource stress induced by expanding desert in the Levant (this volume), and rising sea level in southeast Asia (Gorman, 1977:349), there were apparently no long-term shifts in resource densities that can be correlated with the shift to food-production in highland Mexico (Flannery, 1968:10). The absence of parallels in the pathways toward agriculture among various regions of the world should, I think, be expected given the complex ecological relationships that governed the transition from forager to food-producer. Once the necessary conditions had been satisfied, food-production was probably inevitable. But the pace of this development would have been regionally specific and driven by different forces such as resource shortages, population growth, risk reduction, and the coevolution of man and plants.

Given what may seem to be an overly ecologically oriented or even environmentally deterministic approach to the problem, I think it is worthwhile to note that had it not been for some Neanderthal driven to grinding pigment for ritual purposes, it is unlikely that most of the world would be sustained by agriculture today.

REFERENCES CITED

Alon, G.
   1976   Pollen Analysis of the Faza'el Sites, Southern Jordan Valley. Unpublished
           M.A. thesis, Department of Archaeology, Hebrew University, Jerusalem.

Anderson-Gerfaud, P.
   1983   A consideration of the uses of certain backed and "lustred" stone tools
           from late Mesolithic and Natufian levels of Abu Hureyra and Mureybet
           (Syria). In *Traces d'utilisation sur les outils Néolithiques du Proche Orient*, ed-
           ited by M.-C. Cauvin. Lyon: Maison de l'Orient. Pp. 77−106.

Aurenche, O.
   1981   Essai de demographie archéologique. L' exemple des villages du Proche-
           orient ancien. *Paléorient* 7(1):93−106.

Barnard, A.
   1979   Kalahari Bushman settlement patterns. In *Social and Ecological Systems*,
           edited by R. Burnham and R. F. Ellen. New York: Academic Press.
           Pp. 131−144.

Bar-Yosef, O.
   1970   The Epipaleolithic Cultures of Palestine. Unpublished Ph.D. thesis, Depart-
           ment of Archaeology, Hebrew University, Jerusalem.

   1974   Kebaran and Natufian sites in Wadi Fazael, Jordan Valley, Israel. *Paléorient*
           2:415−428.

   1975   The Epi-Paleolithic in Palestine and Sinai. In *Problems in Prehistory: North
           Africa and the Levant*, edited by F. Wendorf and A. E. Marks. Dallas, Tex.:
           Southern Methodist University Press. Pp. 313−371.

   1977   Section A, Mushabi IV. In *Prehistoric Investigations in Gebel Maghara, North-
           ern Sinai*, edited by O. Bar-Yosef and J. L. Phillips. Qedem 7, Jerusalem:
           Monographs of the Institute of Archaeology, Hebrew University. Pp.
           184−193.

   1980   Prehistory of the Levant. *Annual Review of Anthropology* 9:101−133.

   1981a   The Epi-Paleolithic complexes in the southern Levant. In *Préhistoire du
           Levant*, edited by J. Cauvin and P. Sanlaville. Paris: Editions du CNRS.
           Pp. 389−408.

   1981b   The Pre-Pottery Neolithic period in the southern Levant. In *Préhistoire du
           Levant*, edited by J. Cauvin and P. Sanlaville. Paris: Editions du CNRS. Pp.
           551−570.

1982   The Natufian of the Southern Levant. In *The Hilly Flanks and Beyond*, edited by T. C. Young, P. E. L. Smith, and P. Mortensen. Chicago: University of Chicago Press. Pp. 11–42.

Bar-Yosef, O., P. Goldberg, and T. Leveson
    1974   Kebaran and Natufian sites in Wadi Fazael, Jordan Valley, Israel. *Paléorient* 2:415–428.

Bar-Yosef, O., A. Gopher, and N. Goring-Morris
    1980   Netiv Hagdud: a "Sultanian" mound in the lower Jordan valley. *Paléorient* 6:201–206.

Bar-Yosef, O., and N. Goren
    1973   Natufian remains in Hayonim Cave. *Paléorient* 1:49–68.

Bar-Yosef, O., and N. Goring-Morris
    1977   Geometric Kebaran A occurrences. In *Prehistoric Investigations in Gebel Maghara, Northern Sinai*, edited by O. Bar-Yosef and J. L. Phillips. Qedem 7, Jerusalem: Monographs of the Institute of Archaeology, Hebrew University. Pp. 115–148.

Bar-Yosef, O., and J. L. Phillips
    1977   *Prehistoric Investigations in Gebel Maghara, Northern Sinai*. Qedem 7, Jerusalem: Monographs of the Institute of Archaeology, Hebrew University.

Bar-Yosef, O., and E. Tchernov
    1966   Archaeological finds and fossil faunas of the Natufian and microlithic industries at Hayonim cave, Western Galilee, (Israel). *Israel Journal of Zoology* 15:104–140.

    1970   The Natufian bone industry from Hayonim Cave. *Israel Exploration Journal* 20:141–150.

Bar-Yosef, O., and F. Valla
    1979   L'Evolution du Natoufien. Nouvelles perspectives. *Paléorient* 5:145–152.

Bate, D.M.A.
    1932   A note on the fauna of Athlit Caves. *Royal Anthropological Institute of Great Britain and Ireland* 2:277–279.

Bender, F.
    1968   *Geologie von Jordanien*. Berlin: Gebruder Borntraeger.

Bentley, G. R.
    1985   Hunter-Gatherer energetics and fertility: a reassessment of the !Kung San. *Human Ecology* 13(1):79–104.

Betts, A.
    1982   A Natufian site in the Black Desert, eastern Jordan. *Paléorient* 812:79–82.
    1985   Black Desert Survey, Jordan: third preliminary report. *Levant* 17:29–52.

Billewicz, W. H.
    1979   The timing of post-partum menstruation and breast-feeding: a simple formula. *Journal of Biosocial Science* 11:141–151.

Binford, L. R.
    1968   Post-Pleistocene adaptations. In *New Perspectives in Archaeology*, edited by S. R. Binford and L. R. Binford. Chicago: Aldine. Pp.313–341.
    1971   Mortuary practices: their study and their potential. In *Approaches to the Social Dimensions of Mortuary Practices*, edited by James A. Brown. Memoirs of the Society for American Archaeology No. 25. Pp.6–29.
    1980   Willow smoke and dogs' tails: hunter-gatherer settlement systems and archaeological site formation. *American Antiquity* 45(1):4–20.

Bintliff, J. L.
    1982   Paleoclimatic modeling of environmental changes in the east Mediterra-

nean region since the last glaciation. In *Paleoclimates, Paleoenvironment and Human Communities in the Eastern Mediterranean Region in Later Prehistory*, edited by J. L. Bintliff and W. Van Zeist. Oxford: British Archaeological Reports. Pp. 485–527

Birdsell, J. B.
    1968   Some predictions for the Pleistocene based on equilibrium systems among recent hunter-gathers. In *Man the Hunter*, edited by R. B. Lee and I. Devore. Chicago: Aldine. Pp. 229–240.

Bordes, F.
    1957   La signification du microburin dans le Paléolithique supérieur. *L'Anthropologie* 61:578–582.

Boserup, E.
    1965   *The Conditions of Agricultural Growth*. London: George Allen and Unwin.

Bostanci, E.Y.
    1962   A new Upper Paleolithic and Mesolithic facies at Belbasi Rock Shelter on the Mediterranean coast of Anatolia. *Tagung der Deutschen Gesellschaft für Anthropologie* 8:253–262.

Bottema, S., and W. Van Zeist
    1981   Palynological evidence for the climatic history of the Near East, 50,000–6,000 B. P. In *Préhistoire du Levant*, edited by J. Cauvin and P. Sanlaville. Paris: Editions du CNRS. Pp. 111–132.

Brahimi, C.
    1970   *L'Ibéromaurusien littoral de la région d'Alger*. Mémoires du Centre de Recherches Anthropologiques, Préhistoriques, et Ethnographiques, Tôme XIII, Alger. Paris: Arts et Métiers Graphiques.

Braidwood, L.
    1952   Early food producers: excavations in Iraqi Kurdistan. *Archaeology* 5:157–164.

Braidwood, R.
    1951a   *Prehistoric Men*, 2nd edition. Chicago: Chicago Natural History Museum.
    1951b   From cave to village in prehistoric Iraq. *American Schools of Oriental Research* 124:12–18.
    1960a   The agricultural revolution. *Scientific American* 203:130–148.
    1960b   Levels in prehistory: a model for the consideration of the evidence. In *Evolution After Darwin*. The University of Chicago Centennial. Volume II, The Evolution of Man. Chicago: University of Chicago Press. Pp. 143–151.

Braidwood, R., and L. Braidwood
    1950   Jarmo: a village of early farmers in Iraq. *Antiquity* 24:189–195.

Braidwood, R., and B. Howe
    1960   Prehistoric investigation in Iraqi Kurdistan. In *Studies in Ancient Oriental Civilization* (Vol. 31). Chicago: University of Chicago Press.

Brooks, C. E. P.
    1926   *The Evolution of Climate*, 2nd edition. London: Benn.

Bronson, B.
    1977   The earliest farming: demography as cause and consequence. In *Origins of Agriculture*, edited by C. A. Reed. The Hague: Mouton. Pp. 23–48.

Butler, B. H., E. Tchernov, H. Hietala, and S. Davis
    1977   Faunal exploitation during the Late Epipaleolithic in the Har Harif. In *Prehistory and Paleoenvironments in the Central Negev, Israel* (Vol. 2), edited by A. E. Marks. Dallas, Tex.: Southern Methodist University Press. Pp. 327–346.

Butzer, K. W.

1975   Patterns of environmental change in the Near East during late Pleistocene and early Holocene times. In *Problems in Prehistory: North Africa and the Levant*, edited by F. Wendorf and A. E. Marks. Dallas, Tex.: Southern Methodist University Press. Pp. 389–410.

1978   The late prehistoric environmental history of the Near East. In *The Environmental History of the Near and Middle East Since the Last Ice Age*, edited by William C. Brice. New York: Academic Press. Pp 5–12.

1982   *Archaeology as Human Ecology*. Cambridge: Cambridge University Press.

Butzer, K. W., and C. L. Hanson

1968   *Desert and River in Nubia: Geomorphology and Prehistoric Environments at the Aswan Reservoir*. Madison: University of Wisconsin Press.

Byrd, B.

1984   Personal communication.

1987   Beidha and the Natufian: Variability in Levantine Settlement and Subsistence. Unpublished Ph.D. thesis, University of Arizona, Tucson.

Byrd, B., and G. Rollefson

1984   Natufian occupation in the Wadi El Hasa Southern Jordan. *Annual of the Department of Antiquities* 28:143–150.

Camps, G.

1975   The prehistoric cultures of North Africa: radio-carbon chronology. In *Problems in Prehistory: North Africa and the Levant*, edited by F. Wendorf and A. E. Marks. Dallas, Tex.: Southern Methodist University Press. Pp. 181–192.

Carr-Saunders, A. M.

1922   *The Population Problem*. London: Oxford University Press.

Casteel, R.

1979   Relationships between surface area and population size: a cautionary note. *American Antiquity* 44:803–807.

Cauvin, J.

1977   Les nouvelles fouilles de Mureybet (1971–1974) et leur signification pour les origines de la sédentarisation au Proche-orient. *Annual of the American School of Oriental Research* 44:19–48.

1978   *Les Premiers villages de Syrie-Palestine du IX ème au VII ème millénaire avant J.C.* Lyon: Maison de l'Orient.

Cauvin, M.-C.

1974a   Outillage lithique et chronolgie à Tell àswad (Damascene, Syrie). *Paléorient* 2:429–436.

1974b   L'Industrie natoufienne de Taibe dans le Horn (Syrie). *Bulletin de la Société Préhistorique Française* 71:469–478.

1981   L'Epipaléolithique du Levant. In *Préhistoire du Levant*, edited by J. Cauvin and P. Sanlaville. Paris: Editions du CNRS. Pp. 439–444.

Chapman, R.

1981   The emergence of formal disposal areas and the "problem" of megalithic tombs in prehistoric Europe. In *The Archaeology of Death*, edited by R. Chapman, I. Kinnes, and K. Randsborg. Cambridge: Cambridge University Press. Pp.71–82.

Childe, V. G.

1928   *The Most Ancient East*. London: Routledge and Kegan Paul.

1934   *New Light on the Most Ancient East*. London: Kegan Paul, Trench, Trubner.

1939   *Man Makes Himself*. New York: Oxford University Press.

1952   *New Light on the Ancient Near East*, 4th edition. London: Routledge and Kegan Paul.

Clarke, D. L.
1968   *Analytical Archaeology*. London: Methuen & Co. Ltd.
1979   *Analytical Archaeology: Collected Papers of David L. Clarke*, edited by his colleagues. London: Academic Press.

Close, A. E.
1978   The identification of style in lithic artefacts. *World Archaeology* 10: 223–237.

Cohen, M.
1975   Archaeological evidence for population pressure in pre-agricultural societies. *American Antiquity* 40:471–475.
1977   *The Food Crisis in Prehistory*. New Haven, Conn.: Yale University Press.

Conkey, M. W.
1978   Style and information in cultural evolution: toward a predictive model for the Paleolithic. In *Social Anthropology*, edited by C. L. Redman, M. J. Berman, E. V. Curtin, W. T. Langhorne, Jr., N. M. Versaggi, and J. C. Wanser. New York: Academic Press. Pp. 61–85.
1980   The identification of prehistoric hunter-gatherer aggregation sites: the case of Altamira. *Current Anthropology* 21:609–630.

Coon, C.
1957   *Seven Caves: Archaeological Exploration in the Middle East*. New York: Knopf.

Crognier, E., and M. Dupouy-Madre
1974   Les Natufiens du Nahal Oren, Israel, étude anthropologique. *Paléorient* 2:103–121.

Davis, S.
1974   Animal remains from the Kebaran site of En Gev I, Jordan Valley, Israel. *Paléorient* 2(2):453–462.
1981   The effects of temperature change and domestication on the body size of Late Pleistocene to Holocene mammals of Israel. *Paleobiology* 7:101–114.

Davis, S., and F. R. Valla
1978   Evidence for domestication of the dog 12,000 years ago in the Natufian of Israel. *Nature* 276:608–610.

De La Campa, E. M.
1966   Fauna malacologica, In *Excavaciones en la Terraza de "El Khiam" (Jordania)* (Vol.2), edited by J. G. Echegaray. Madrid: Instituto Español de Prehistoria. Pp. 165–182.

Degerbol, M.
1961   *Proceedings of the Prehistoric Society* 3:35–55.

de Morgan, J.
1926   *La Préhistoire Orientale*. Vol. II. Paris: P. Geuthner.

Divale, W. T.
1974   Migration, external warfare and matrilocal residence. *Behavioral Science Research* 2:77–133.

Divale, W. T., and M. Harris
1976   Population, warfare, and the male supremacist complex. *American Anthropologist* 78:521–538.

Drucker, P.
1965   *Cultures of the North Pacific Coast*. San Francisco: Chandler.

Dunnell, R. C.
1971   *Systematics in Prehistory*. New York: The Free Press.

Echegaray, J. G., ed.
1964   *Excavaciones en la Terraza de "El-Khiam" (Jordania)* (Vol.1). Madrid: Insti-
        tuto Español de Prehistoria.
1966   *Excavaciones en la Terraza de "El-Khiam" (Jordania)* (Vol.II). Madrid: Insti-
        tuto Español de Prehistoria.

El-Moslimany, A. P.
1986   Ecology and Late Quaternary history of the Kurdo-Zagrosian oak forest
        near Lake Zeribar, western Iran. *Vegatatio* 68:55–63.

Ember, M., and C. R. Ember
1971   The conditions favoring matrilocal versus patrilocal residence. *American An-
        thropologist* 73(3):571–594.

Emiliani, C.
1972   Quaternary paleotemperatures and the duration of high-temperature inter-
        vals. *Science* 178:398–401.

Emiliani, C. and N. Shackleton
1974   The Brunhes Epoch: isotopic paleotemperatures and geochronology. *Sci-
        ence* 183:511–514.

Erinç, S.
1978   Changes in the physical environment in Turkey since the end of the Last
        Glacial. In *The Environmental History of the Near and Middle East Since the
        Last Ice Age*, edited by William C. Brice. New York: Academic Press. Pp.
        87–110.

Ewing, J. F.
1949   The treasures of Ksar Akil. *Thought* 24:255–288.

Farrand, W. R.
1979   Chronology and paleoenvironment of Levantine prehistoric sites as seen
        from sediment studies. *Journal of Archaeological Science* 6:369–392.

Fenenga, F.
1953   The weights of chipped stone projectile points: a clue to their functions.
        Southwestern Journal of Anthropology 9:309–323.

Ferembach, D.
1970   Etude anthropologique des ossements humains Proto-Néolithiques de Zawi
        Chemi Shanidar. *Sumer* 26:21–64.
1977   Les Natoufiens de Palestine. In *Eretz-Israel* (vol.13), edited by B. Arensburg
        and O. Bar-Yosef. Jerusalem: Hebrew University. Pp.240–251.

Flannery, K. V.
1968   The Olmec and the Valley of Oaxaca: a model for interregional interaction
        in formative times. In *Dumbarton Oaks Conference on the Olmec*, edited by
        E.P. Benson. Washington, D.C.: Dumbarton Oaks Research Library and
        Collection. Pp. 79–118.
1969   Origins and ecological effects of early domestication in Iran and the Near
        East. In *The Domestication and Exploitation of Plants and Animals*, edited by P.
        J. Ucko and G. W. Dimbleby. London: Duckworth. Pp. 73–100.
1972   The origins of the village as a settlement type in Meso-America and the
        Near East: A comparative study. In *Man, Settlement and Urbanism*, edited
        by P. J. Ucko, R. Tringham, and G. W. Dimbleby. London: Duckworth. Pp.
        23–53
1973   The origins of agriculture. *Annual Review of Anthropology* 2:271–310.
1986   The research problem. In *Guila Naquitz, Archaic Foraging and Early Agricul-
        ture in Oaxaca, Mexico*. Orlando, Fl.: Academic Press. Pp. 7–10.

Flint, R. F.
  1971   *Glacial and Quaternary Geology.* New York: Wiley.
Frisch, R. E.
  1974   Critical weight at menarche: initiation of the adolescent growth spurt and
           control of puberty. In *Control of Onset of Puberty*, edited by M. M. Grumbach,
           G. D. Grove, and F. E. Meyer. New York: Wiley. Pp. 403–423.
  1975   Demographic implications of the biological determinants of female fecund-
           ity. *Social Biology* 22:17–22.
Frisch, R. E. and R. Revelle
  1970   Height and weight at menarche and a hypothesis of critical body weights
           and adolescent events. *Science* 169:397–399.
Fujimoto, T.
  1979   The Epi-Paleolithic assemblages of Douara Cave. In *Paleolithic Site of Douara
           Cave and Paleogeography of the Palmyra Basin in Syria*, edited by K. Hanihara
           and T. Akazawa. Tokyo: University of Tokyo Press. Pp. 47–75.
Garrard, A. N., B. Byrd, and A. Betts
  1986   Prehistoric environment and settlement in the Azraq Basin: an interim re-
           port on the 1984 excavation season. *Levant* 18:5–24.
Garrod, D. A .E.
  1932   A new Mesolithic industry: the Natufian of Palestine. *Journal of the Royal
           Anthropological Society* 62:257–269.
  1942   Excavations at the Cave of Shukbah, Palestine, 1928. *Proceedings of the Pre-
           historic Society* 8:1–20.
  1954   Excavations at the Mughraret El-Kebara, Mount Carmel, 1931: the Aurig-
           nacian industries. *Proceedings of the Prehistoric Society* 43:155–192.
  1958   The Natufian culture: the life and economy of a Mesolithic people in the
           Near East. *Proceedings of the British Academy* 43:211–227.
Garrod, D. A. E., and D. M. A. Bate
  1937   *The Stone Age of Mount Carmel* (Vol. 1). Oxford: Clarendon Press.
Gobert, E. G.
  1962   La préhistoire dans la zone littorale de la Tunisie. *Quaternaria* 6:271–308.
Goldberg, P.
  1976   Pleistocene geology of the Avdat/Aqev area. In *Prehistory and Paleoenviron-
           ments in the Central Negev, Israel* (Vol.1), edited by A. E. Marks. Dallas, Tex.:
           Southern Methodist University Press. Pp 25–55.
  1977   Late quaternary stratigraphy of Gebel Maghara. In *Prehistoric Investigations
           in Gebel Maghara, Northern Sinai*, edited by O. Bar-Yosef and J. L. Philips.
           Qedem 7, Jerusalem. Monographs of the Institute of Archaeology, Hebrew
           University. Pp 11–31.
  1981   Late Quaternary stratigraphy of Israel: an eclectic view. In *Préhistoire du
           Levant*, edited by J. Cauvin and P. Sanlaville. Paris: Editions du CNRS. Pp.
           55–66.
Goldstein, L.
  1981   One-dimensional archaeology and multi-dimensional people: spatial or-
           ganization and mortuary analysis. In *The Archaeology of Death*, edited by R.
           Chapman, I. Kinnes, and K. Randsborg. Cambridge: Cambridge University
           Press. Pp. 71–82.
Good, R.
  1947   *The Geography of Flowering Plants.* London: Longmans, Green and Co.
Goodman, D. L. Martin, G. J. Armelogos, and G. Clark
  1984   Indications of stress from bone and teeth. In *Paleopathology at the Origins of*

Agriculture, edited by M. N. Cohen and G. J. Armelogos. New York: Academic Press. Pp. 13–49.

Goody, J.
1970 Causal inferences concerning inheritance and property. *Human Relations* 24:295–314.
1976 *Production and Reproduction*. Cambridge: Cambridge University Press.

Goring-Morris, N.
1978 Ma'aleh Ziq, a Geometric Kebaran A site in the Central Negev, Israel. *Paléorient* 4:267–272.
1980 Upper Paleolithic and Kebaran Sites in Wadi Fazael, Jordan Valley. Unpublished M.A. thesis, Institute of Archaeology, Hebrew University.
1987 *At the Edge: Terminal Pleistocene Hunter-Gatherers in the Negev and Sinai*. Oxford: British Archaeological Reports.

Gorman, C.
1977 *A Priori* models and Thai prehistory: a reconsideration of the beginnings of agriculture in Southeastern Asia. In *Origins of Agriculture*, edited by C. A. Reed. The Hague: Mouton. Pp. 321–356.

Gould, R.
1982 To have and have not: the ecology of sharing among hunter-gatherers. In *Resource Managers: North American and Australian Hunter-Gatherers*, edited by N. M. Williams and E. S. Hienn, AAAS Selected Symposium No.67. Boulder, Co.: Westview, Pp. 69–92.

Hall, S. A.
1980 Paleoenvironmental synthesis of Hominy Creek Valley: pollen and land snail evidence. In *The Prehistory and Paleoenvironment of Hominy Creek Valley*, edited by D. O. Henry. Tulsa, Okla.: Laboratory of Archaeology, Department of Anthropology, University of Tulsa. Pp. 44–54.

Hammel, E. A.
1964 Territorial patterning of marriage relationships in a coastal Peruvian Village. *American Anthropologist* 66(1):67–74.

Harlan, J. R.
1967 A wild wheat harvest in Turkey. *Archaeology* 20:197–201.

Harris, D. R.
1977 The origins of agriculture: alternative pathways toward agriculture. In *Origins of Agriculture*, edited by C. A. Reed. The Hague: Mouton. Pp. 173–249.
1978 Settling down: an evolutionary model for the transformation of mobile bands into sedentary communities. In *The Evolution of Social Systems*, edited by J. Friedman and M. L. Rowlands. London: Duckworth. Pp. 401–417.

Harris, M.
1977 *Cannibals and Kings: The Origins of Cultures*. New York: Random House.
1980 *Culture, People, Nature*. New York: Crowell.

Hassan, F. A.
1977 The dynamics of agricultural origins in Palestine: a theoretical model. In *Origins of Agriculture*, edited by C. A. Reed. The Hague: Mouton. Pp. 589–609.
1981 *Demographic Archaeology*. New York: Academic Press.

Hayden, B.
1981 Technological transitions among hunter-gatherers. *Current Anthropology* 22(5):519–549.

Hecker, H.
1982   Domestication revisited: its implications for faunal analysis. *Journal of Field Archaeology* 9:217–236.

Heinz, H. J.
1979   The nexus complex among the !Xo Bushman of Botswana. *Anthropus* 74:30–48.

Henry, D. O.
1973a   The Natufian of Palestine: Its Material Culture and Ecology. Unpublished Ph.D. thesis, Department of Anthropology, Southern Methodist University, Dallas.

1973b   The Natufian site of Rosh Zin, Negev, Israel: preliminary report. *Palestine Exploration Quarterly* 105:129–140.

1974   The utilization of the microburin technique in the Levant. *Paléorient* 2:389–398.

1975   The fauna in near Eastern archaeological deposits. In *Problems in Prehistory: North Africa and the Levant*, edited by F. Wendorf and A. E. Marks. Dallas, Tex.: Southern Methodist University Press. Pp. 379–385.

1976   Rosh Zin: a Natufian settlement near Ein Ardat. In *Prehistory and Paleoenvironments in the Central Negev, Israel* (Vol.1), edited by A. E. Marks. Dallas, Tex.: Southern Methodist University Press. Pp. 317–348.

1977   An examination of the artifact variability in the Natufian of Palestine. In *Eretz-Israel* (Vol.13), edited by B. Arensburg and O. Bar-Yosef. Jerusalem: Hebrew University. Pp. 229–239.

1981   An analysis of settlement patterns and adaptive strategies of the Natufian. In *Préhistoire du Levant*, edited by J. Cauvin and P. Sanlaville. Paris: Editions du CNRS. Pp. 420–432.

1982   The prehistory of southern Jordan and relationships with the Levant. *Journal of Field Archaeology* 9(4):417–444.

1983   Adaptive evolution within the Epipaleolithic of the Near East. In *Advances in World Archaeology* (Vol.2), edited by F. Wendorf and A. E. Close. London: Academic Press. Pp. 99–160

1985   Preagricultural sedentism: the Natufian example. In *Prehistoric Hunter-Gatherers*, edited by T. D. Price and J.A. Brown. Orlando, Fl.: Academic Press. Pp. 365–384.

1987a   Prehistory and paleoenvironments of Jordan: an overview. *Paléorient* 12(2):5–26.

1987b   Topographic influences on Epipaleolithic land-use patterns in southern Jordan. In *Studies in the History and Archaeology of Jordan* (Vol.3), edited by A.Hadidi. London: Routledge and Kegan Paul, pp. 21–28.

Henry, D. O., and S. Davis
1974   The 1974 excavation of Ha-Yonim Terrace (Israel), a brief report. *Paléorient* 2(1):195–197.

Henry, D. O., and A. N. Garrard
1988   Tor Hamar: An Epipaleolithic rockshelter in southern Jordan. *Palestine Exploration Quarterly* 120:1–25.

Henry, D. O., F. A. Hassan, K. C. Henry, and M. Jones
1983   An investigation of the prehistory of southern Jordan. *Palestine Exploration Quarterly* 115:1–24.

Henry, D. O., and Arl. Leroi-Gourhan
1976   The excavation of Hayonim Terrace: an interim report. *Journal of Field Archaeology* 3:391–406.

Henry, D. O., Arl. Leroi-Gourhan, and S. Davis
1981   Hayonim Terrace: Late Pleistocene changes in environment and economy. *Journal of Archaeological Science* 8:33–58

Henry, D. O., and A. F. Servello
1974   Compendium of carbon-14 determinations derived from Near Eastern prehistoric deposits. *Paléorient* 2:19–44.

Henry, D. O., and P. Turnbull, A. Emery-Barbier, and Arl. Leroi-Gourhan
1985   Archaeological and faunal remains from Natufian and Timnian sites in southern Jordan. *Bulletin of the American Schools of Oriental Research* 257: 45–64.

Hillman, G.
1975   Appendix A: The plant remains from Tell Abu Hureyra in Syria: a preliminary report. *Proceedings of the Prehistoric Society* 41:70–73.

Hodder, I.
1979   Economic and social stress and material culture patterning. *American Antiquity* 44(3):446–454.

Hole, F.
1971   Comment on: origins of food production in Southwest Asia (G. Wright). *Current Anthropology* 12(45):472–473.

1984   A reassessment of the Neolithic Revolution. *Paléorient* 10:49–60.

(in press) A two-part, two-stage model of domestication. In *The Walking Larder: Patterns of Domestication, Pastoralism, and Predation*, edited by Juliet Clutton-Brock. Southampton: Archaeological Congress.

Hooijer, D.
1961   The fossil vertebrates of Ksar Akil, a paleolithic rock shelter in Lebanon. *Zoologische Verhandelingen* 49:4–67.

Hopf, M.
1969   Plant remains and early farming in Jericho. In *The Domestication and Exploitation of Plants and Animals*, edited by P. J. Ucko and G. W. Dimbleby. London: Duckworth. Pp. 355–359.

Horowitz, A.
1971   Climate and vegetational developments in north-eastern Israel during Upper Pleistocene-Holocene times. *Pollen et Spores* 13(2):255–278.

1974   *The Late Cenozoic Stratigraphy and paleogeography of Israel.* Institute of Archaeology, Tel-Aviv University.

1976   Late quaternary paleoenvironments of prehistoric settlements. In *Prehistory and Paleoenvironments in the Central Negev, Israel* (Vol.1), edited by A. E. Marks. Dallas, Tex.: Southern Methodist University Press. Pp. 57–68.

1977   Pollen spectra from two early Holocene prehistoric sites in the Har Harif (west Central Negev). In *Prehistory and Paleoenvironments in the Central Negev, Israel* (Vol.2), edited by A. E. Marks. Dallas, Tex.: Southern Methodist University Press. Pp. 323–326.

1979   *The Quaternary of Israel.* New York: Academic Press.

Hours, F.
1974   Remarques sur l' utilisation de listes types pour l'étude du Paléolithique supérieur et de l' Epipaléolithique du Levant. *Paléorient* 2:3–18.

Howe, B.
1983   Karim Shahir. In *Prehistoric Archaeology Along the Zagros Flanks*, edited by L S. Braidwood, B. Howe, C. A. Reed, and P. J. Watson. Chicago: University of Chicago Press. Pp. 23–154.

Howell, N.

1979 *Demography of the Dobe !Kung*. New York: Academic Press.

Jelliffe, D. B., and P. Jelliffe

1974 Letter: Universal growth standards for preschool children. *Lancet* 2:47.

Jochim, M. A.

1976 *Hunter-Gatherer Subsistence and Settlement: A Predictive Model*. New York: Academic Press.

Jones, M.

1983 The Qalkhan and Hamran. Unpublished Ph.D. thesis, Department of Anthropology, Southern Methodist University, Dallas.

Kaufman, D.

1976 Typological and Technological comparisons of Two Epi-Paleolithic Assemblages from the coastal Plain of Israel. Unpublished M.A. thesis, University of Tel-Aviv.

1983 A Mushabian site in the Nahal Zin. In *Prehistory and Paleoenvironments in the Central Negev, Israel* (Vol.3), edited by A. E. Marks. Dallas, Tex.: Southern Methodist University. Pp. 333–342.

1986 A reconsideration of the adaptive change in the Levantine Epipaleolithic. In *The End of the Paleolithic in the Old World*, edited by L. G. Straus, Oxford: Bar International Series. Pp. 117–127.

1987 Excavations at the Geometric Kebaran site of Neve David, Israel. *Quärtar* 37/38:189–199.

Kaufman, D., and A. Ronen

1976 Epipaleolithic sites near Nahal Hadera, central coastal plain of Israel. *Tel Aviv* 3:16–30.

Kenyon, K.

1959 Earliest Jericho. *Antiquity* 33:5–9.

1960 Excavations at Jericho, 1957–1958. *Palestine Exploration Quarterly* 92:1–21.

1981 *Excavations at Jericho* (Vol.3). London: British School of Archaeology in Jerusalem.

Kirkbride, D.

1958 A Kebaran rockshelter in Wadi Madamagh, near Petra, Jordan. *Man* 63:55–58.

1966 Five seasons at the Pre-Pottery Neolithic village of Beidha in Jordan. *Palestine Exploration Quarterly* 98:8–72.

Kloos, P.

1963 Marital residence and local endogamy: environmental knowledge or leadership. *American Anthropologist* 65:854–862.

Knodel, J.

1977 Breast feeding and population growth. *Science* 198:1111–1124.

Konner, M., and C. Worthman

1980 Nursing frequencies, gonadal function and birth-spacing among !Kung hunter-gatherers. *Science* 207:788–791.

Koucky, F. and R. Smith

1986 Lake Beisan and the prehistoric settlement of the northern Jordan Valley. *Paléorient* 12,2:27–36.

Kraybill, N.

1977 Pre-agricultural tools for the preparation of foods in the Old World. In *Origins of Agriculture*, edited by C. A. Reed. Mouton: The Hague. Pp. 485–522.

Kroeber, A. L.
> 1939   *Cultural and Natural Areas of Native North America*. University of California, Publications in American Archaeology and Ethnology 38. Berkeley.
> 1976   *Handbook of the Indians of California*. New York: Dover Publications.

Lamb, H. H.
> 1975   Our understanding of global wind circulation and climatic variations. *Bird Study* 22:121–141.

Lancaster, J.B.
> 1976   Women, horticulture, and society in Sub-Saharan Africa. *American Anthropolgist* 78(3):539–564.

Lee, R. B.
> 1969   !Kung Bushmen subsistence—an input-output analysis. In *Environment and Cultural Behavior*, edited by A. P. Vayda. New York: Natural History Press. Pp. 47–79.
> 1972   Work effort, group structure and land use in contemporary hunter-gatherers. In *Man, Settlement and Urbanism*, edited by P. J. Ucko, R. Tringham, and G. W. Dimbleby. London: Duckworth. Pp. 177–185.
> 1979   *The !Kung San: Men, Women and Work in a Foraging Society*. Cambridge: Cambridge University Press.

Lee, R. B., and I. Devore
> 1968   *Man the Hunter*. Chicago: Aldine.

Legge, A. J.
> 1972   Prehistoric exploitation of the gazelle in Palestine. In *Papers in Economic Prehistory*, edited by E. S. Higgs. Cambridge: Cambridge University Press. Pp. 119–124.
> 1975   The fauna of Tell Abu Hureyra: preliminary analysis. *Proceedings of the Prehistoric Society* 41:74–76.

Leroi-Gourhan, Arl.
> 1969   Pollen grains of gramineae and cerealia from Shanidar and Zawi Chemi. In *The Domestication and Exploitation of Plants and Animals*, edited by P. J. Ucko and G. W. Dimbleby. London: Duckworth. Pp. 143–148.
> 1971   Pollens et terrasses marines au Liban. *Quaternaria* 15:249–59.
> 1978   Some palynological diagrams from Near Eastern archaeological sites. In *History of environmental conditions of Southwest Asia from the Last Pleniglacial till today*. Tubingen Symposium, February, 1978, Tubingen.
> 1980   Les analyses polliniques au moyen-orient. *Paléorient* 6:79–92.
> 1981   Le Levant à la fin du Pleistocène et à l'Holocène d'après la palynologie. In *Préhistoire du Levant*, edited by J. Cauvin and P. Sanlaville. Paris: Editions du CNRS. Pp. 107–10.

Levinson, D., and M. J. Malone
> 1980   *Toward Explaining Human Culture*. New Haven, Conn.: HRAF Press.

MacNeish, R. S.
> 1964   Ancient Mesoamerican civilization. *Science* 143:531–537.
> 1967   A summary of the subsistence. In *Environment and Subsistence: The Prehistory of the Tehuacan Valley* (Vol.1), edited by D. S. Byers. Austin, Tex.: University of Texas Press. Pp. 290–309.

Marks, A. E.
> 1973   The Harif point, a new tool type from the terminal Epi-Paleolithic of the Central Negev, Israel. *Paléorient* 1:99–102.
> 1975   An outline of prehistoric occurrences and chronology in the Central Negev, Israel. In *Problems in Prehistory: North Africa and the Levant*, edited by

F. Wendorf and A. E. Marks. Dallas, Tex.: Southern Methodist University Press. Pp. 351–362.

1976   Site D5, a Geometric Kebaran "A" occupation in the Nahal Zin. In *Prehistory and Paleoenvironments in the Central Negev, Israel* (Vol. 1), edited by A. E. Marks. Dallas, Tex.: Southern Methodist University Press. Pp. 227–293.

1977a   *Prehistory and Paleoenvironments in the Central Negev, Israel. Volume II: The Avdat/Aqev Area and the Har Harif.* Dallas, Tex.: Southern Methodist University Press.

1977b   The Epi-Paleolithic of the Central Negev: current status. In *Eretz-Israel* (Vol.13), edited by B. Arensburg and O. Bar-Yosef. Jerusalem: Hebrew University. Pp. 227–228.

1977c   Introduction: preliminary overview of Central Negev Prehistory. In *Prehistory and Paleoenvironments in the Central Negev, Israel* (Vol.2), edited by A. E. Marks. Dallas, Tex.: Southern Methodist University Press. Pp. 3–34.

Marks, A. E., H. Crew, R. Ferring, and J. Phillips
1972   Prehistoric sites near Har Harif. *Israel Exploration Journal* 22(2–3):73–85.

Marks, A. E., and D. A. Friedel
1977   Prehistoric settlement patterns in the Avdat/Aqev area. In *Prehistory and Paleoenvironments in the Central Negev, Israel* (Vol.2), edited by A. E. Marks. Dallas, Tex.: Southern Methodist University Press. Pp. 131–158.

Marks, A. E., and P. Larson
1977   Test excavations at the Natufian site of Rosh Horesha. In *Prehistory and Paleoenvironments in the Central Negev, Israel* (Vol.2), edited by A. E. Marks. Dallas, Tex.: Southern Methodist University Press. Pp. 191–232.

Marks, A. E., J. Phillips, H. Crew and R. Ferring
1971   Prehistoric sites near 'En-'Avdat in the Negev. *Israel Exploration Journal* 21:13–24.

Marks, A. E., and T. R. Scott
1976   Abu Salem: type site of the Harifian industry of the southern Levant. *Journal of Field Archaeology* 3(1):43–60.

Marks, A. E., and A. H. Simmons
1977   The Negev Kebaran of the Har Harif. In *Prehistory and Paleoenvironments in the Central Negev, Israel* (Vol.2), edited by A. E. Marks. Dallas, Tex.: Southern Methodist University Press. Pp. 233–270.

Marshall, L.
1976   *The !Kung of Nyae Nyae.* Cambridge, Mass.: Harvard University Press.

McArthur, J., B. Bullen, I. Beitins, M. Pagano, T. Badger, and A. Klibanki
1980   Hypothalamic amenorrhea in runners of normal body composition. *Endocrine Research Communications* 7(1):13–25.

McBurney, C.B.M.
1968   The cave of Ali Tappeh and the Epi-Paleolithic in N.E. Iran. *Proceedings of the Prehistoric Society* 23:385–418.

McNicoll, A., W. Ball, S. Bassett, P. Edward, D. Petves, T. Potts, L. Randle, L. Villiers, and P. Watson
1985   *Preliminary report on the University of Sydney's fifth season of excavation at Pella in Jordan.* Annual of the Department of Antiquities of Jordan, 28.

Mellaart, J.
1975   *The Neolithic of the Near East.* London: Thames and Hudson.

Meyers, J. T.
1971   The origins of agriculture: an evaluation of three hypotheses. In *Prehistoric Agriculture*, edited by S. Struever. Garden City, N. Y.: Natural History Press. Pp. 101–125.

Mienis, H.
1977   Marine molluscs from the Epi-Paleolithic and Harifian of the Har Harif, Central Negev, (Israel). In *Prehistory and Paleoenvironments in the Central Negev, Israel* (Vol.2), edited by A. E. Marks. Dallas, Tex.: Southern Methodist University Press. Pp. 347–353.

Moore, A. M. I.
1975   The excavation of Tell Abu Hureyra in Syria: a preliminary report. *Proceedings of the Prehistoric Society* 41:50–77.
1979   A pre-Neolithic farmers' village on the Euphrates. *Scientific American* 241: 62–70.
1982   Agricultural origins in the Near East—a model for the 1980's. *World Archaeology* 14:224–236.
1985   The development of Neolithic societies in the Near East. In *Advances in World Archaeology*, edited by F. Wendorf and A. E. Cose. New York: Academic Press. Pp. 1–70.

Mortenson, P.
1970   A preliminary study of the chipped stone industry from Beidha. *Acta Archaeologia* 41:1–54.
1972   Seasonal camps and early villages in the Zagros. In *Man, Settlement and Urbanism*, edited by P. J. Ucko, R. Tringham, and G. W. Dimbleby. London: Duckworth. Pp. 293–297.

Mosley, W.H.
1977   The effects of nutrition on natural fertility. Paper presented at Seminar on Natural Fertility, Institut National d' Etudes Demographiques, Paris.

Muheisan, M.
1983   La Préhistoire en Jordanie, Recherches sur l' Epipaléolithique, L'exemple du gisement Kharraneh IV. Unpublished Ph.D. dissertation. Bordeaux: Université de Bordeaux.

Murdock, G. P.
1949   *Social Structure*. New York: Macmillan.
1967   *Ethnographic Atlas*. Pittsburgh, Pa.: University of Pittsburgh Press.

Mussi, M.
1976   The Natufian of Palestine: the beginnings of agriculture in a paleoethnological perspective. *Origini* 10: 89–107.

Neev, D., and K. O. Emery
1967   The Dead Sea. *Bulletin of the Geological Survey of Israel* 41:1–147.

Neuville, R.
1934   Le préhistorique de Palestine. *Revue Biblique* 43:237.
1951   *Le Paléolithique et le Mésolithique du désert de Judée*. Archives de l'Institut de Paléontologie Humaine 24. Paris: Masson.

Niklewsky, J., and W. Van Zeist
1970   A Late Quaternary pollen diagram from northwestern Syria. *Acta Botanica Neerlandica* 19:737–754.

Noy, T.
1971   *Halutza Dunes: Prehistoric Survey*. Jerusalem: Israel Museum.

Noy, T., A. J. Legge, and E. S. Higgs
1973   Recent excavations at Nahal Oren, Israel. *Proceedings of the Prehistoric Society* 39:75–99.

Noy, T., J. Schuldenrein, and E. Tchernov
1980   Gilgal, a Pre-Pottery Neolithic A site in the lower Jordan Valley. *Israel Exploration Journal* 30:63–82.

Orni, E., and E. Efrat
  1966   *Geography of Israel*, 2nd edition, Jerusalem: Israel Program for Scientific Translation.

Olszewski, D.
  1986   *The North Syrian Epipaleolithic*. Oxford: British Archaeological Reports International Series.

Payne, J. C.
  1983   The flint industries of Jericho. In *Jericho IV*, edited by K. M. Kenyon and T. A. Holland. Jerusalem: British School of Archaeology. Pp. 622–758.

Peak, H., and Fleure, H.
  1927   *Peasants and Potters*. London: Oxford University Press.

Perkins, D.
  1966   The fauna from Madamagh and Beidha. *Palestine Exploration Quarterly*: 66–67.

Perrot, J.
  1951   La Terrasse d' El-Khiam. In *Le Paléolithique et le Mésolithique du désert de Judée*, edited by R. Neuville. Paris: Masson. Pp. 134–178.
  1960   Excavations at Eynan (Ein Mallaha), preliminary report on the 1959 season. *Israel Exploration Journal* 10(1):14–22
  1962   Palestine-Syria Celicia. In *Courses Toward Urban Life*, edited by R. J. Braidwood and G. R. Willey. Chicago: Aldine. Pp. 147–164.
  1966   Le Gisement Natufian de Mallaha ('Eyan), Israel. *L'Anthropologie* 70: 437–484.

Pfeiffer, J. E.
  1969   *The Emergence of Man*. New York: Harper & Row.

Phillips, J. L.
  1973   *Two Final Paleolithic sites in the Nile Valley and Their External Relations*. Cairo: Geological Survey of Egypt Paper No. 57.
  1975   Iberomaurusian related sites in the Nile Valley. In *Problems in Prehistory: North Africa and the Levant*, edited by F. Wendorf and A. E. Marks. Dallas, Tex.: Southern Methodist University Press. Pp. 171–180.
  1977   The Harifian. In *Prehistoric Investigations in Gebel Maghara, Northern Sinai*, edited by O. Bar-Yosef and J. L. Phillips. Qedem 7, Jerusalem: Monographs of the Institute of Archaeology, Hebrew University. Pp. 199–218.

Phillips, J. L., and O. Bar-Yosef
  1974   Prehistoric sites near Nahal Lavan, Western Negev, Israel. *Paléorient* 2:343–482.

Phillips, J. L., and K. W. Butler
  1973   A ⟨⟨Silsilian⟩⟩ occupation site (GS-2B-II) of the Kom Ombo Plain, Upper Egypt: geology, archaeology and paleoecology. *Quaternaria* 17:343–386.

Phillips, J. L., and E. Mintz
  1977   The Mushabian. In *Prehistoric Investigations in Gebel Maghara, Northern Sinai*, edited by O. Bar-Yosef and J. L. Phillips. Qedem 7, Jerusalem: Monographs of the Institute of Archaeology, Hebrew University. Pp. 149–163.

Pianka, E. R.
  1970   On r and K selection or b and d selection? *American Naturalist* 106: 581–588.

Prior, J. C., K. Cameron, B. Hoyuen, and J. Thomas
  1982   Menstrual cycle changes with Marathon training: norulation and short luteal phase. *Canadian Journal Of Applied Sport Sciences* 7:173–177.

Smith, P., O. Bar-Yosef, and A. Sillen
  1985   Archaeological and skeletal evidence for dietary change during the Late
          Pleistocene/Early Holocene in the Levant. In *Paleopathology at the Origins of
          Agriculture*, edited by M. N. Cohen and G. J. Armelagos. New York: Aca-
          demic Press. Pp. 101–130.

Smith, P. E. L.
  1968   A revised view of the Later Paleolithic of Egypt. In *La Préhistoire: problèmes
          et tendances*. Paris: Editions du CNRS. Pp. 391–399.
  1972   Changes in population pressure in archaeological explanation. *World Ar-
          chaeology* 4:5–18.

Smith, P. E. L., and T. C. Young, Jr.
  1983   The force of numbers: Population pressure in the Central Western Zagros
          12,000–4,500 B.C.. In *The Hilly Flanks and Beyond*, edited by T. C. Young,
          Jr., P. E. L. Smith, and P. Mortensen. Chicago: University of Chicago Press.
          Pp. 141–161.

Solecki, R. L.
  1964   Zawi Chemi Shanidar, a post-Pleistocene village site in Northern Iraq. *Sixth
          International Congress of the Quaternary*. Warsaw, 1961. Pp. 405–412.
  1969   Milling tools and the Epi-Paleolithic in the Near East. *Etudes sur le Quater-
          naire dans le monde*, VIIIème Congres, Pp. 989–994.
  1981   *An Early Village Site at Zawi Chemi Shanidar*. In *Bibliotheca Mesopotamia*
          (Vol.13), edited by Giorgio Buccellati. Malibu, Ca.: Undena.

Solecki, R. S.
  1964   Shanidar Cave: a Late Pleistocene site in northern Iraq. *Sixth International
          Congress of the Quaternary*, Warsaw, 1961. Pp. 413–423.

Solecki, R. S., and M. Rubin
  1958   Dating of Zawi Chemi, an early village site at Shanidar, Northern Iraq. *Sci-
          ence* 127:1446.

Stekelis, M., and G. Haas
  1942   Preliminary report on soundings in prehistoric caves in Palestine (Mug-
          haret al-Watwat; Mugharet an-Nugtah; Mugharet Wadi-Fallah; Mugharet
          Abu-Usba; Iraq el-Barud). *Bulletin American Schools of Oriental Research*
          86:2–10.
  1952   The Abu-Usba Cave, *Israel Exploration Journal* 13:1–12.

Stekelis, M., and T. Yizraeli
  1963   Excavations at Nahal Oren: preliminary report. *Israel Exploration Journal*
          13:1–2.

Steward, J.
  1938   *Basin-Plateau Aboriginal Socio-political Groups*. Bureau of American Eth-
          nology, Bulletin 120.

Stordeur, D.
  1981   La Contribution de l'industrie de l'os à la délimination des ares culturelles:
          l'exemple du Natoufien. In *Préhistoire du Levant*, edited by J. Cauvin and
          P. Sanlaville. Paris: Editions du CNRS. Pp. 433–438.

Tanner, N. A.
  1964   The adolescent growth-spurt and development age. In *Human Biology*, ed-
          ited by G. A. Harrison, J. S. Weiner, J. M. Tanner, and N. A. Barnicott.
          London: Oxford University Press. Pp. 321–339.

Tchernov, E.
  1976   Some Late Quaternary faunal remains from the Avdat-Aqev area. In *Pre-
          history and Paleoenvironments of the Central Negev, Israel* (Vol. 1), edited by

A. E. Marks. Dallas, Tex.: Southern Methodist University Press. Pp. 69–74.

1981 The biostratigraphy of the Middle East. In *Préhistoire du Levant*, edited by J. Cauvin and P. Sanlaville. Paris: Editions du CNRS. Pp. 67–98.

Tixier, J.

1963 *Typologie de l'Epipaléolithique du Maghreb*. Mémoires du Centre de Recherches Anthropologiques, Préhistoriques et Ethnologiques, Alger. Paris: Arts et Métiers Graphiques.

Trigger, B. G.

1980 *Gordon Childe: Revolutions in Archaeology*. New York: Columbia University Press.

Trussel, J.

1978 Menarche and fatness: re-examination of the critical body composition hypothesis. *Science* 200:1506–1509.

Turnbull, C. M.

1968 The importance of flux in two hunting societies. In *Man the Hunter*, edited by R. Lee and I. Devore. Chicago: Aldine. Pp. 132–137.

Turnbull, P., and C. A. Reed

1974 The fauna from the terminal Pleistocene of Palegawra cave: Zarzian occupation site in Northeast Iraq. *Fieldiana: Anthropology* 63:81–146.

Turville-Petre, F.

1932 Excavations in the Mugharet el Kebarah. *Journal of the Royal Anthropological Institute* 62:270–276.

Valla, F. R.

1975 *Le Natufien, une culture préhistorique en Palestine*. Paris: Cahiers de la Revue Biblique.

1981 Les Etablissements Natoufiens dans le nord d'Israel. In *Préhistoire du Levant*, edited by J. Cauvin and P. Sanlaville. Paris: Editions du CNRS. Pp. 409–420.

1984 *Les industries de silex de Mallaha (Eynan)*. Mémoires et Travaux du Centre de Recherche Français de Jérusalem, 30 Paris: Association Paléorient.

Valla, F. R., I. Gilead, and O. Bar-Yosef

1979 Prospection préhistorique dans le Neguev septentrional. *Paléorient* 5:221–232.

Valla, F. R., O. Bar-Yosef, P. Smith, E. Tchernov, and J. Desse.

1986 Un nouveau sondage sur la terrasse d'el Ouad, Israel. *Paléorient* 12(1):21–38.

Vallois, H. V.

1936 Les ossements Natoufiens d'Erq el-Ahmar (Palestine). *L'Anthropologie* 46:529–539.

Van Ginneken, J. K.

1974 Prolonged breast feeding as a birth spacing method. *Studies in Family Planning* 5:501–508.

Van Loon, M.

1968 The Oriental Institute excavations at Mureybat, Syria; preliminary report on the 1965 campaign. *Near Eastern Studies* 27:265–282.

Van Zeist, W.

1967 Late Quaternary vegetation history of western Iran. *Review of Paleobotany and Palynology* 2:301–311.

1970 The Oriental Institute excavation at Mureybet, Syria: preliminary report on the 1965 campaign, part II: the paleobotany. *Journal of Near Eastern Studies* 29:167–176.

Van Zeist, W., and S. Bottema
    1977   Palynological investigations in western Iran. *Paleohistoria* 19:19–85.
Van Zeist, W., and S. Bakker-Herres
    1979   Some economic and ecological aspects of the plant husbandry of Tell As-wad. *Paléorient* 5:161–169.
Vaufrey, R.
    1951   Etude paléontologique. Mammiferes. In *Le Paléolithique et le Mésolithique du désert de Judée* (Vol.1), edited by R. Neuville. Paris: Masson. Pp.198–233.
Vita-Finzi, C., and E. S. Higgs
    1970   Prehistoric economy in the Mount Carmel area of Palestine: site catchment analysis. *Proceedings of the Prehistoric Society* 36:1–37.
Waechter, J.
    1949   The Mesolithic Age in the Middle East. Unpublished Ph.D. thesis, Cambridge University.
Warren, M. P.
    1980   The effects of exercise on pubertal progession and reproductive function in girls. *Journal of Clinical Endocrinology and Metabolism* 51:1150–1157.
Watanabe, H.
    1972   *The Ainu Ecosystem*. Tokyo: University of Tokyo Press.
Wendorf, F.
    1968   *The Prehistory of Nubia* (two vol). Dallas, Tex: Fort Burgwin Research Center and Southern Methodist University Press.
Wendorf, F., and R. Schild
    1976   *Prehistory of the Nile Valley*. New York: Academic Press.
Wendorf, F., R. Schild, N. El Hadidi, A. E. Close, M. Kobusiewiz, H. Wieckowska, B. Issawi, and H. Haas
    1979   Use of barley in the Egyptian Late Paleolithic. *Science* 205 (4413): 1341–1347.
Wenke, R. J.
    1984   *Patterns in Prehistory*. New York: Oxford University Press.
Whyte, R. O.
    1977   The botanical Neolithic revolution. *Human Ecology* 5(3):209–222.
Wiessner, P.
    1974   A functional estimater of population from floor area. *American Antiquity* 39(2):343–350.
    1979   Reply to Casteel. *American Antiquity* 44(4):808–810.
    1983   Style and social information in Kalahari San projectile points. *American Antiquity* 48(2):253–276.
Williams, B. J.
    1974   A model of band society. *American Antiquity* 39(4), Part 2, Memoir 29.
Wilmsen, E.
    1977   Seasonal effects of dietary intake on Kalahari San. *Proceedings of the Federation of American Societies of Experimental Biology* 37:65–72.
Wobst, M.
    1974   Boundary conditions for Paleolithic social systems: a simulation approach. *American Antiquity* 39(2):147–178.
    1977   Stylistic behavior and information exchange. In *Papers for the Director: Research Essays in Honor of James B. Griffin*, edited by C. Cleland. Ann Arbor, Mich.: Museum of Anthropology. Pp. 317–342.
    1978   The archaeo-ethnology of hunter-gathers, or the tyranny of the ethnographic record in archaeology. *American Antiquity* 43:303–309.

Wright, G. A.
1971   Origins of food production in southeast Asia: survey of ideas. *Current Anthropology* 12:447–470.
1978   Social differentiation in the early Natufian. In *Social Anthropology*, edited by C. L. Redman, M. J. Berman, E. V. Curtin, W. T. Langhorne, Jr., N. H. Versaggi, and J. C. Wanser. New York: Academic Press. Pp. 201–224.

Wright, H. E., Jr.
1968   Natural environment of early food production north of Mesopotamia. *Science* 161:334–339.
1970   Environmental changes and the origin of agriculture in the Near East. *Bioscience* 20(4):210–217.
1977   Environmental change and the origins of agriculture in the Old and New Worlds. In *Origins of Agriculture*, edited by C. A. Reed. The Hague: Mouton. Pp. 281–318.

Yellen, J.
1977   *Archaeological Approaches to the Present*. New York: Academic Press.

Yizraeli, T.
1967   Mesolithic hunters' industries at Ramat Matred (the Wilderness of Zin), first report. *Palestine Exploration Quarterly* 99:78–85.

Zeuner, F. E.
1959   *The Pleistocene Period: Its Climate, Chronology and Faunal Successions* (2nd ed.). London: Hutchinson.

Zohary, D.
1962   *Plant Life of Palestine*. New York: Ronald Press Company.
1969   The progenitors of wheat and barley in relation to domestication and agricultural dispersal in the Old World. In *The Domestication and Exploitation of Plants and Animals*, edited by P. J. Ucko and G. W. Dimbleby. London: Duckworth. Pp. 47–66.

APPENDIX A:
MUSHABIAN COMPLEX ASSEMBLAGES

TABLE A.1
Sinai Mushabian

	Mushabi[a] I		Mushabi[a] XIV Lev. 1		Mushabi[a] XIV Surf.		Nahal[b] Hadera		Nahal[b] Hadera II		Mushabi[a] V excav.		Mushabi[a] V Surf.		Mushabi[a] XIX		Mushabi[c] IV		Nahal[d] Lavan IV	
	N	%	N	%	N	%	N	%	N	%	N	%	N	%	N	%	N	%	N	%
Major tool classes																				
Scrapers	25	1	2	1	5	2	74	14	116	21	8	1	0	0	3	1	31	8	20	20
Burins	14	1	6	2	9	4	46	9	34	6	3	0	1	1	0	0	7	2	2	3
Notch-dent.	148	5	13	5	20	8	91	17	56	10	39	4	16	11	10	2	79	19	26	26
Bkd. bldts.	2498	82	215	79	166	66	112	21	244	43	725	80	105	74	506	79	138	33	16	16
Geometrics	28	1	5	2	11	4	16	3	21	4	72	8	15	11	69	11	80	19	23	23
Others	312	10	31	11	40	16	199	37	94	17	58	6	5	4	53	8	88	21	12	12
Total	3025	100	272	100	251	100	538	101	565	101	905	99	142	101	641	101	423	100	99	100
Varieties of backed bladelets																				
Arched	339	26	98	50	88	67	nd	nd	nd	nd	92	19	18	30	63	14	11	17	nd	nd
Straight	33	3	6	3	0	0	nd	1	nd	2	14	4	4	6	0	0	0	0	nd	nd
Scalene	740	58	42	22	21	16	nd	9	nd	18	234	48	10	17	84	19	16	25	nd	nd
La Mouillah	160	13	48	25	23	17	20	67	43	68	145	30	28	47	294	67	37	58	pr	pr
Total	1272	100	192	100	132	100	30	nd	63	nd	485	101	60	100	441	100	64	100	nd	nd
Varieties of geometric microliths																				
Trapezes	0	0	0	0	6	55	5	38	8	40	49	68	3	20	65	94	23	32	0	0
Triangles	7	25	0	0	4	36	2	15	9	45	19	26	11	74	4	6	23	32	0	0
Lunates	21	75	5	100	1	9	6	46	3	14	4	6	1	6	0	0	27	37	23	100
Total	28	100	5	100	11	100	13	99	20	100	72	100	15	100	69	100	73	101	23	100
Microburins																				
IMbt	922	23	147	35	110	30	nd	nd	nd	nd	825	48	234	62	683	52	244	39	27	21
rIMbt	41		43		40		nd		nd		60		75		57		53		nd	

[a] Phillips and Mintz, 1977; [b] Kaufman, 1976; [c] Bar-Yosef, 1977; [d] Phillips and Bar-Yosef, 1974. nd = no data, pr = present.

TABLE A.2
Negev Mushabian

	G9[a]		K9[a]		G14[a]		Ira 23[b]		D101B[c]		K6[a]		G3[a]		K5[a]		K7[a]	
	N	%	N	%	N	%	N	%	N	%	N	%	N	%	N	%	N	%
Major tool classes																		
Scrapers	11	8	53	14	14	3	17	5	26	17	8	1	6	6	23	8	19	5
Burins	5	4	5	1	2	0	10	3	4	3	3	1	1	1	2	1	4	1
Notch-dent.	15	11	90	23	30	6	85	25	9	6	70	17	31	29	94	35	96	25
Bkd. bldts.	67	48	153	39	357	76	125	37	85	52	237	59	43	40	87	32	89	24
Geometrics	0	0	0	0	6	1	4	1	2	1	8	2	3	2	15	6	32	9
Others	43	30	90	23	60	13	98	29	32	20	72	18	23	21	51	19	131	35
Total	141	101	391	100	469	99	339	100	158	99	398	99	107	99	272	101	371	99
Varieties of backed bladelets																		
Arched	0	0	1	0	0	0	pr	pr	8	22	4	15	0	0	5	21	0	0
Straight	0	0	3	13	9	13	pr	pr	22	61	6	23	4	57	12	50	6	35
Scalene	9	100	20	83	61	87	pr	pr	5	14	16	62	3	43	7	29	11	65
La Mouillah	0	0	0	0	0	0	pr	pr	1	3	0	0	0	0	0	0	0	0
Total	9	100	24	100	70	100	nd	nd	36	100	26	100	7	100	24	100	17	100
Varieties of geometric microliths																		
Trapezes	0	0	0	0	3	50	nd	nd	2	100	0	0	0	0	1	7	0	0
Triangles	0	0	0	0	2	33	nd	nd	0	0	1	13	0	0	3	20	2	6
Lunates	0	0	0	0	1	17	nd	nd	0	0	7	87	3	100	11	73	30	94
Total	0	0	0	0	6	100	pr	pr	2	100	8	100	3	100	15	100	32	100
Microburins																		
lMbt	30	18	131	25	154	25	85	20	45	22	86	18	32	23	65	19	92	20
rlMbt		23		84		70		nd		73		76		84		71		65

[a]Marks and Simmons, 1977; [b]Valla, et al., 1979; [c]Kaufman, 1983. nd = no data, pr = present.

TABLE A.3
Madamaghan

	Tor[a] Hamar		J436[b]	
	N	%	*N*	%
Major tool classes				
Scrapers	83	8	9	7
Burins	16	2	0	0
Notch-dent.	59	6	7	5
Bkd. bldts.	538	52	94	69
Geometrics	15	1	11	8
Others	331	32	15	11
Total	1042	101	43	100
Varieties of backed bladelets				
Arched	207	41	19	44
Straight	194	39	5	12
Scalene	0	0	1	2
La Mouillah	102	20	18	42
Total	503	100	43	100
Varieties of geometric microliths				
Trapezes	6	40	11	100
Triangles	4	27	0	0
Lunates	5	33	0	0
Total	15	100	11	100
Microburins				
IMbt	1081	51	34	20
rIMbt		66		49

[a]Henry and Garrard, 1988; [b]unpublished.

APPENDIX B:
GEOMETRIC KEBARAN COMPLEX
ASSEMBLAGES

TABLE B.1
Group I

	El[a] Khiam Level 9 N	El[a] Khiam Level 9 %	Hefsibah[b] B2 N	Hefsibah[b] B2 %	Hefsibah[b] B3 N	Hefsibah[b] B3 %	Hefsibah[b] B4 N	Hefsibah[b] B4 %	Hefsibah[b] C N	Hefsibah[b] C %	Lagama[c] Ic N	Lagama[c] Ic %	Mushabi[c] XIV Level 2 N	Mushabi[c] XIV Level 2 %	Hayonim[d] Terrace D N	Hayonim[d] Terrace D %
Major tool classes																
Scrapers	258	17	152	9	24	4	20	3	2	2	0	0	1	1	34	4
Burins	173	12	131	8	48	9	190	33	22	25	3	2	0	0	30	3
Notch-dent.	81	6	16	1	1	0	8	1	0	0	23	17	2	1	50	6
Bkd. bldts.	374	25	1195	71	442	79	315	54	46	53	37	28	99	48	369	41
Geometrics	20	1	136	8	30	5	20	3	12	14	44	33	96	48	318	35
Others	577	39	65	4	18	3	31	5	5	6	25	19	3	2	102	11
Total	1483	100	1695	101	563	100	584	99	87	100	132	99	201	100	903	100
Varieties of backed bladelets																
Arched	nd	nd	nd	nd	nd	nd	nd	nd	nd	nd	8	67	1	1	nd	nd
Straight	nd	nd	nd	nd	nd	nd	nd	nd	nd	nd	3	25	95	99	nd	nd
Scalene	nd	nd	nd	nd	nd	nd	nd	nd	nd	nd	0	0	0	0	nd	nd
La Mouillah	nd	nd	nd	nd	nd	nd	nd	nd	nd	nd	1	8	0	0	nd	nd
Total	nd	nd	nd	nd	nd	nd	nd	nd	nd	nd	12	100	96	100	nd	nd
Varieties of geometric microliths																
Trapezes	18	90	nd	nd	nd	nd	nd	nd	nd	nd	40	91	95	100	131	86
Triangles	2	10	nd	nd	nd	nd	nd	nd	nd	nd	0	0	0	0	7	5
Lunates	0	0	nd	nd	nd	nd	nd	nd	nd	nd	4	9	0	0	15	10
Total	20	100	nd	nd	nd	nd	nd	nd	nd	nd	44	100	95	100	153	101
Microburins																
IMbt	0	0	7	6.5	1	.1	0	0	0	0	3	2.2	3	1.4	25	2.7
rIMbt	0	0	nd	nd	nd	nd	0	0	0	0	nd	nd	nd	nd	nd	nd

[a]Echegaray, 1964, 1966; [b]Ronen, et al., 1975; [c]Bar-Yosef and Goring-Morris, 1977; [d]Henry and Leroi-Gourhan, 1976. nd = no data.

TABLE B.2
Group II

	Douara Cave Unit A[a]		Douara Cave Unit B[a]		D101C[b]		D5[c]		Nahal Lavan II[d]		Lagama N IV[e]		Lagama N VII[e]		Ma'aleh Ziq[f]	
	N	%	N	%	N	%	N	%	N	%	N	%	N	%	N	%
Major tool classes																
Scrapers	10	8	1	2	14	15	111	11	19	3	9	10	16	1	33	3
Burins	13	10	5	11	0	0	12	1	3	0	0	0	0	0	1	1
Notch-dent.	5	4	2	4	3	3	107	10	44	7	9	10	27	2	34	3
Bkd. bldts.	43	34	19	41	39	41	492	47	195	29	28	30	363	29	364	35
Geometrics	35	28	10	22	14	15	109	10	369	54	35	37	640	51	500	48
Others	21	17	9	20	26	27	213	21	51	8	13	14	220	18	119	11
Total	127	101	46	100	96	101	1044	100	681	101	94	101	1266	101	1051	101
Varieties of backed bladelets																
Arched	nd	nd	nd	nd	nd	nd	231	47	nd	nd	1	100	2	100	nd	nd
Straight	nd	nd	nd	nd	nd	nd	206	42	nd	nd	0	0	0	0	nd	nd
Scalene	nd	nd	nd	nd	nd	nd	55	11	nd	nd	0	0	0	0	nd	nd
La Mouillah	nd	nd	nd	nd	nd	nd	0	0	nd	nd	0	0	0	0	nd	nd
Total	nd	nd	nd	nd	nd	nd	492	100	nd	nd	1	100	2	100	nd	nd
Varieties of geometric microliths																
Trapezes	35	100	10	100	15	100	111	100	369	100	18	100	484	99	nd	nd
Triangles	0	0	0	0	0	0	0	0	0	0	0	0	4	1	nd	nd
Lunates	0	0	0	0	0	0	0	0	0	0	0	0	0	0	nd	nd
Total	35	100	10	100	15	100	111	100	369	100	18	100	488	100	nd	nd
Microburins																
IMbt	14	10	6	12	nd		25	2	9	1	3	7	110	8	0	
rIMbt		18		17	nd			17		2		13		20	0	

[a]Fujimoto, 1979; [b]Simmons, 1977; [c]Marks, 1976; [d]Phillips and Bar-Yosef, 1974; [e]Bar-Yosef and Goring-Morris, 1977; [f]Goring-Morris, 1978. nd = no data.

TABLE B.2 (cont.)
Group II cont.

	J31[a] N	J31[a] %	Kharaneh[b] Phase C N	Kharaneh[b] Phase C %	Nahal Lavan[c] VI N	Nahal Lavan[c] VI %	Nahal Lavan[c] 105 N	Nahal Lavan[c] 105 %	Mushabi[d] XVII N	Mushabi[d] XVII %	Mushabi[d] XVIII N	Mushabi[d] XVIII %	J201[a] B N	J201[a] B %	J201[a] A N	J201[a] A %	J203[a] lower layer N	J203[a] lower layer %
Major tool classes																		
Scrapers	3	2	15	7	2	2	17	5	0	0	0	0	15	4	7	4	1	1
Burins	0	0	6	3	0	0	0	0	0	0	0	0	1	0	0	0	1	1
Notch-dent.	5	3	6	3	4	4	2	1	2	4	1	3	24	6	6	3	1	1
Bkd. bldts.	94	63	173	77	20	20	38	11	24	53	10	33	255	60	104	58	55	78
Geometrics	15	10	12	5	69	69	272	81	17	38	18	60	70	16	35	19	5	7
Others	32	21	14	6	5	5	7	2	2	4	1	3	63	15	27	15	8	11
Total	149	99	226	101	100	100	336	100	45	99	30	99	428	101	179	99	71	99
Varieties of backed bladelets																		
Arched	nd	nd	8	31	nd	nd	nd	nd	nd	nd	nd	nd	3	1	nd	nd	nd	nd
Straight	nd	nd	15	58	nd	nd	nd	nd	nd	nd	nd	nd	216	99	nd	nd	nd	nd
Scalene	nd	nd	3	12	nd	nd	nd	nd	nd	nd	nd	nd	0	0	nd	nd	nd	nd
La Mouillah	nd	nd	0	0	nd	nd	nd	nd	nd	nd	nd	nd	0	0	nd	nd	nd	nd
Total	nd	nd	26	101	nd	nd	nd	nd	nd	nd	nd	nd	219	100	nd	nd	nd	nd
Varieties of geometric microliths																		
Trapezes	15	100	12	100	nd	nd	nd	nd	17	100	14	100	70	100	35	100	5	100
Triangles	0	0	0	0	nd	nd	nd	nd	0	0	0	0	0	0	0	0	0	0
Lunates	0	0	0	0	nd	nd	nd	nd	0	0	0	0	0	0	0	0	0	0
Total	15	100	12	100	nd	nd	nd	nd	17	100	14	100	70	100	35	100	5	100
Microburins																		
lMbt	0	0	0	0	0	0	0	0	0	0	4	12	1	1	0	0	0	0
rlMbt	0	0	0	0	0	0	0	0	0	0		22		1	0	0	0	0

[a]Jones, 1983; [b]Muheisan, 1983; [c]Phillips and Bar-Yosef, 1974; [d]Bar-Yosef and Goring-Morris, 1977. nd = no data.

TABLE B.3
Group III

	Nahal[a] Oren VII Lower		Nahal[a] Oren VII Upper		Ein Gev[b] IV		Kefar[b] Darom 27	
	N	%	N	%	N	%	N	%
Major tool classes								
Scrapers	49	21	15	8	153	19	22	15
Burins	23	10	14	8	23	3	23	16
Notch-dent.	0	0	4	3	136	17	15	10
Bkd. bldts.	72	31	36	20	123	15	51	35
Geometrics	64	27	45	25	106	13	10	7
Others	27	12	64	36	232	33	23	16
Total	235	101	178	100	803	100	144	99
Varieties of backed bladelets								
Arched	nd	nd	nd	nd	nd	nd	nd	nd
Straight	nd	nd	nd	nd	nd	nd	nd	nd
Scalene	nd	nd	nd	nd	nd	nd	nd	nd
La Mouillah	nd	nd	nd	nd	nd	nd	nd	nd
Total	nd	nd	nd	nd	nd	nd	nd	nd
Varieties of geometric microliths								
Trapezes	4	7	8	16	1	1	nd	nd
Triangles	36	59	31	63	105	99	nd	nd
Lunates	21	34	10	20	0	0	nd	nd
Total	61	100	49	99	106	100	nd	nd
Microburins								
IMbt	5	2	0	0	1016	55.8	3	2
rIMbt		8		0		82.5		nd

[a]Noy, et al., 1975; [b]Bar-Yosef, 1970.

TABLE B.4
Group IV

	El[a] Khiam Level 8		El[a] Khiam Level 7		J202[b] Lower Unit 6		J202[b] Upper Unit 6		J203[b] Upper		Kharaneh IV[c] Sondage III, Couche II	
	N	%	N	%	N	%	N	%	N	%	N	%
Major Tool Classes												
Scrapers	52	10	21	9	11	5	5	4	16	3	14	4
Burins	143	28	66	28	3	2	2	2	0	0	4	1
Notch-dent.	22	4	13	5	14	7	31	27	24	5	7	2
Bkd. bldts.	34	7	22	9	114	56	24	21	332	71	68	19
Geometrics	14	3	10	4	25	12	26	22	65	14	210	59
Others	244	48	106	45	36	18	28	24	28	6	54	15
Total	509	100	238	100	230	100	116	100	465	99	357	100
Varieties of backed bladelets												
Arched	nd	nd	nd	nd	2	2	2	5	nd	nd	nd	nd
Straight	nd	nd	nd	nd	86	98	39	95	nd	nd	nd	nd
Scalene	nd	nd	nd	nd	0	0	0	0	nd	nd	nd	nd
La Mouillah	nd	nd	nd	nd	0	0	0	0	nd	nd	nd	nd
Total	nd	nd	nd	nd	88	100	41	100	nd	nd	nd	nd
Varieties of geometric microliths												
Trapeze	1	7	4	40	18	72	2	8	47	85	87	80
Triangles	3	21	0	0	0	0	0	0	0	0	1	1
Lunates	10	71	6	60	7	28	24	92	8	15	21	19
Total	14	99	10	100	25	100	26	100	55	100	109	100
Microburins												
IMbt	32	6	29	11	27	12	34	23	28	6	0	0
rIMbt		40		48		19		41		7		0

[a]Echegaray, 1966; [b]Jones, 1983; [c]Muheisan, 1983.

APPENDIX C:
NATUFIAN COMPLEX ASSEMBLAGES

TABLE C.1
Natufian

	Hayonim Interior[a]		Hayonim Exterior[a]		Rosh Zin[b]		Rosh Horesha[c]		Erq el Ahmar[d]		El Wad B1[e]		El Wad B2[e,f]		Shukbah[g]		Ira 10[h]		Abu Usba[i]	
	N	%	N	%	N	%	N	%	N	%	N	%	N	%	N	%	N	%	N	%
Major tool classes																				
Scrapers	65	18	52	23	90	10	34	3	83	21	41	1	76	1	101	12	6	2	68	32
Burins	86	24	82	36	136	15	238	21	24	6	124	3	151	2	42	5	24	8	55	26
Notch-dent.	49	14	24	10	227	25	192	17	4	1	41	1	76	1	8	1	41	14	14	7
Bkd. bldts.	13	4	14	6	90	10	158	14	63	16	579	14	1364	18	143	17	59	20	19	9
Geometrics	31	9	5	2	336	37	465	41	189	48	2768	67	5076	67	387	46	79	27	42	20
Others	113	32	54	23	28	3	45	4	30	8	579	14	833	11	160	19	81	28	13	6
Total	357	100	231	100	907	100	1132	100	393	100	4132	100	7576	100	841	100	290	99	212	100
Varieties of backed bladelets																				
Arched	nd	nd	nd	nd	13	25	28	33	nd	nd	nd	nd	nd	nd	nd	nd	nd	nd	nd	nd
Straight	nd	nd	nd	nd	38	75	57	67	nd	nd	nd	nd	nd	nd	nd	nd	nd	nd	nd	nd
Scalene	nd	nd	nd	nd	0	0	0	0	nd	nd	nd	nd	nd	nd	nd	nd	nd	nd	nd	nd
La Mouillah	nd	nd	nd	nd	0	0	0	0	nd	nd	nd	nd	nd	nd	nd	nd	nd	nd	nd	nd
Total	nd	nd	nd	nd	51	100	85	100	nd	nd	nd	nd	nd	nd	nd	nd	nd	nd	nd	nd
Varieties of geometric microliths																				
Trapezes	nd	nd	nd	nd	11	3	22	3	nd	nd	1	1	nd	nd	nd	nd	nd	nd	nd	nd
Triangles	nd	nd	nd	nd	57	17	85	9	nd	nd	4	5	nd	nd	nd	nd	nd	nd	nd	nd
Lunates	nd	nd	nd	nd	349	80	855	88	nd	nd	69	94	nd	nd	nd	nd	nd	nd	nd	nd
Total	nd	nd	nd	nd	417	100	962	100	nd	nd	74	100	nd	nd	nd	nd	nd	nd	nd	nd
Microburins																				
lMbt	0	nd	0	nd	793	47	1168	50	0	nd	311	7	nd	nd	0	nd	359	55	15	7
rlMbt	nd	nd	nd	nd		80		55	nd	nd		10	nd	nd	nd	nd		82		31

[a]Bar-Yosef and Tchernov, 1966; [b]Henry, 1973a, 1977; [c]Henry, 1973a; [d]Neuville, 1951; [e]Garrod and Bate, 1937; [f]Valla, 1984; [g]Garrod, 1932; [h]Valla, et al., 1979; [i]Stekelis and Haas, 1952.

TABLE C.1 (cont.)
Natufian cont.

	Hayonim/ Terrace B1-D [j] N	%	Wadi Judayid [k] N	%	Fazael IV [l] N	%	Tabaqa Surface [m] N	%	Hatula [n] N	%	Nahal Oren VI N	%	Nahal Oren V N	%	Ein Mallaha "ancien" [o] N	%	Ein Mallaha "recent" [o] N	%	Ein Mallaha "final" [o] N	%
Major tool classes																				
Scrapers	67	6	3	2	12	1	33	20	43	3	4	1	10	2	36	2	15	1	38	2
Burins	35	3	1	1	1	.1	3	2	25	2	29	9	45	8	183	10	96	8	106	5
Notch-dent.	146	14	24	16	163	14	42	25	32	2	49	16	116	22	225	13	196	16	357	18
Bkd. bldts.	409	38	6	4	243	21	49	29	167	11	113	36	122	23	707	40	507	42	764	37
Geometrics	151	14	96	62	243	21	49	29	167	11	68	22	83	15	125	7	72	6	170	8
Others	269	25	24	15	299	26	32	18	729	49	52	17	163	30	485	28	333	27	606	30
Total	1077	100	154	100	1143	99	169	100	1483	100	315	101	539	100	1761	100	1219	100	2041	100
Varieties of backed bladelets																				
Arched	50	16	1	17	nd	nd	nd	nd	nd	nd	nd	nd	nd	nd	nd	nd	nd	nd	nd	nd
Straight	264	84	5	83	nd	nd	nd	nd	nd	nd	nd	nd	nd	nd	nd	nd	nd	nd	nd	nd
Scalene	0	0	0	0	nd	nd	nd	nd	nd	nd	nd	nd	nd	nd	nd	nd	nd	nd	nd	nd
La Mouillah	0	0	0	0	nd	nd	nd	nd	nd	nd	nd	nd	nd	nd	nd	nd	nd	nd	nd	nd
Total	314	100	6	100	nd	nd	nd	nd	nd	nd	nd	nd	nd	nd	nd	nd	nd	nd	nd	nd
Varieties of geometric microliths																				
Trapezes	20	13	0	0	nd	nd	nd	nd	16	2	7	10	6	7	12	10	13	18	10	6
Triangles	25	17	4	4	nd	nd	nd	nd	17	2	10	15	10	12	12	10	5	7	14	8
Lunates	106	70	92	96	nd	nd	nd	nd	696	96	51	75	67	81	101	80	54	75	146	86
Total	151	100	96	100	nd	nd	nd	nd	719	100	68	100	83	100	125	100	72	100	170	100
Microburins																				
lMbt	408	27.5	74	32.5	nd	nd	nd	nd	6	.4	13	4.0	48	8.2	52	2.9	54	4.2	253	11.0
rlMbt		65.8		43.5		nd		nd		.8		16.1		36.6		2.9		42.9		59.0

[j] Henry and Leroi-Gourhan, 1976; [k] Henry, et al., 1985; [l] Bar-Yosef, et al., 1974; [m] Byrd and Rollefson, 1984; [n] Ronen and Lechevallier, 1985; [o] Valla, 1984.

TABLE C.2
Harifian

	G12[a]		G8[a]		G20[a]		K3[a]		Lagama[b] IV		Mushabi[b] III		Mushabi[b] XX		Mushabi[b] XV		Lavan[c] 110		Ira[d] 25	
	N	%	N	%	N	%	N	%	N	%	N	%	N	%	N	%	N	%	N	%
Major tool classes																				
Scrapers	652	11	149	18	54	28	106	32	6	3	10	3	23	5	6	4	8	7	26	11
Burins	43	1	22	3	3	2	5	2	0	0	3	0	4	1	0	0	1	1	4	2
Notch-dent.	814	14	146	18	14	7	81	25	11	5	7	2	20	4	17	11	8	7	16	7
Bkd. bldts.	1034	18	161	20	44	24	21	6	26	12	51	14	98	21	14	9	9	8	49	21
Geometrics	1268	22	67	8	2	1	2	1	4	2	16	4	19	4	8	5	1	1	74	32
Others	2011	34	277	33	75	38	113	34	164	78	290	77	295	65	108	71	95	77	69	28
Total	5822	100	822	100	192	100	328	100	211	100	377	100	459	100	153	100	122	101	238	101
Varieties of backed bladelets																				
Arched	206	41	65	77	10	36	14	82	18	64	10	63	15	8	nd	nd	nd	nd	nd	nd
Straight	301	59	49	23	18	64	3	18	10	36	6	38	17	27	nd	nd	nd	nd	nd	nd
Scalene	0	0	0	0	0	0	0	0	0	0	0	0	14	22	nd	nd	nd	nd	nd	nd
La Mouillah	0	0	0	0	0	0	0	0	0	0	0	0	28	43	nd	nd	nd	nd	nd	nd
Total	507	100	54	100	28	100	17	100	28	100	16	101	74	100	nd	nd	nd	nd	nd	nd
Varieties of geometric microliths																				
Trapezes	54	4	4	6	1	50	0	0	0	0	1	6	1	5	3	38	0	0	nd	nd
Triangles	450	36	21	33	0	0	0	0	0	0	6	38	1	5	1	12	0	0	nd	nd
Lunates	739	60	38	60	1	50	2	100	4	100	9	56	17	90	4	50	1	100	nd	nd
Total	1243	100	63	99	2	100	2	100	4	100	16	100	19	100	8	100	1	100	nd	nd
Microburins																				
IMbt	3674	38.7	530	39.2	75	28.1	73	18.2	88	29.4	249	39.8	147	24.3	98	39.0	23	15.4	181	43
rIMbt		68.5		87.3		64.6		90.1		53.0		65.2		46.8		41.5		25.6		nd

[a]Scott, 1977; [b]Phillips, 1977; [c]Phillips, et al., 1974; [d]Valla, et al., 1979.

INDEX